The Political Economy of Integration

This book assesses South America's most ambitious attempt at economic integration, Mercosur. It explains the main—and inherent—weaknesses of the integration effort, through explicit comparison with the European experience with integration. Jeffrey Cason argues that the three main reasons for Mercosur's limited success are weak domestic political institutions in the member countries, vulnerability in the global political economy, and a serious imbalance in the economic and political weight of the member countries.

In addition to providing this overarching explanation for Mercosur's limitations, the book tells the story of Mercosur's genesis, development, and frustrations. This book provides both an explanatory framework for understanding Mercosur and a story. It considers how Mercosur emerged, why it was greeted with great enthusiasm (and huge trade growth), and how it hit stumbling blocks as it sought to be more than it was capable of being. The book also focuses on how and why developing countries are inherently limited in any economic integration project.

Jeffrey W. Cason is Dean of International Programs and the Edward C. Knox Professor of International Studies and Political Science at Middlebury College, Vermont.

Routledge Studies in the Modern World Economy

1 **Interest Rates and Budget Deficits**
A study of the advanced economies
Kanhaya L Gupta and Bakhtiar Moazzami

2 **World Trade after the Uruguay Round**
Prospects and policy options for the twenty-first century
Edited by Harald Sander and András Inotai

3 **The Flow Analysis of Labour Markets**
Edited by Ronald Schettkat

4 **Inflation and Unemployment**
Contributions to a new macroeconomic approach
Edited by Alvaro Cencini and Mauro Baranzini

5 **Macroeconomic Dimensions of Public Finance**
Essays in honour of Vito Tanzi
Edited by Mario I. Blejer and Teresa M. Ter-Minassian

6 **Fiscal Policy and Economic Reforms**
Essays in honour of Vito Tanzi
Edited by Mario I. Blejer and Teresa M. Ter-Minassian

7 **Competition Policy in the Global Economy**
Modalities for co-operation
Edited by Leonard Waverman, William S. Comanor and Akira Goto

8 **Working in the Macro Economy**
A study of the US labor market
Martin F. J. Prachowny

9 **How Does Privatization Work?**
Edited by Anthony Bennett

10 **The Economics and Politics of International Trade**
Freedom and trade: Volume II
Edited by Gary Cook

11 **The Legal and Moral Aspects of International Trade**
Freedom and trade: Volume III
Edited by Asif Qureshi, Hillel Steiner and Geraint Parry

12 **Capital Markets and Corporate Governance in Japan, Germany and the United States**
Organizational response to market inefficiencies
Helmut M. Dietl

13 **Competition and Trade Policies**
Coherence or conflict
Edited by Einar Hope

14 **Rice**
The primary commodity
A. J. H. Latham

15 **Trade, Theory and Econometrics**
Essays in honour of John S. Chipman
Edited by James C. Moore, Raymond Riezman, James R. Melvin

16 **Who benefits from Privatisation?**
Edited by Moazzem Hossain and Justin Malbon

17 **Towards a Fair Global Labour Market**
Avoiding the new slave trade
Ozay Mehmet, Errol Mendes and Robert Sinding

18 **Models of Futures Markets**
Edited by Barry Goss

19 **Venture Capital Investment**
An agency analysis of UK practice
Gavin C. Reid

20 **Macroeconomic Forecasting**
A sociological appraisal
Robert Evans

21 **Multimedia and Regional Economic Restructuring**
Edited by Hans-Joachim Braczyk, Gerhard Fuchs and Hans-Georg Wolf

22 **The New Industrial Geography**
Regions, regulation and institutions
Edited by Trevor J. Barnes and Meric S. Gertler

23 **The Employment Impact of Innovation**
Evidence and policy
Edited by Marco Vivarelli and Mario Pianta

24 **International Health Care Reform**
A legal, economic and political analysis
Colleen Flood

25 **Competition Policy Analysis**
Edited by Einar Hope

26 **Culture and Enterprise**
The development, representation and morality of business
Don Lavoie and Emily Chamlee-Wright

27 **Global Financial Crises and Reforms**
Cases and caveats
B.N. Ghosh

28 **Geography of Production and Economic Integration**
Miroslav N. Jovanovi?

29 **Technology, Trade and Growth in OECD Countries**
Does specialisation matter?
Valentina Meliciani

30 **Post-Industrial Labour Markets**
Profiles of North America and Scandinavia
Edited by Thomas P Boje and Bengt Furaker

31 **Capital Flows without Crisis**
Reconciling capital mobility and economic stability
Edited by Dipak Dasgupta, Marc Uzan and Dominic Wilson

32 **International Trade and National Welfare**
Murray C Kemp

33 **Global Trading Systems at Crossroads**
A post-Seattle perspective
Dilip K. Das

34 **The Economics and Management of Technological Diversification**
Edited by John Cantwell, Alfonso Gambardella and Ove Granstrand

35 **Before and Beyond EMU**
Historical lessons and future prospects
Edited by Patrick Crowley

36 **Fiscal Decentralization**
Ehtisham Ahmad and Vito Tanzi

37 **Regionalisation of Globalised Innovation**
Locations for advanced industrial development and disparities in participation
Edited by Ulrich Hilpert

38 **Gold and the Modern World Economy**
Edited by MoonJoong Tcha

39 **Global Economic Institutions**
Willem Molle

40 **Global Governance and Financial Crises**
Edited by Meghnad Desai and Yahia Said

41 **Linking Local and Global Economies**
The ties That bind
Edited by Carlo Pietrobelli and Arni Sverrisson

42 **Tax Systems and Tax Reforms in Europe**
Edited by Luigi Bernardi and Paola Profeta

43 **Trade Liberalization and APEC**
Edited by Jiro Okamoto

44 **Fiscal Deficits in the Pacific Region**
Edited by Akira Kohsaka

45 **Financial Globalization and the Emerging Market Economies**
Dilip K. Das

46 **International Labor Mobility**
Unemployment and Increasing returns to scale
Bharati Basu

47 **Good Governance in the Era of Global Neoliberalism**
Conflict and depolitization in Latin America, Eastern Europe, Asia and Africa
Edited by Jolle Demmers, Alex E. Fernández Jilberto & Barbara Hogenboom

48 **The International Trade System**
Alice Landau

49 **International Perspectives on Temporary Work and Workers**
Edited by John Burgess and Julia Connell

50 **Working Time and Workers' Preferences in Industrialized Countries**
Finding the balance
Edited by Jon C. Messenger

51 **Tax Systems and Tax Reforms in New EU Members**
Edited by Luigi Bernardi, Mark Chandler and Luca Gandullia

52 **Globalization and the Nation State**
The impact of the IMF and the World Bank
Edited by Gustav Ranis, James Vreeland and Stephen Kosak

53 **Macroeconomic Policies and Poverty Reduction**
Edited by Ashoka Mody and Catherine Pattillo

54 **Regional Monetary Policy**
Carlos J. Rodríguez-Fuentez

55 **Trade and Migration in the Modern World**
Carl Mosk

56 **Globalisation and the Labour Market**
Trade, technology and less-skilled workers in Europe and the United States
Edited by Robert Anderton, Paul Brenton and John Whalley

57 **Financial Crises**
Socio-economic causes and institutional context
Brenda Spotton Visano

58 **Globalization and Self Determination**
Is the nation-state under siege?
Edited by David R. Cameron, Gustav Ranis and Annalisa Zinn

59 **Developing Countries and the Doha Development Round of the WTO**
Edited by Pitou van Dijck and Gerrit Faber

60 **Immigrant Enterprise in Europe and the USA**
Prodromos Panayiotopoulos

61 **Solving the Riddle of Globalization and Development**
Edited by Manuel Agosín, David Bloom, George Chapelier and Jagdish Saigal

62 **Foreign Direct Investment and the World Economy**
Ashoka Mody

63 **The World Economy**
A global analysis
Horst Siebert

64 **Production Organizations in Japanese Economic Development**
Edited by Tetsuji Okazaki

65 **The Economics of Language**
International analyses
Edited by Barry R. Chiswick and Paul W. Miller

66 **Street Entrepreneurs**
People, place and politics in local and global perspective
Edited by John Cross and Alfonso Morales

67 **Global Challenges and Local Responses**
The East Asian experience
Edited by Jang-Sup Shin

68 **Globalization and Regional Integration**
The origins, development and impact of the single European aviation market
Alan Dobson

69 **Russia Moves into the Global Economy: Breaking Out**
John M. Letiche

70 **The European Economy in an American Mirror**
Barry Eichengreen, Michael Landesmann and Dieter Stiefel

71 **Working Time Around the World**
Trends in working hours, laws, and policies in a global comparative perspective
Jon C. Messenger, Sangheon Lee and Deidre McCann

72 **International Water Treaties**
Negotiation and cooperation along transboundary rivers
Shlomi Dinar

73 **Economic Integration in the Americas**
Edited by Joseph A. McKinney and H. Stephen Gardner

74 **Expanding Frontiers of Global Trade Rules**
The political economy dynamics of the international trading system
Nitya Nanda

75 **The Macroeconomics of Global Imbalances**
European and Asian perspectives
Edited by Marc Uzan

76 **China and Asia**
Economic and financial interactions
Edited by Yin-Wong Cheung and Kar-Yiu Wong

77 **Regional Inequality in China**
Trends, explanations and policy responses
Edited by Shenggen Fan, Ravi Kanbur and Xiaobo Zhang

78 **Governing Rapid Growth in China**
Equity and institutions
Edited by Ravi Kanbur and Xiaobo Zhang

79 **The Indonesian Labour Market**
Shafiq Dhanani, Iyanatul Islam and Anis Chowdhury

80 **Cost-Benefit Analysis in Multi-level Government in Europe and the USA**
The case of EU cohesion policy and of US federal investment policies
Alessandro Ferrara

81 **The Economic Geography of Air Transportation**
Space, time, and the freedom of the sky
John Bowen

82 **Cartelization, Antitrust and Globalization in the US and Europe**
Mark LeClair

83 **The Political Economy of Integration**
The experience of Mercosur
Jeffrey W. Cason

The Political Economy of Integration

The experience of Mercosur

Jeffrey W. Cason

Routledge
Taylor & Francis Group
LONDON AND NEW YORK

First published 2011
by Routledge
2 Park Square, Milton Park, Abingdon, Oxon OX14 4RN

Simultaneously published in the USA and Canada
by Routledge
711 Third Avenue, New York, NY 10017

Routledge is an imprint of the Taylor & Francis Group, an informa business

Typeset in Times New Roman by Swales & Willis Ltd, Exeter, Devon
First issued in paperback in 2013

British Library Cataloguing in Publication Data
A catalogue record for this book is available
from the British Library

Library of Congress Cataloging in Publication Data
A catalog record for this book has been requested

ISBN: 978–0–415–74615–1 (pbk)
ISBN: 978–0–415–77885–5 (hbk)
ISBN: 978–0–203–84625–4 (ebk)

Table of contents

Tables and figures

Tables

Figures

Acknowledgments

This book is the product of a long-standing interest in Latin American trade, and in particular the ways in which Latin American countries have attempted to use trade to achieve development objectives. Trade has long been a contentious issue in Latin America, and one that looms large in the minds of policy makers and the population alike. Trade is a hot political issue everywhere, but especially so in the Latin American context. This is my attempt to come to grips with that politics in the context of Latin American integration.

As I have carried out the research for this book over the years, many colleagues in the United States, Brazil, Argentina, and Uruguay have helped me understand Latin American integration from their own perspectives. At times, they may not have realized the impact they had on my thinking about the topic, and certainly they were always willing to let me test out my ideas. Among the people who helped me, through conversation and other exchanges, in ways large and small, are: Paulo Roberto de Almeida, Kit Ashby, Jorge Balbis, Nora Balzarotti, Victor Blatt, Atílio Borón, Clovis Brigagão, Jorge Campbell, Zairo Cheibub, Norberto Colominas, Gerónimo de Sierra, Wilson Fernández, Julio Gambina, Fernando González, José Augusto Guilhon Albuquerque, Belela Herrera, Jorge Lavopa, Flávia Campos de Mello, Marcílio Marques Moreira, Reginaldo Mattar Nasser, Gustavo Moreno, Janina Onuki, Jorge Papadopulos, Marcelo Pereira, Eduardo Piazza, Diego Piñeiro, Bruno Podestá, Fernando Porta, Tim Power, Marcelo Rossal, Jorge Schvarzer, Bill Smith, Fernando Sotelino, Malusa Stein, Miguel Teubal, Janice Tirelli, João Paulo Cândia Veiga, and Tullo Vigevani. They may be surprised at some of my interpretations, in the end, but they may also recognize some of our conversations here. And as is always the case with such acknowledgments, any errors are my own.

I have also benefitted from the research assistance of a number of Middlebury undergraduates over the years, who worked with me at different stages of this project. They include Jennifer Burrell, David Haglund, Vinay Jawahar, Mateal Lovaas, Laura Potter, and Ayse Zarakol. Gail Borden and Liz Ross also helped with the production of the figures, and Charlotte Tate helped coordinate the work of several of the research assistants. My colleagues in the political science department at Middlebury College provided me with valuable feedback at several stages during the writing of this book. I was also able to try out these ideas with talks at a number of Latin American universities, and appreciate the comments and feedback that I received at the Universidade Federal de Santa Catarina (Florianópolis), the Universidade Federal Fluminense (Niterói), the Universidad ORT (Montevideo), the Universidad de la República (Montevideo), and the Pontifícia Universidade Católica de São Paulo.

I also received generous support to conduct research associated with this book from the American Philosophical Society, the Ada Howe Kent program at Middlebury College, and two Fulbright grants. In the case of both Fulbright grants, I was fortunate to be able to teach courses related to the political economy of integration, and learned a great deal from my students and colleagues at the Universidad de la República in Montevideo and the Universidade Federal de Santa Catarina in Florianópolis. My hosts at both institutions—Luis Behares in Montevideo and Fernando Ponte in Florianópolis—greatly facilitated my own personal integration with their respective academic cultures, and deserve a special thank you for their help and friendship. Eduardo Gómes has also been a long-standing confidante and collaborator (and host!) over the years. He's heard me try out these ideas in numerous fora, and has always given me insightful feedback.

A section of Chapter 5 draws on an article I previously published (Cason 2000a) in the *Journal of Interamerican Studies and World Affairs*, and I am grateful to the journal (since renamed *Latin American Politics and Society*) for permission to use portions of that article here. Tom Sutton and Simon Holt were of great assistance in seeing this project through on the Routledge end of things, as well. I would also like to thank Anita Kakar for her help in making my prose more readable, and Dan Crepps for helping me with the final proofing of the manuscript. Throughout the book, all translations from Portuguese or Spanish sources are mine.

Being able to share the process of writing this book with my family—even when they didn't know this is what they were sharing—has been a pleasure. Most particularly, in the last stage of fieldwork for this book, I was able to share a year in Brazil with Gail, Elias, Sophia, and Gabriel. One might note that taking a family abroad ultimately slowed down the writing of the book itself, but that's not the way I see it. Rather, having them with me during some of the research and writing process made it a wonderful adventure and a much more satisfying way to spend my time, in the end. Finally, I have enjoyed sharing fleeting glimpses of the book with my wider family along the process, and in particular with my parents—all four of them. I dedicate this book to them, for all that they have given me through the years.

Introduction

Ever since Latin American countries achieved their independence in the early nineteenth century, leaders have dreamed of integrating the region into a single nation. Simón Bolívar, for example, wrote in 1815 in his Letter from Jamaica that "more than anyone, I desire to see [Latin] America fashioned into the greatest nation in the world, greatest not so much by virtue of her area and wealth as by her freedom and glory" (1965 [1815]: 67). Over time, of course, nations developed distinct national identities, and these identities are keenly felt and not particularly amenable to easy alteration, despite the homogenizing influences of globalization. An Ecuadorian has little to do with an Argentine, in terms of political culture, racial/ethnic makeup, and cultural outlook, and much the same could be said about most any pair of Latin American countries. A dream of unity is just that, a dream. A United States of Latin America is not on anyone's radar screen.

Despite this obvious fact, Latin American countries attempted to bring their economies closer together for most of the second half of the twentieth century and into the new millennium. These efforts began in earnest in the early 1960s. At their core, the Latin American integration projects were meant to push the development process forward. They emerged after Latin American countries began to industrialize following the shock of the Great Depression. This import-substitution industrialization (ISI) developed gradually in the interwar period, and by the 1950s most nations in the region came to see their future in increasing industrial development, moving away from their traditional dependence on mineral and agricultural exports. ISI involved relatively high tariffs, subsidies for industrialists, and (in some nations) relatively higher wages for workers, since local business generally did not have to worry about keeping prices down to compete with imports (Hirschman 1971; Kaufman 1990). These ISI models had a wide array of problems, including recurrent balance-of-payments crises and a stop-and-go quality of economic growth that unleashed substantial political conflict, but they did survive for many decades. There were also multiple attempts to save ISI, and a reluctance to dump it, largely because political constituencies had grown up to support ISI, and thus had a vested interest in seeing it continue.

Economic integration was seen as one way to continue holding on to the ISI model. After all, one of the problems with ISI in Latin America was the small size of the domestic markets in most countries in the region. Policy makers in the region hoped to use Latin American integration—first embodied in the Latin American Free Trade Association (LAFTA) agreement signed in 1960—to expand the market for their ISI development strategies. There was hope that the Latin American integration process could repeat the success and growth of Europe, whose integration process by then was well underway. It is no accident that calls for Latin American integration emerged after the success of Europe; in many ways, the European process of integration was considered a model.

Alas, Europe was not a model for Latin America. Europe was at the center of the international political economy; Latin America was still mired in poverty and severe inequality. The European nations that embarked on the European Community project were all democracies; the Latin American nations were at times (relatively) democratic, and at times they were ruled by military dictatorships. Europe was largely industrialized; Latin America still mostly exported primary products, and industrialization was at relatively early stages in the region. Europe was at the center of the Cold War struggle; Latin America, while an important battleground in the Cold War, did not receive anything close to a Marshall Plan with its own Alliance for Progress.

Consequently, the hopes for Latin American integration were not realized. For a variety of reasons, including recurrent balance-of-payments crises in many large Latin American countries, the complexity of negotiating free trade among so many nations, and political instability in the region, Latin American integration under the auspices of LAFTA stagnated before it could gain any momentum. There was then an attempt to be more modest, two decades later, when the Latin American Integration Association (Asociación Latinoamericana de Integración—ALADI) was formed. This renewed attempt was both limited and badly timed, since just after Latin America started the ALADI process, the debt crisis struck in 1982. With most countries struggling to meet their debt service obligations, it was rather difficult to think of liberalizing imports, even imports coming from fellow Latin American countries. In addition, most of Latin America was still committed to its old statist, ISI strategy. Openness did not come easily. Indeed, the 1980s are commonly referred to as the "lost decade" of Latin American development.

But this "lost decade" was not so lost when it came to integration, as it turned out. In 1985, Brazil and Argentina embarked on a process of economic integration that eventually culminated in the formation of Mercosur (Mercado Común del Sur—Common Market of the South; Mercosul in Portuguese). Mercosur also includes Uruguay and Paraguay as full members (with Venezuela hoping for full membership), as well as associate members in much of the rest of South America. The integration process was beset by many problems early on, but did lead to the most successful integration process in Latin America. Despite its many problems and limitations that will be explored in this book, Mercosur has created an integration process that would be very difficult and painful to reverse. No other Latin American integration process can boast this sort of (limited) success, either in the growth of trade that has occurred among its members or in its impressive inflow of foreign investment.

When it comes to explaining how Mercosur developed, there have been a number of attempts to compare the Mercosur process to the European Union (EU) (Caetano and Perina 2000; González-Oldekop 1997), but much of the work done on the Mercosur integration project has been piecemeal. Some of the work has focused on small parts of the integration process, analyzing specific decisions, for example. Quite a few economists have become interested in the process, and have focused on issues like trade diversion and trade creation (Yeats 1998; Bonelli and Hahn 2000). Others have focused on legal aspects of the integration process and other "technical" issues (Pimentel 1998; Basso 1997; Porrata-Doria 2005). There are also some who have attempted to understand the politics of Mercosur (Hirst 1996a; Ginesta 1999; Lavagna 1998; Roett 1999). In the end, however, there is to date no overall accounting of how and why Mercosur developed as it did, in English. In addition, because of the stagnation of the process recently, there has been much less scholarly attention paid to Mercosur in the last several years. But the stagnation of this process is part of what needs explaining, as the stagnation has structural causes.

In exploring the Mercosur integration process, I ask several questions in this book: In what ways is the Mercosur process like other integration processes? In what ways is it different? How can we explain these similarities and differences? In refining these questions, I focus on two issues: primarily, I explain the particular institutional choices that the Mercosur nations have made over the course of the integration process. Secondarily, I focus on what Keohane and Hoffmann refer to broadly as "institutional" concerns: "how political processes and practices have changed" over the course of integration (1991: 4). In both areas, there are significant similarities and differences between Mercosur and the EU.

In the book, I focus on two levels of analysis: national-level actors (states, labor, and business primarily) and the international political economy. When it comes to the interests of national actors, I focus on the preferences of these actors in state and society, as well as the interaction between these actors. At the international level, I consider transnational economic linkages such as trade and investment patterns and political factors such as the end of the Cold War and pressures from other countries and blocs toward the Mercosur countries. Based on this analysis, I describe the pattern of Mercosur (and developing country) integration as *vulnerable integration*. This is not to say that Mercosur has always seen integration thwarted because of its vulnerability; indeed, sometimes, the factors that have led to Mercosur's vulnerability have even pushed the integration process forward. More often than not, however, vulnerability has had negative consequences.

At its core, vulnerable integration, as experienced by Mercosur, can be summarized as follows: developing or emerging countries embark on integration projects with a number of disadvantages, including weak political institutions, underdeveloped and clientelistic relationships between state and civil society actors, and heavy dependence on foreign capital for investment and the financing of current account deficits. These disadvantages lead countries to limit their integration projects to commercial liberalization, and they make developing countries especially unwilling to give up sovereignty to or even pool it with supranational institutions. As a consequence, while the integration project may proceed for a time, it is frequently threatened by international economic shocks and the possibility that political leaders in the integrating countries will renege on their commitments to integrate. Since there is a) no supporting supranational institutional structure to protect integration in bad times and b) underdeveloped civil society support for integration, it is much less likely to have staying power or to be able to weather a crisis. In addition, because of the aforementioned unwillingness to give up or pool sovereignty, integration in Mercosur has remained mostly an affair of commercial liberalization. Any efforts to "deepen" the integration process to encompass other issues, such as labor codes or consumer regulations, are usually frustrated.

The limitations of Mercosur are evident when compared to integration in the EU. One of the major differences between the EU and Mercosur integration experiences is the motivation for integration. Those writing about Europe have emphasized either economic interests or political processes when attempting to explain how European integration came about and evolved. While economic interests and political processes also played an important role in South American integration, these processes operated quite differently. As Monica Hirst reports, Mercosur was adopted over the objections of large segments of the business sector, who only eventually came to accept it as an "inevitable evil," something they were powerless to prevent (1996a: 193) Business was not clamoring for more integration on any large scale (some firms excepted); business was still mostly comfortable with continued ISI, even if there were serious questions about the viability and evident exhaustion of the old model. Kingstone (1999), for example, makes the case that business, at least in Brazil, was ripe for a new economic strategy after the ISI model was apparently exhausted, but integration was not high on the list of alternative strategies. Fundamentally, as will become evident in the empirical chapters, South American integration was a political decision, and it came in a top-down fashion.

At first glance, then, the South American decision to integrate might be seen to confirm some European-based arguments about the primacy of political or ideological factors on integration decisions. This is only the case, however, if we disregard the differences between how politics operated in the two regions. First, unlike Europe, Mercosur has no strong federalist impulse, despite the rhetorical homage occasionally paid to Bolívar and other figures who have preached Latin American unity. Second, the South American nations suffer from relatively underdeveloped civil societies and interest groups. It is not that interest groups and civil society do not exist in Latin America, but they are relatively unorganized, and attempts to influence the policy-making process generally have come not from organized interest groups but through clientelistic connections between the state and society that lead to relatively weak civil societies.

The lack of federalist ideology or an interest in pooling sovereignty (especially in Brazil) has meant that South American integration has been particularly uninstitutionalized. There are no supranational bureaucrats with even the slightest power to set the agenda for integration. This lack of institutionalization has had interesting effects on Mercosur's ability to move forward—at times, the lack of institutional constraints has made striking new bargains possible, while at other times it has led to stagnation in the integration process, particularly when there have been disputes between the integrating partners. With few institutional mechanisms in place to resolve conflicts, integration has repeatedly floundered in times of crisis.

In the end, those hypotheses about European integration that are the most general are the most useful, but by their very generality are not particularly satisfying. The most useful of these is what Keohane and Hoffmann refer to as the "preference-convergence hypothesis." In referring to the Single European Act, they argue that its ratification resulted "from a convergence of national interests around a new pattern of economic policymaking . . . [M]embers of a regional organization must regard themselves as having a great deal in common, distinguishing themselves from outsiders" (Keohane and Hoffmann 1991: 23–24). As they go on to note, however, such conclusions are not especially satisfactory unless the analyst can take them further and explain just how and why the interests of the most important actors changed. In the empirical chapters of this book, this will be one of my primary tasks, and what will become evident is that the most important actors in the Mercosur story are quite different from the important actors in Europe.

Organization of the book

Chapter 1 puts the Mercosur integration process in a comparative context. I discuss the relevant literature on European integration, and while I do not enter into the debates on European integration specifically or draw conclusions about them, I focus on the main elements of European integration that are relevant for Mercosur. After all, any integration project will confront issues such as the reduction of national sovereignty over economic policies, the economic costs and benefits of integration, and a broader geopolitical context. It then uses this literature to understand integration in Mercosur, and draws out similarities and differences between them. The chapter fleshes out the "vulnerable integration" model that Mercosur has experienced. In discussing this model of integration, I emphasize in particular the dependence of emerging markets on foreign capital, their weak political institutions, the disorganized nature of civil society, and the ways in which Mercosur has been particularly vulnerable to international political and economic trends.

Chapter 2 lays the groundwork for the specific analysis of Mercosur. Integration in the region needs to be understood in the context of its long historical trajectory of failures and fleeting successes. Integration is never just an economic project; at its core, in Latin America especially, integration has always been a political project, even when economic interests have been prominent. This chapter considers the roots of Latin American integration, which lie in the nineteenth century, and then considers the failed efforts to promote integration when ISI policies started to run into problems in the post-war period. It concludes by focusing on Argentine-Brazilian relations, and the various efforts that were made toward cooperation between these two countries that eventually led to Mercosur.

The next three chapters explore the Mercosur process in detail. Chapter 3 focuses on the decision-making process that surrounded the signing of the Treaty of Asunción, which established Mercosur in 1991. It considers both international factors that influenced this decision as well as the domestic politics that surrounded the decision and made it possible. In this chapter, I emphasize how, on a domestic level, different "visions" of integration were present in the respective states, business, and labor in each country. The focus, in this regard, will be on how these conflicting visions allowed for eventual agreement on the decision to move forward in the integration process. The evidence provides support for the preference-convergence hypothesis mentioned earlier, showing how interests converged enough to make agreement on Mercosur possible.

Chapter 4 focuses on the decision to form a customs union in the region, with the signing of the Protocol of Ouro Preto in 1994. In some ways, the decision to move towards a customs union was astounding; after all, the proposed timeline for achieving this step was extraordinarily rapid, especially when compared to European integration. It was, in fact, rather remarkable that this was achieved, and this accomplishment depended in large part on the political leadership of the Mercosur countries. At the same time, the consolidation of the customs union was assisted by international factors, and in this chapter I make the argument that vulnerability in integration can be an advantage.

Chapter 5 considers the problems associated with consolidation in the Mercosur bloc. There is a widespread sense, recently, that the integration process has lost both steam and focus. Mercosur has faced enormous challenges, both because it quite self-consciously did not establish any supranational institutions along the lines of the European Commission, and because the international economic climate of the late 1990s and early twenty-first century constantly buffeted the region, calling into question the viability of deepening integration. With this adverse international context and the institutional weaknesses of Mercosur, there was a sense that this integration project had hit a wall and was unlikely to progress further.

The final chapter considers the future of integration in Mercosur and the potential for integration in emerging countries. Here I return to the challenges facing a vulnerable integration project like Mercosur. These challenges include the dependence on foreign investment for the success of integration, the institutional shortcomings in countries that are weak or relatively unconsolidated democracies, and an international political and economic environment that discourages state intervention in the economy. The lessons of Mercosur are relevant both for the countries that make up this particular economic bloc and for other developing or emerging countries that are contemplating integration projects in an increasingly globalized world.

1 Understanding integration

The European model and a South American case

Without a doubt, Europe stands as the integration model for the rest of the world. It has moved, in fits and starts, up the ladder of integration, going from a free trade area to a customs union to a common market and now to a monetary union. This was not an easy task, and at numerous points in the process, it appeared that the European integration project would be derailed. Indeed, although there are still plenty of unresolved issues as the EU expands (and there always will be), the EU has remade the European political economy over the last half century. There is obviously a voluminous literature on this European project, some of which will be referred to here, but this book will not analyze that progress in detail.

Instead, it focuses on South American integration. In debates in the region about the direction that Latin American integration should take, Europe is a constant reference. Depending on the analyst, Mercosur is sometimes portrayed as lacking in key institutional areas when it is compared to Europe, while for others it is viewed as somehow superior, both because it has integrated much more rapidly and more "pragmatically" (see, *inter alia*, González-Oldekop 1997; Calvete 2000; Peña 1999; Casella 2000; Duina 2007).

Regardless as to how it is viewed in comparison, Europe is clearly a primary reference point for Mercosur. Some of the literature on the European integration process is in fact a good starting point for understanding Mercosur, even though the two processes are quite different. This chapter will make the case that Mercosur integration is fundamentally different in kind from European integration. In the introduction, I laid out the main arguments that led to these differences, and recapitulate them briefly here: a combination of weak political institutions and structural position in the international political economy has led to particular institutional choices and political practices in Mercosur. These institutional choices and political practices make Mercosur much more vulnerable to a wide variety of shocks that originate both outside the region and within the Mercosur countries themselves.

This argument will not rehash old debates on dependency that were popular in the 1960s and 1970s, particularly in Latin American studies. Indeed, one of the arguments here is that Latin American integration has been surprisingly successful, and the international political economy does not condemn poor nations to eternal poverty. Rather, it attempts to understand how structural position in the international political economy and different political institutions affect integration. Given the very different structural positions of Europe and Latin America—as well as their substantially different institutions—it would be surprising to find that integration would occur in both places with similar dynamics. As Ernst Haas noted in his classic study of European integration more than 50 years ago, "I would have little hesitation in applying the technique of analysis here used to the study of integration under NATO, the Scandinavian setting, the Organisation for European Economic Cooperation, or Canadian–United States relations. I would hesitate to claim validity for it in the study of regional political integration in Latin America, the Middle East, or South-East Asia (Haas 1958: xvi). Not only are Europe and South America in different places in the international political economy, but they have strikingly different political institutions and quite different civil society organizations. These differences make the dynamics of Latin American integration quite distinct. Indeed, I argue that Latin American integration simply cannot be like its European counterpart.

To get better leverage on understanding the case of Mercosur, this chapter considers how some of the debates on European integration inform the Mercosur process. The goal here is to establish a framework for the historical and political detail to follow. I am mostly concerned here with the incentives and disincentives to integrate, the role of international factors in the integration process, the role of civil society in the politics of integration, and finally, the institutions that support or impede integration. I turn to these specific issues after laying out the framework I use to compare integration processes.

A framework for comparing integration experiences

As noted earlier, a good bit of the work on Mercosur uses the EU as a frame of reference. Much of this work, however, does not go beyond noting that a) the experiences are different and/or b) that Mercosur should be more like the EU. While a) is certainly correct, it does not explain much, especially because the focus of analysis is so fuzzy. Here I present a framework that concentrates on what I consider the most important elements of the integration process. On the one hand, I try to explain particular political and institutional choices, and consequently focus on a number of key decision points in the integration process, as Moravcsik (1998a) did in his wide-ranging study of the EU. On the other hand, as noted in the introduction, I am interested in Keohane and Hoffmann's broader "institutional" concerns, the ways in which political processes and practices change over the course of integration.

It is important as well to show how these variables are linked and affect one another. It is useful to illustrate their connections graphically, as in Figure 1.1. In the right section of the graph (labeled "The Array of Integration Outcomes"), I depict what is involved in an initial decision to integrate, as well as what happens when there is a decision to "go forward" in the integration process. Though obviously simplified, I break the integration decision down to the *depth* of the integrating ambition, the *breadth* of the issues covered by the integration decision, and the *institutionalization* that results from the integration decision.

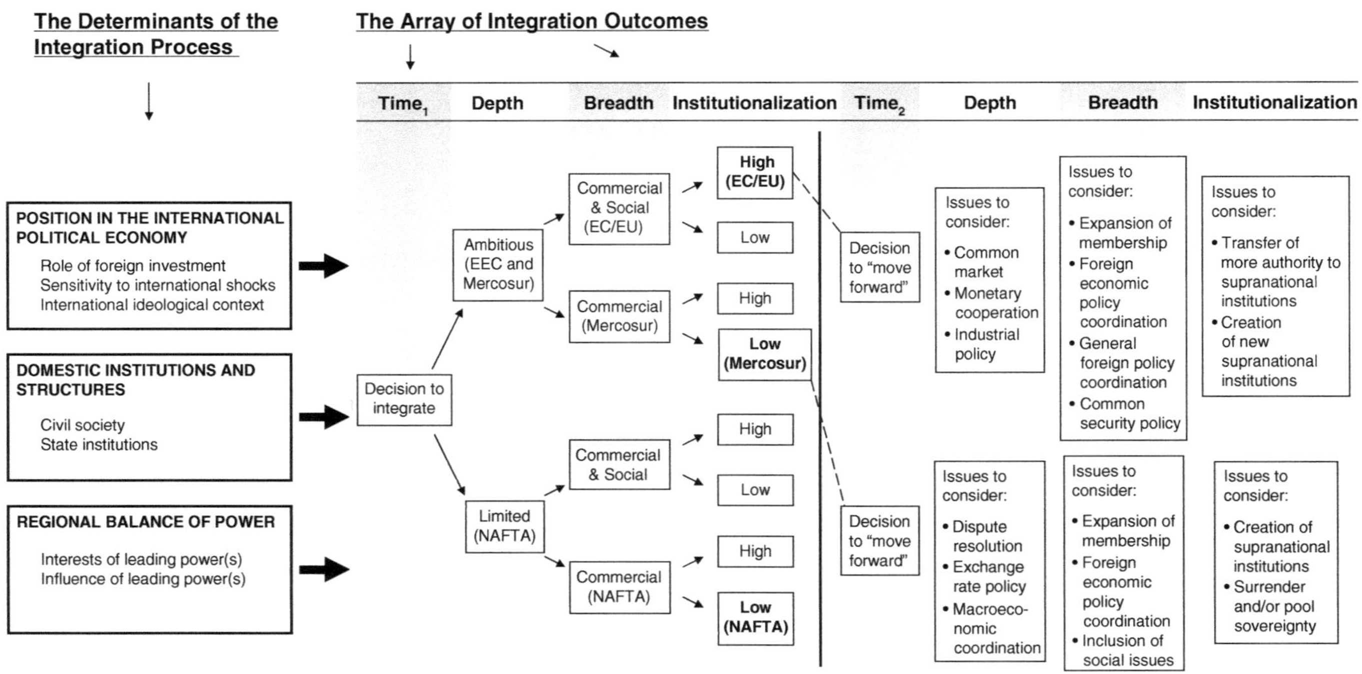

Figure 1.1 A model of the regional integration process

Source: Author.

When I discuss *depth*, I refer to the overall goals of a particular regional integration agreement. In order of increasing depth, these would be 1) a free trade area (which provides for free exchange of goods and services between parties to the agreement); 2) a customs union (which includes the former but also has a common external tariff on goods coming from outside the parties to the agreement); 3) a common market (which has a customs union and also the free flow of factors of production, including labor); 4) an economic union (which, in addition to a common market has harmonization of economic policies among member countries); and 5) complete economic integration (which has complete unification of all economic policies) (Nye 1971a: 27–30; Balassa 1967).

Clearly, different economic integration schemes have different goals from the outset. Some, such as the North American Free Trade Area (NAFTA), as it name indicates, is only interested in the first level of economic integration, and the unrealized Free Trade Area of the Americas (FTAA) had similar goals. On the other hand, the European Community/Union and Mercosur were much more ambitious; Mercosur's name—*Common Market* of the South—reflects this ambition. That said, the ambition of any integration effort does not necessarily match up to reality, as numerous failed attempts at integration indicate. In addition, leaders who sign such accords may be deliberately vague on what they intend and hope to accomplish, either because they disagree among themselves or because their constituencies in their home countries are divided on what integration should accomplish. Nevertheless, this depth dimension is important, as it is important to gauge the intentions (or the range of intentions) of countries that agree to pursue integration.

The *breadth* dimension is related to the depth dimension. By breadth, I do not mean the geographic scope of integration—a frequent use of the term—but rather the scope of policy areas that are subject to negotiation among integration partners. Most commonly, there is a distinction between strictly commercial negotiations and those that concentrate—in addition to commercial matters—on social issues such as labor, environmental standards, or broader economic cooperation. NAFTA, for example, brought in environmental and labor standards, though only in a weak and subsidiary way. The EU, in contrast, has found itself regulating such issues as a matter of course. And it is here that Mercosur begins to diverge significantly from the EU; nothing beyond commercial integration has ever been on the table. It has not been completely ignored in the politics of integration, as will become clear later, but these issues have never been incorporated into formal agreements among the Mercosur member states. In addition, while the EU nations regularly consult with one another on matters of macroeconomic coordination, and most have adopted a common currency, the economic turbulence of South America of the last two decades made this all but impossible in Mercosur.

Finally, the *institutionalization* dimension concerns the degree to which the integration process brings with it the creation of new entities to regulate the integration process. In this dimension I include the creation of supranational institutions that will a) have an interest in seeing the integration process move forward; b) have some power to influence the direction of integration; and c) take on some functions previously performed by sovereign national governments. It is in this dimension that we observe the degree to which sovereignty among integrating nations is pooled and/or given up. To qualify as "high" on the institutionalization dimension, it is not enough to have formed a transnational bureaucracy or to have assigned some national government bureaucrats the task of managing integration; institutions must have substantial power to affect the integration process or be able to speak for the nations making up the organization collectively. Here, again, the EU differs sharply from Mercosur. The former has seen the gradual growth—from the beginning of the integration process—of supranational institutions with influence; Mercosur, in contrast, has had no such institutions.

In analyzing integration, I am not concerned just with the initial choices made by policy makers, or just with their subsequent choices; I am also concerned with how initial and subsequent decisions affect political processes and how political practices change with integration. I attempt to incorporate both of these concerns in the third section (on the right) of Figure 1.1. In this section of the figure, instead of incorporating a decision tree, I present the context of the two alternatives to integration that I have identified. Above, the experience of the EU is represented. Decisions made earlier—to be broad in its integration focus and to institutionalize this integration with supranational institutions—led to a particular set of issues when it comes to "moving forward" in the integration process. When it comes to depth, the new issues included industrial policy and monetary policy, in effect moving toward economic union. Until economic integration advanced substantially, such issues were considered the province of national governments, and integration changed this. On the other hand, Mercosur, with its much less well-institutionalized and narrower integration focus, found itself concentrating on issues that were handled in the early stages of European integration.

When it comes to breadth, at subsequent stages there is a bit more commonality, as any ambitious economic integration project will probably confront two important issues: whether to expand to additional countries and how to coordinate foreign economic policy. Indeed, both the EU and Mercosur confronted these matters. Other matters of breadth, however, differ, since a more institutionalized and broader integration process will already have confronted them; here, most importantly, is the question of whether or not to include social issues on the agenda of integration, still in very early stages in Mercosur. The EU, by contrast, has matters such as security cooperation and common defense policy on the table. In Mercosur, they are not.

Finally, when it comes to the institutionalization dimension, the difference between the two integration patterns is especially stark: since the EU has already developed—and had developed from the beginning—supranational institutions, the question there is how far to take this process of supranationalization and to what extent the member nations will tolerate this process (Banchoff and Smith 1999). In Mercosur, which avoided any semblance of supranational institutions with authority from the beginning, the issue is very different and more vexing. Having succeeded, to a reasonable degree, with integration *without* such institutions, it is difficult to come to terms with the possibility of having them, given the costs for individual governments to giving such institutions greater authority.

On the left side of Figure 1.1, "The determinants of the integration process," I focus on the variables that I identify as most important in influencing the path of integration chosen. Here, specifically, I focus on three independent variables. First, I focus on the position of the region in the international political economy. This encompasses three broad elements: a region's dependence on foreign investment in key sectors of the economy, the region's sensitivity to international shocks, and the international ideological context, which is transmitted through the advice of international financial institutions and its contacts with foreign countries and companies. Generally speaking, the more a region's fortunes are influenced by happenings outside the bloc's borders, the greater the likelihood of the regional integration scheme standing on shaky ground.

The second independent variable in this framework concerns the strength of domestic institutions in countries that are undergoing a process of regional integration. Here the focus is on the strength of state institutions and those in civil society. The general argument here is that stronger institutions in both arenas will lead to a more robust integration project. Conversely, weaker institutions will make it more difficult to come to agreements (since states will not necessarily be able to follow through on commitments that are made at the negotiating table), and will make them less sustainable in the long run, if groups in civil society are unable to provide a strong base of support for integration as it unfolds.

The final independent variable focuses in particular on the relative weight of the principle partners in an integration project. Here, the focus is twofold. First, we need to understand the specific interests of the key governments in any integration scheme, and specifically focus on their preferences when it comes to the depth, breadth, and institutionalization dimensions discussed earlier. We cannot necessarily read directly from those preferences to final outcomes, particularly since preferences may change during the negotiation process, and governments themselves are likely to be divided when it comes to those preferences. But we can get a fairly good understanding for how integration will proceed by considering these preferences. The second major dimension here concerns the relative weight of the major partners in an integration project. To the extent that there are partners with relatively equal economic weight, the greater the likelihood that there will be an integration that requires some devolution of sovereignty to supranational institutions. Conversely, the greater the weight of a single player in an integration scheme, the greater the likelihood that integration will not advance very far along the dimension of institutionalization.

It will help, at this point, to flesh out this more abstract discussion with some specific focus on the Mercosur process, with an eye toward constructing an argument about the inherent vulnerability of Mercosur as a regional bloc. To begin with the international context, there are three principal ways in which the international environment has increased the vulnerability and development of Mercosur. Developing countries continue to depend heavily on foreign investment in the most dynamic sectors of their economies. This is not to say that more developed countries do not depend on this sort of investment; of course they do. But the difference is qualitative. Attracting foreign investment from outside Europe has never been a driving motivation behind European integration. In Mercosur it has been, and the foreign firms that have invested in the Mercosur countries have become major players in the process. In Mercosur, integration has been part and parcel of an effort to avoid being marginalized in the international political economy. Leaders have made this point repeatedly, and policies have followed this search for outside capital. Indeed, some of the most important conflicts that have emerged in the Mercosur integration process have been over the distribution of foreign investment in the region. For example, one of the most contentious conflicts in Mercosur integration in the 1990s was policy in the automobile sector, as Brazil and Argentina competed over who would get more of the investment in the sector. Needless to say, there are no Brazilian or Argentine auto firms; all of this investment comes from outside the region.

The particular importance of international capital has a significant influence on the direction of integration: MNC firms are quite interested in integration, because it allows them to rationalize their productive facilities. And they are, by and large, only interested in commercial integration; they are quite loath to see social policy or worker rights part of any integration process. In other words, they are an important actor in the Mercosur integration process, and they want commercial integration.

The second way in which the international context affects Mercosur is the sensitivity of developing countries to things that happen in the international political economy, which makes them particularly vulnerable to economic developments beyond their borders. All countries are vulnerable in this "globalized" age—as the world financial meltdown of 2008–2009 made clear—but the effects are often (though not always) felt more profoundly in developing countries. For example, the 1994 devaluation in Mexico—through its myriad political and economic effects—profoundly affected the Mercosur process and Latin America in general. The Asian financial crisis had effects around the world, but they were arguably more acute in developing countries, which saw their currencies under attack as a response to what happened in Asia. This latter crisis also had profound effects on the Mercosur process. When the Asian flu reached Brazil in late 1998 and early 1999, and Brazil was forced to devalue its currency by some 40 percent, this had an enormous impact on the competitiveness of Argentine exports to Brazil, which suddenly got much more expensive. Indeed, this devaluation of the Brazilian *real* had repercussions for years to come, and when Argentina itself got deeper into crisis in 2001 and 2002, Mercosur took an enormous hit.

To draw a more specific linkage between this sensitivity and the institutionalization of integration, we can point to one of the direct causes of a lack of supranational institutions in Mercosur. To some degree, the lack of supranational institutions is meant, quite self-consciously, to increase the flexibility in the process by *not* tying the hands of the integration partners, since they know unexpected shocks may present themselves; the only thing that they tied themselves into—in the Treaty of Asunción—was the automatic reduction of tariffs within the block. This reinforces a point that this analysis will make repeatedly: integration in Mercosur remains, and will most likely remain, only on the commercial level and will not attempt to address other issues, which might require more authority for supranational institutions.

The third element in the international context—ideas that are embedded in both multilateral and national institutions—rounds out an understanding of how international factors influence integration projects. In this sense, timing matters when it comes to the prospects for regional integration. European integration occurred at a point in time when the world was not so "globalized," and even though that process also faced serious vulnerabilities at early stages of integration, the European countries had more instruments at their disposal when it came to fending off threats to their integration project. In the early stages of European integration, the member countries still had many policy instruments available that allowed them to shield their economies from international shocks, such as effective capital controls and much greater protectionism. Such instruments are not available in the post-Cold War international political economy, where a liberal international ideology reigns supreme and old-style protectionism is illegitimate. Furthermore, European integration occurred at a time when the welfare state was still legitimate; though it is still legitimate there, it is also under attack, and in any case, Mercosur countries have for the most part embraced the neoliberal model of political economy, which has the impact of further limiting the willingness of their governments to negotiate social policy as part of their integration effort.

The second cluster of determinants of regional integration projects is domestic institutions and structures. Civil society is relatively underdeveloped in the Mercosur countries, which has two consequences. On the one hand, it is rather difficult for governments attempting to push integration forward to mobilize key actors in civil society on behalf of integration. Second, it means that there is relatively little participation of civil society in the integration process, which means that when integration is threatened (as it has been on numerous occasions in Mercosur), the constituency that is willing to fight hard politically in favor of integration is limited, thus increasing the probability that integration can be derailed.

To the extent that civil society is organized in the Mercosur nations, it is by far most organized in the business sector. Labor is particularly weak, and even when governments that supposedly had labor support were elected—such as Carlos Menem in Argentina—nearly all of their policies have been business-friendly and labor-hostile. Business does participate in the integration negotiations; labor never does, nor does it really have a place at the table, and leaders do not pay a political cost for not giving them a place at the table.

In addition to civil society institutions, state institutions are generally weak in the Mercosur countries. I do not mean to imply that all sectors of the state are feeble—and I will point out where there are strong state institutions later—but overall, state capacity is limited in the Mercosur countries. The literature outlining this particular facet of Latin American politics is extensive, and generally the arguments provided in these analyses focus on the implications of this lack of institutionalization for domestic politics. But this lack of institutionalization has important implications for regional integration. After all, if the available institutions are unable to handle domestic political pressures, they would be even less able to respond to pressures from the international political economy and regional integration. As a consequence, one of the defining aspects of Mercosur has been its extraordinary reliance on presidential diplomacy at almost every stage of the process, and its consistently underdeveloped supranational institutional infrastructure. After all, what model from domestic politics would policy makers rely on for supranational institutions, if many of those institutions are themselves weak?

Finally, my third set of determinants focuses on the overwhelming weight of Brazil in the Mercosur process. It is fair to say that in the case of European integration, at the beginning in particular, the major players were Germany and France, and they were relatively balanced. This is not the case in Mercosur, where Brazil accounts for around 80 percent of the gross domestic product (GDP) in the region, and its influence is outsized when compared to Argentina, the other major power in Mercosur. This means, for purposes of understanding the integration process, that the much more powerful nation is going to be extremely unlikely to allow its freedom to act constrained. As a consequence, the creation of supranational institutions is unlikely.

In making this observation, it is essential to understand the particular interests of Brazil. Integration would not have happened if the Brazilians did not want it to happen. And they wanted it to happen, in particular, because they want to be the leader of South America, and they want to be the leader of the bloc that is the counterweight to the US in the hemisphere. But it is not interested in being put in a constraining set of institutions or policy dictates, which goes a long way toward explaining why there is no discussion of supranational institutions coming from them, and very little discussion of social policy in the bloc.

To draw some of these different arguments together and to summarize the overall argument I make before continuing with a more detailed analysis of the relevant theoretical literature: Mercosur embarked on its integration project with a number of disadvantages, including weak political institutions, underdeveloped and clientelistic relationships between state and civil society actors, and heavy dependence on foreign capital for investment and the financing of current account deficits. As a consequence, Mercosur limited itself to commercial liberalization, and the member countries were unwilling to give up or pool sovereignty to supranational institutions. Because of this, Mercosur was frequently threatened by international economic shocks and the possibility that political leaders in the integrating countries would renege on their commitments to integrate. Any efforts to "deepen" the integration process to encompass other issues, such as labor codes or consumer regulations, were usually frustrated.

Before moving on to a more direct confrontation between the European literature on integration and the Mercosur case, it is necessary to consider a potential objection to the preceding analysis: Is Mercosur simply less developed as an economic and political bloc because it has had much less time to develop than the EU? After all, the EU has confronted many problems over the course of its history, and its agreement on the Single European Act (SEA) and the Maastricht Treaty was hardly predictable to analysts in the 1970s. The answer here is that it is not simply a question of *time*; Mercosur is different in *type*. For a variety of reasons, Mercosur could never have been like the EU. A short digression to discuss the European experience with integration will make this clear.

Explaining European integration

The literature explaining European integration is extensive. The classic works on the phenomenon date from the late 1950s and early 1960s, when it was becoming clear that a new political process was taking root and expanding; it was indeed a brand new phenomenon in the modern world (Haas 1958; Lindberg 1963; Haas 1964; Lindberg and Scheingold 1971). Different from earlier nineteenth-century projects of national unification, the launching of the European Coal and Steel Community in 1951, followed by the formation of the European Economic Community in 1957, involved the creation of what Karl Deutsch referred to as a "pluralistic security community" that created new supranational institutions (1954). Coming after the devastation of World War II, the new organizations were meant in many ways to create a new community that would not go to war again. Joining traditional rivals France and Germany in particular was meant to accomplish this goal.[1]

Initially, the literature on integration was filled with optimism. After all, the process seemed to be going forward with remarkable speed, and it accompanied the swift economic recovery of war-devastated economies in the 1950s. European economies grew rapidly during the 1950s, which certainly contributed to this optimism and dynamic integration. It is relatively easy to engage in integration when economies are growing rapidly, since with rapid growth, there are simply fewer losers in the process.

But integration encountered many problems and stumbling blocks. France, in particular, put the brakes on the process in the 1960s when, under the leadership of Charles DeGaulle, it slowed the process considerably and was unwilling to give up authority to supranational institutions. Economic stagnation after the first oil shock in 1973 also contributed to the slowdown in integration, and this slowdown continued until the mid-1980s, when there was a burst in activity toward greater union and cooperation, culminating in the Single European Act in 1986 and the Maastricht Treaty in 1992 (Keohane and Hoffmann 1991; Moravcsik 1998a; Cameron 1992; McAllister 1997).

Now, more than 50 years of economic integration in Europe has produced an economic union that is unprecedented and impressive, and European monetary union is a culminating event in this process. But it took a long time to get there. The process had many ups and downs, which is of course natural in any process of integration, given the costs associated with it and the vicissitudes of the international economy and domestic responses to them.

The ups and downs of the integration process were accompanied by ups and downs in the attention paid to integration by political scientists (Caporaso and Keeler 1995). The theoretical thrust of this attention also varied, depending on whether integration was experiencing expansion or stagnation. Generally speaking, the literature on European integration has been divided between the proponents of neofunctionalism and those who fell into the intergovernmentalist camp. The neofunctionalists generally could be considered the optimists on integration, those who thought that the integration process was being overtaken by a transnational dynamic that was pushing integration forward in spite of the interests of states. The key concept in this regard was "spillover," whereby integration in one area led to integration in another. As Haas described the process,

> From the initially merged sectors, a demonstrable process of expanding group expectations among industrialists, dealers, and trade unions emerges. A spill-over into as yet unintegrated economic areas and a concern over political techniques appropriate for the control of new and larger problems is manifest. And in the process of reformulating expectations and demands, the interest groups in question approach one another supranationally while their erstwhile ties with national friends undergo deterioration. At the level of political parties a similar process takes place . . . Finally, the spill-over process asserts itself in the relations among civil servants, national government offices, central banks and technical advisors.
>
> (1958: 313)

In other words, integration unleashed a brand new dynamic, which was increasingly beyond the control of states.

Intergovernmentalists, on the other hand, argued that the European integration process, new as it might be, still hewed to old patterns of international politics (Hoffmann 1966; Hoffmann 1982; Keohane and Hoffmann 1991; Moravcsik 1991). According to this interpretation, states still have the primary role in the international political economy, and generally, integration successes and failures can be explained by the preferences and power of states in this process. Especially recently, this interpretation also placed substantial emphasis on the domestic politics associated with integration, noting how domestic forces might hold back or push the integration process forward. This approach sees relatively little influence for transnational bureaucrats who want to see integration advance. At any rate, when integration was stagnating, from the 1970s through the early 1980s, these debates were largely exhausted, with little that was new or exciting to analyze (Haas 1975).

When European integration moved forward in the mid-1980s and early 1990s, political scientists once again turned their attention to the European integration process. According to Caporaso and Keeler, "To a striking extent . . . the new debates parallel the old" (1995: 43). That said, attempts have been made to overcome old (and sometimes false) divisions between the two camps. Analysts recognized that theoretical fashion tends to follow success or failure in the integration process. In the end, however, as Keohane and Hoffmann point out,

> It is worth noting that imperfect scholarly memories have stereotyped the debate of the late 1960s between neofunctionalists and statists . . . Haas never believed that spillover was automatic. Nor did the critics see a resurgence of

> integration as impossible. Hoffmann argued in 1966 that "one can conceive of a set of circumstances in which a speedy forward march could succeed." The question is not so much "Will European integration succeed?" as "Under what conditions can integration progress?"
>
> (1991: 39)

And we should recognize that there is an inherent tension in any integration process between the interests of states, supranational bureaucrats, and non-state actors who want to see integration progress or slow down. At different points in time, different forces will be preeminent, and some actors will change their preferences (and political action) in response to changes that occur in the international political economy, the domestic political economy, or in the integration process itself. The challenge for any analysis of integration is to weave all of these elements together to both explain a specific case and arrive at general propositions about integration processes.

I do not attempt to come to any conclusions about European integration here. Instead, I provide evidence of an *alternative* model of integration, based on Mercosur. To the extent that integration theory relies on an analysis of the EU, generalizations are limited, since the EU cannot be presumed to be a model for all integration processes. One of the problems for any analysis has been that most other attempts at integration have ended in failure. To some degree, NAFTA is an exception, but it is quite a different animal from the EU. Mercosur, on the other hand, has ambitions similar to the EU: a customs union, to be followed by a true common market, as noted earlier.

In the end, how does the Mercosur case help in our understanding of integration processes generally? At first glance, it would seem that the debates between neofunctionalists and intergovernmentalists would have little relevance. After all, there are few important transnational bureaucrats in the Mercosur integration process; Mercosur nations have made a conscious effort, to this point, to avoid supranational institutions such as the European Commission. Indeed, the process has been not only intergovernmental, but particularly *presidential*, depending, to an extraordinary degree on the preferences and commitments of presidents to the process.

That said, spillover—as noted earlier, perhaps the key conceptual contribution of the neofunctionalists—can operate without supranational institutions quite easily. I follow Joseph Nye's understanding of how spillover might work, where "imbalances created by the functional interdependence or inherent linkages of tasks can press political actors to redefine their common tasks." As Nye notes, "The redefinition of tasks need not mean an upgrading of common tasks. The response can also be negative" (1971b: 200, 201). Indeed, Latin America has experienced quite negative outcomes when it comes to spillover, as the subsequent analysis will show.

The dynamics of integration

Clearly, not all issues that were relevant in the European integration process have been relevant in the Mercosur case. For example, instead of Cold War dynamics being at the forefront, with Mercosur the nations dealt with post-Cold War dynamics. In addition, whereas European integration got its start at a point when tariffs throughout the world were relatively high—even though trade was increasing rapidly—Mercosur faced an international economic environment that was much more open and developing countries were under strong pressures to liberalize their economies generally. Furthermore, agricultural policy was much less important in Mercosur than it was in Europe.[2] And, finally, even though Europe was still recovering economically from a devastating war when its integration process began, it was at the center of the world economy. Mercosur was not.

Integration, however, involves processes that are more abstract as well, and this section focuses on them, since they were relevant both to Europe and the Mercosur countries. I first consider incentives and disincentives to countries contemplating or experiencing integration. The next section looks at the international context, which is always relevant to nations experiencing integration. The third area that I discuss is the role of civil society in the integration process. Finally, I focus on institutions—both national and supranational—that influence the pace and direction of integration.

Why integrate? Incentives in the integration process

Perhaps the core question confronting any government contemplating integration is this: Why should it give up sovereignty over its economic policy voluntarily?

Before the end of World War II, sovereignty was more or less a sacred concept in international relations, at least for powerful nations in the international political arena. The stronger nations in the international political economy did not tolerate many intrusions on their sovereignty, and sovereignty was one of the key ordering principles in international relations. Of course, weaker nations (and Latin America is emblematic of this phenomenon) did not enjoy as many of the perquisites of sovereignty, as they were subject to pressure from outside political and economic forces that often undermined this sovereignty. In more extreme instances, Latin American nations would see their sovereignty compromised by direct political and military intervention in their affairs, by the United States in particular (Smith 2008). Nevertheless, at least rhetorically, the concept was held as sacred and essential.

In part because of the experience of the Great Depression and World War II, however, sovereignty has been reduced in the post-war period. World War II saw savagery and war crimes beyond anyone's imagination, which led to new principles in the international community that would allow for intervention in the internal affairs of sovereign nations under some extreme circumstances. The United Nations Charter, in Articles 41 and 42, allowed such intervention. Though intervention has seldom occurred, it did introduce a new element in international law that made the concept of sovereignty less sacred than before.

At any rate, violations of the sovereignty principle to intervene in international conflicts or to protect against human rights violations would almost always be involuntary—the country that saw its sovereignty violated would not be welcoming international intervention. In contrast, with economic integration, giving up sovereignty was voluntary. The post-war period witnessed an expansion of cooperative arrangements in the international political economy because of the experience of the interwar period. This interwar period was one of enormous economic dislocation, in part brought on by a lack of international economic cooperation among the main powers (Kindleberger 1986; Gilpin 1987). The leaders who designed the institutions governing the international political economy at Bretton Woods hoped that with the creation of new institutions, the economic chaos of the interwar period, and its unfortunate political implications, could be avoided. The World Bank, the International Monetary Fund (IMF), and the (proposed) International Trade Organization (later General Agreement on Tariffs and Trade [GATT], then later the World Trade Organization) were meant to provide stability in a rocky international environment, committing the member states to certain rules of the game in a post-war international economic order (Gilpin 1987; Spero and Hart 2009).

In particular, the IMF and the GATT were meant to impose binding constraints on nations that agreed to submit to their rules. If a nation was experiencing balance-of-payments problems, it would receive help from the IMF, but only on the condition that it carried out certain reforms. And the GATT imposed reductions in tariff rates (and later non-tariff barriers), obliging countries to change their trade policies more or less permanently, with the understanding that other nations would do the same, and thus it placed restrictions on national economic policies. These arrangements are not iron clad—nations often violate their promises to the IMF, and many countries have gotten around GATT rules through mechanisms such as voluntary export restraints negotiated bilaterally (Kahler 1992; Yoffie 1983). Generally speaking, however, these international institutions have provided a check on purely self-interested behavior in the international political economy (Keohane 1984).

An economic integration process takes this forfeiture of sovereignty several steps further. By signing the Treaty of Rome in 1957, the European nations were agreeing that they would no longer be able to increase tariffs placed on their partners and would instead be required to reduce them. As integration proceeded further, this forfeiture of policy instruments expanded to monetary policy and regulatory policy, which was quite contentious. After all, the agreement to establish a common currency in the EU was hardly a cakewalk, and many political forces in the European nations fought hard against it (Smith 1999; Moravcsik 1998b).

Why did nations in Europe agree to give up sovereignty? Obviously, leaders saw advantages to integration, which I discuss later. That said, they would have been unwilling to do so unless their neighbors did. Consequently, one of the most important elements in any process of integration is the need to tie the hands of one's partners as well as one's own. Even if countries viewed integration as beneficial, they would not have agreed to integrate unless their surrender of sovereignty was associated with a similar surrender by their partners (Wooley 1992). As a consequence, the Europeans developed rules to guarantee that their partners would not renege on their commitments.

Assuming an ability to tie ones neighbors to the set of liberalization measures associated with economic integration, it is still necessary to understand why this would occur. In the most basic sense, some, such as Moravcsik, argue that economic integration moves forward because nations think that an integration process will benefit them economically. Not all firms or workers will be winners in an integration process; by its very nature, economic integration produces losers. Economists generally extol the virtues of free trade, but they do recognize that there are losers in those sectors that are less internationally competitive.[3] As a consequence, most integration efforts die on the drawing board, victims of anticipated or actual political resistance to freer trade.[4] When they are successful, most of the negotiations in any economic integration process focus on the distribution of gains and losses. The gains and losses cannot be known precisely beforehand; economic integration, like most public policy, has its share of unexpected consequences. What matters here is the *perception* of the potential gains and losses for the key players, particularly in the business sector. If many of them think integration will benefit them, they will support it and attempt to make it a reality. And if many of them think they will lose, integration is much less likely.

Economically, some degree of complementarity is essential for integration to occur. In Europe after World War II, this complementarity existed, which certainly had the effect of pushing integration forward. Over time, as Europe internalized the integration process, the benefits became obvious. Once trade was fully liberalized and the customs union complete in the late 1960s, the political tasks became more difficult, as Europe confronted whether to move toward a true common market and monetary union. Theoretically, these further advances in integration were seen as quite beneficial, but the length of time before they were accomplished (more than two decades after the customs union was complete) speaks to the difficulty of agreeing to them.[5]

The international context

Economic factors alone do not make an integration process go forward. If they did, then neoclassical economists would have their paradise of a free-trading world. But as these economists often note with disdain, "politics gets in the way." And, of course, politics will never go away.[6] To understand when and why economic integration goes forward, a study of its contextual political factors is crucial.

Even if policy makers judge economic integration as beneficial, and a majority of firms within potential integration partners think that integration would be a good idea, international conditions can prevent it. Sworn enemies are not likely to integrate economically, even if the economic benefits of such a process are obvious. International conditions can also push an integration process forward, and since they are often cited in the European case as a strong motivating force for integration, their positive effects are the focus here.

Two of the most common assertions associated with European integration are that it was embarked on 1) to avoid another war between France and Germany and 2) to strengthen the Western alliance in the post-war period. The arguments are based on a simple logic: leaders in Europe in the post-war period, and particularly those in France and Germany, saw advantages to tying their economies together, to create an interdependence that would make future war difficult. If integration were to succeed, more interests in France and Germany would see their fates intertwined positively, thus making their political leaderships less likely to engage in hostile actions with their neighbors. Visionary leadership saw integration as a way to preserve peace.

This impulse to integrate for peace was reinforced by the nature of global competition during the Cold War. The United States in particular was interested in seeing Europe strengthened in the post-war period, which led to the Marshall Plan and the creation of the North Atlantic Treaty Organization (NATO). The United States saw benefits to an economically stronger Europe, which would be able to resist threats from domestic Communist Parties in Western Europe, solidifying liberal democracy in the Western alliance.[7]

These "international context" arguments are largely geopolitical. There is another factor that is sometimes viewed as even more important: the international *economic* context. During the early years of European integration, most analysts ignored this international economic context, preferring instead to focus on the domestic politics associated with integration, or at most on the international economic relations among those nations making up the economic grouping. As countries grew more economically interdependent in the 1950s and 1960s—a consequence of the increase in international trade sponsored by GATT, as well as increasing investment by (particularly United States) multinational corporations—political scientists turned their attention toward this international economic context (Gilpin 1987; Keohane and Nye 1972; Keohane and Nye 1977). At times, indeed, they accorded it a great deal of explanatory power in their theories that purported to explain changes in economic policy.[8]

While the international economic context was frequently invoked in studies of developing countries, this was less frequently the case with the EU. It was most commonly used to explain the revival of momentum in the integration process in the 1980s. During the 1980s, there was a large-scale shift in the international ideological climate in favor of market-oriented solutions to the economic problems facing countries in both the developed and developing world (Biersteker 1995). In the European case, this was most obvious in the transformation of French economic policy after the failure of its "Keynesianism in one country" policy after the Socialist Party victory in the 1981 elections. Once France failed miserably in this experiment—a failure usually attributed to the international economic context—and got with the neoliberal program, accelerated integration became much more feasible. But, as Keohane and Hoffmann argue, "events in the world political economy were important influences on the governmental decisions associated with the Community's revival . . . [but are] not sufficient to explain the sudden strengthening of European institutions during the 1980s" (1991: 22). As they argue, if international conditions were primary, they probably would have acted at a much earlier stage to change the dynamics of EU in a more positive direction, but they did not. So the international economic context is really only one possible conditioning element in the process of integration.

This interpretation is probably not far off the mark, particularly for an area at the core of the international political economy. What will become apparent in analyzing Mercosur is that the international context is far weightier in developing countries, and cannot be considered merely "contextual" or "conditioning." What might be a blip on the screen for more diversified economies at the heart of the international system can become a tidal wave for developing countries. They are much more dependent on inflows of foreign investment to grow, and if anything happens to limit those inflows—say, a currency crisis in Mexico that suddenly makes investors much more wary about investing in almost all countries in Latin America—integration becomes more tenuous.

Civil society in the integration process

Economic incentives to integrate always exist, though they are usually not enough to move a process forward. The international context is always a background, and sometimes a foreground, condition that integrating nations must consider. But integration simply will not occur if civil society—and in particular business—is not willing to go along with the integration effort. Civil society makes up the "facts on the ground" that make integration real.

At the same time, the role of civil society is much more ambiguous and conflicted, in large part because there will always be parts of civil society that favor integration, and other parts that do not. In any given country contemplating integration, political leaders will face competing pressures. At times the decision to move forward is relatively easy, if a large portion of civil society is behind the effort. In many cases, however, there will be no clear message from civil society, and it is at this time that national or supranational leadership can play a particularly important role in advancing regional integration.

This leadership must take civil society into account, obviously, since leaders will not be acting in a vacuum. Thus, it is necessary to understand the preferences of key groups in civil society. Here, I will focus on business and labor. Although there are many other organizations in civil society that will express positions on integration, and sometimes act politically on those positions, for purposes of integration in Mercosur, at least, business (in particular) and labor (to a lesser degree) have been the main actors. As noted earlier, agriculture played a much larger role in European integration than it does in Mercosur, and many other interest groups have been involved in the European integration process from a very early stage.[9] This has not been the case, however, in Mercosur.

It is also important to note that when an integration process begins, civil society support for the process is not necessarily easy to find. As a consequence, at the early stages of integration, it is much more likely that national and supranational leadership will be key. After all, because of the uncertainties associated with integration, and because no one has actually benefited from it yet, there are only *potential* allies in an integration process. Many will be reticent about integration because they do not know what its consequences will be; as always, change is difficult to engineer. Some will be able to imagine a different future, but more will probably be concerned with the potential negative consequences of a new economic arrangement.

Early on, then, states and/or supranational authorities are crucial in the process. Even so, leaders will tend to take a fair measure of how their nations, and presumably civil societies, would benefit or lose when it comes to integration. After all, these leaders will not sell their countries down the river in an integration process; they will have a fairly good idea of what integration would do to their economies. Again, as noted earlier, these leaders will not act in a vacuum when it comes to pursuing integration. And since they have a fairly good idea of who would benefit and lose from integration, these leaders most likely know who their potential constituency would be. As time goes on in the integration process, the constituencies in favor of accelerated integration do indeed emerge. Businesses that are able to take advantage of the integration process emerge as champions of the process itself; some argue that in European integration, business was crucial in pushing the SEA project forward (Cameron 1992). In the end, as subsequent chapters demonstrate, civil society is crucial in any integration project, even when international factors are weighty, as in Mercosur.

Institutions in the integration process

Integration relies on a wide array of institutions to progress. Institutions regulate the speed of integration. They regulate how leaders and bureaucrats of different nations negotiate with one another. They determine if and how disputes are settled among integrating partners. They regulate who can participate in integration processes. Simply put, institutions are fundamental. To keep things simple, here I divide these institutions into those that are national and those that are supranational. It is important to keep in mind, from the outset, that many more of these institutions are involved in the integration process in Europe than in Mercosur.

The crucial national institutions include cabinet ministries, political parties, national courts, national parliaments, and national bureaucracies. The most crucial cabinet ministries tend to be those involved with foreign affairs or economic matters, though as integration deepens, other ministries—such as defense or interior ministries—may become involved, in effect confirming spillover expectations. This process is not automatic or inevitable, but has occurred in Europe. In addition, in the European case, this participation of a wide variety of cabinet ministers in the integration process has been institutionalized through the Council of Ministers, which must approve all decisions made by the European Commission (George 1996: Chapter 1). Through this mechanism, national institutions are an integral part of the European integration process.

National bureaucracies also are charged with implementing decisions on integration reached by the political leadership. Political parties take positions on integration and attempt to put them into practice if they are elected through national parliaments. Courts rule on the application of region-wide regulations. In all cases, the strength and efficiency of these institutions will have an important impact on the course of integration.

Whereas national institutions, whether developed or underdeveloped, must always be taken into account when analyzing integration, supranational institutions may or may not exist. In the EU the European Commission was created with the Treaty of Rome. Although it has not had an independent authority to enact important new measures (since they must be approved by the Council of Ministers, which acts on the basis of national preferences), the Commission has at times been quite proactive in pushing integration forward.[10] For my purposes, whether or not it has been decisive in major decisions about European integration is not important. Clearly, the Commission matters, and just as clearly, there is no parallel institution in Mercosur.

In addition to a supranational bureaucracy that might propose new initiatives or administer the integration process, another important supranational player is a supranational court system. Such a system can have the authority to resolve disputes between the partners in an integration process and determine the status of community-wide regulations, as well as the relationship between national and community-wide law. In the European case, the European Court of Justice has played an important role in establishing the legitimacy and authority of Community law (Shapiro 1992).

A final supranational institution that may be relevant in an integration process is a supranational parliament. Such a parliament can help to redress the problem of a "democratic deficit" in the integration process, when an increasing number of decisions are taken outside the authority of national governments (Neunreither 1994; Smith 1996). This supranational parliament has achieved some greater authority over time in the EU, though the transfer of sovereignty to this institution has been quite slow.

The Mercosur case: vulnerable integration

Mercosur integration has been different, and different enough, that I identify it as a separate category of integration, what I have called vulnerable integration. If other parts of the developing world were to engage in serious integration efforts, they would likely face many of the same pressures and dynamics associated with Mercosur. In effect, Mercosur can be seen as a prototype for developing or emerging country integration. Most developing countries are in a relatively exposed position when it comes to foreign investment, and most of them have underdeveloped political institutions.

There is, I argue, an interaction between international factors and domestic factors that leads to the particular model of integration that I have identified for Mercosur. On the international level, it is not necessary here to rehearse the old debates about "dependency" and "interdependence" (Gunder Frank 1967; Cardoso and Faletto 1979; Evans 1979; Caporaso 1980; Baldwin 1980; Packenham 1992; Keohane and Nye 1977; Katzenstein 1975; Rosecrance and Stein 1973).[11] Those debates were often politically charged, and the political charge did not necessarily lead to greater understanding. No one would deny, in the fields of international relations or comparative politics that a country's structural position in the world economy has a substantial effect on its policies and possibilities. The degree to which a country's position affects its development possibilities is more open to debate.[12]

Some might point out that the largest impediment to a successful development strategy lies with the policy makers in individual countries (Wade 1990; Edwards 1995). Others might argue that the international political economy is more often constraining and leaves developing or emerging countries at the mercy of decisions taken elsewhere (Stallings 1992). The approach adopted here is more along the lines of that used by many political scientists and sociologists who view development and economic policy as a function of the constraints and opportunities presented by both the international environment and domestic institutions and economic structure.[13] At some points in time, the opportunities will be greater, while at others the constraints will be extraordinarily confining. The way these opportunities or constraints will present themselves is determined by a variety of factors, including changes in the international system, domestic political alignments and institutions, available ideologies, and the quality and direction of political leadership.

When it comes to supranational institutions, as noted earlier, Mercosur does not have any to speak of. This is not accidental. It is both a response to the vulnerability of integration and contributes to its vulnerability. It is a consequence of the vulnerability in that the Mercosur countries realized that tying their hands too much—given their position in the world economy—could very well lead to problems. They were worried that a lack of flexibility would make it difficult to progress in the integration project. And it would have.

Of course, this flexibility has its downside. It means that the entire integration process is much less predictable and therefore vulnerable. As noted earlier, one of the main reasons that European nations have agreed to have these institutions is to tie the hands of their integration partners to guarantee that they will keep their word when it comes to the commitments they have made. There is no such constraint, other than loud public or private protest, on the actions of Mercosur nations, which makes the process inherently more unstable.

Therefore, the lack of supranational institutions means that individual nations are much freer to take unilateral action when it suits their interests. The Brazilians in particular have been prone to this sort of behavior, as will be shown later, and because of its hegemony in the region, other countries have simply had to live with this behavior (Cason 2000a). Nevertheless, this has put great strain on the regional alliance at a number of points. Consequently, there has been an increasing demand from some nations in Mercosur (particularly Uruguay and Argentina) to establish supranational institutions, largely to constrain Brazil's behavior. To this point, nothing has been accomplished, and for the reasons outlined before, it is highly unlikely that Mercosur will develop strong supranational institutions.

Conclusions

As will become clear in the chapters to follow, the vulnerable integration model developed here emerges from a close examination of the Mercosur case, and I will argue that the processes that we observe in Mercosur would be quite similar for other developing regions attempting to carry out integration. What will become apparent is that while Mercosur has been relatively successful—especially given Latin America's miserable track record in integration—it has limits that arise from the way it integrated. It chose to focus only on commercial issues from the beginning, and it chose to avoid supranational institutions, and in these fundamental ways was very different from the EU.

Why did it focus only on commercial issues? As I have argued, it did so for several reasons. First, the launching of Mercosur occurred at a time when neoliberal, free-market ideology ruled in Latin America, and the presidents in Brazil and Argentina who signed the Treaty of Asunción were committed to such an ideology. In addition, because of the external shocks that it has faced since it emerged, Mercosur has often been on the defensive, and leaders and negotiators in the principal Mercosur nations have concerned themselves with protecting what had been accomplished in the commercial realm. Finally, those civil society actors that might have preferred a broader agenda have been unable to organize behind a clear and coherent agenda, and policy makers have not been forced to take them into account.

Why did it avoid supranational institutions? First, the structural weakness of Latin American nations in the international political economy made them quite wary of such institutions. In addition, the heavyweight in Mercosur, Brazil, was from the beginning unwilling to give up sovereignty to such institutions, and insisted on having flexibility to deal with whatever might emerge during the integration process. Also, given the institutional weakness of the integration partners themselves, it is hard to imagine them creating, from scratch, *new* institutions that would somehow outperform domestic institutions that had their own problems.

In other words, there are both structural and contingent reasons that Mercosur developed as it did. One of the important arguments here, however, is that these initial choices in integration have important consequences later on. It is very difficult for Mercosur to go beyond its initial mandate and put social issues on the integration agenda, particularly given the weaknesses of the institutions in the member states. And because it is unlikely to construct a supranational infrastructure to support integration, it remains particularly vulnerable to new shocks emanating from either the international or domestic political economies. As a consequence, Mercosur is extremely unlikely to deepen, and will remain largely a commercial integration venture.

The following chapters will flesh out these arguments in a number of different ways. In addition to telling the story of Mercosur, I analyze the preferences and political action of state elites and actors in civil society, mostly in the two more important partners in Mercosur, Argentina and Brazil. In many ways, these preferences were determined by the position of the individual nations (and the region as a whole) in the international political economy; they emerged from a particular set of economic and political constraints. In the end, the preferences of state elites and civil society actors combined in such a way to lead to relatively coherent national strategies when it came to integration, and grand rhetoric aside, these strategies recognized the limitations of trying to integrate the Mercosur economies.

2 A long-standing dream

Historical experience with regional integration in Latin America

Integration has a long history of failure in Latin America. Attempts at integration have also had a wide variety of motivations. These motivations have included the desire to unite politically to increase the political influence of the region, the ambition to unite economically to fend off foreign powers and influence, the desire to use economic integration to develop the region, and the hope that economic integration would lead to greater political stability and consolidated democracy. In other words, integration has frequently been asked to accomplish great things.

The fact that integration was asked to do so many things was also its downfall before the relative success of Mercosur. Indeed, Latin American integration before Mercosur failed because of the high expectations, which could never be fulfilled, placed on it by its proponents. A variety of factors led to these unfulfilled expectations, and they are related to the vulnerable integration model outlined in the previous chapter. The most important factors leading to the failures in Latin American integration before Mercosur were the domestic institutional weaknesses of the countries trying to integrate, different levels of development among the integrating countries, different goals for integration among the integrating partners, and Latin America's vulnerability in the international economy. Some of these difficulties have been overcome with the Mercosur project, but several—institutional weaknesses and vulnerability in the international economic system—remain, and make any deepening of integration in Mercosur extraordinarily difficult.

To understand the degree to which Mercosur was successful and how it is limited, it is instructive to look briefly at the Latin American experience with integration prior to the launching of Mercosur, which I do in this chapter, in five sections. First, I look at the integration hopes of those political and military leaders who fought for their independence and that of their descendants in the early twentieth century. I then turn to the first serious effort towards integration in the region, the Latin American Free Trade Association (LAFTA) that was promoted by the Economic Commission for Latin America (Comisión Económica para América Latina—ECLA/CEPAL) to facilitate development in the region and its eventual failure. The third section focuses on LAFTA's successor, the Latin American Integration Association (Asociación Latinoamericana de Integración—LAIA/ALADI), which was a limited attempt to deal with LAFTA's failures. The fourth section discusses the initial and limited success of more modest integration between Argentina and Brazil in the mid-1980s, which coincided and was influenced by the transition to democracy in both countries. This program, known as the Argentine-Brazilian Economic Integration Program (Programa de Integración y Cooperación Económica Argentina-Brasil—ABEIP/PICE) also stalled like previous integration efforts, which is described in the final section. This final section also explains how the ABEIP set the stage for greater integration between Brazil and Argentina, eventually leading to Mercosur.

Dreams of integration

Those familiar with Latin American development will know that integration is not a new phenomenon. After all, Latin America was once integrated, in two pieces more or less, in the Spanish and Portuguese colonial empires. That is not to say that all of the pieces of the Spanish empire in the Americas had much contact with one another; each had a connection with the metropolis, but they did not necessarily have much contact with one another. Nevertheless, they were in colonial times bound together. It would not have been a huge leap at the time to see at least these two parts of Latin America become separate states. And one piece of the Iberian empires in the Americas—Brazil—stayed intact as a state after independence, though it was not a republic until 1888.

The Spanish American colonies were less fortunate, dividing themselves into many separate states, going to war with one another with some frequency, and, as a consequence, allowing themselves to be divided and conquered, though not in a formal colonial fashion. Indeed, during much of the nineteenth century, the nations of Latin America could hardly have been called integrated nations. Local control of political and economic organization, led by *caudillos*, was generally the rule. Whereas the United States found ways of integrating its territories—first after the Articles of Confederation proved a failure, and then after the bloody Civil War—Latin America was far less successful. This left the region vulnerable to outside influence, and indeed, much of the nineteenth century for Latin America was a story of outside domination, infighting, and an inability to do anything for the economy except support extractive and agricultural economic activities.[1]

This pattern of development in Latin America also had political implications. It reinforced extraordinarily unequal patterns of development, which manifested themselves, politically, in authoritarian societies. This pattern was demonstrated both in the smaller states that emerged from the Spanish empire and in the former Portuguese empire, even though the latter remained a single state.

One might ask: If Latin America had been able to remain united (in at least two parts) after independence, would things have turned out differently? The evidence from Portugal's former empire in Latin America does not lead one towards optimism, but it is certainly true that those who fought for independence in Latin America hoped that it would. Leaders such as Simón Bolívar had a vision of a united Latin America, which would certainly have changed the balance of power in the Americas. At the same time, Bolívar was quite aware that this would be difficult, if not impossible, to achieve. The difficulty was driven home at the Congress of Panamá in 1826, when Bolívar hoped to establish a confederation of Latin American nations. This was, according to Milenky, "the final expression of the romantic solidarity of the independence movement" (1973: 8; see also Mace 1988). Since the governments of several Latin American nations did not even come to the Congress, it was evident that any hopes for Latin American unity in the immediate post-independence period were unlikely to be fulfilled.

There were many dreams of integration in the post-independence period, but over the course of more than a century, these dreams could not be realized. During the nineteenth century, there was extraordinary political conflict in much of Spanish America, as leaders attempted to establish authority in the new nation states, often unsuccessfully. Military dictatorships were the rule in the region, and they were hardly interested in pursuing economic or political integration, particularly when they were having enough problems establishing control over their territories. Thus, after the initial enthusiasm associated with independence, any sort of integration dream faded deep into the background.

In Portuguese America, administrative control was more centralized than in Spanish America, and the territory itself was more connected. In the end, Brazil was able to maintain territorial unity in the post-independence period. This is not unrelated to the fact that Brazil was the only independent monarchy in the Americas, which insisted upon a certain centralized control.

In addition, during the nineteenth century and much of the early twentieth century, Latin American was integrated into the world economy through primary product exports. It was the age of liberalism in Latin America, and elites were concerned with their primary product exports to the more important parts of the world economy. Practically speaking, there was little interest in moving towards any sort of integration in the hemisphere. The focus was on rich markets, and not one another.[2] Although there was some fear in the newly independent nations of Latin America that there would be attempts at reconquest from the European powers, Milenky notes that,

> Fear alone was not strong enough to overcome the divisive forces at work within and among the several Latin American countries during the nineteenth century. Economically, they became oriented toward Europe or the United States rather than toward each other . . . What remained of continental sentiment became the property of the intellectuals, and lost what few ties it had once had with concrete economic or political action.
>
> (1973: 8)

Indeed, the desire for integration among independence leaders was very much in the ideological realm, where it stayed for more than a century.

Even though the desire for Latin American integration remained in the ideological realm, the hope for unity in the region did not die. During the nineteenth century, the reasons for integration were sometimes expressed vaguely. In the twentieth century, however, the desire for integration—and the arguments for it—became much more explicit. The goals of integration were both political and economic. In the economic sphere, there was a desire to achieve greater independence from the more powerful and developed countries in the world economy. In the political sphere, there was a similar refrain, which in fact had been felt in the nineteenth century as well: Latin America hoped to achieve, through integration, a greater degree of political independence from Europe, and later the United States. Importantly, integration was also seen by some as a potential answer to the development dilemmas of Latin America. It was viewed as a way not only to achieve greater independence from the more powerful countries in the global economy, but as a way to encourage faster growth and more diversified economies through regional import substitution.

In the late nineteenth and early twentieth century, as nations (at least in some places in the region) consolidated their authority, and as at least some limited democracy was put in practice in some countries, a new sense of regional identity began to take hold. In particular, there was also an increasing sense of identity in the region in opposition to outside interests. Much of this identity, "anti-imperialist" in ideology, was focused against the United States or Europe, depending on the nations that had dominated particular countries. In Mexico and Cuba, for example, the anti-imperialist ire was focused on the United States; in Argentina, the major imperial power was the British. In the end, however, a development strategy that favored integration could not really take off until leaders and policy makers in the Latin American nations had a clear consciousness about *development.* This only occurred gradually in the middle of the twentieth century with the emergence of import-substitution industrialization (ISI) after the onset of the Great Depression. Even then, an understanding of what state intervention could do for development emerged slowly and piecemeal, and some nations were much quicker to get to this point of self-conscious development strategy than others.

Before the onset of ISI, the sense of Latin American identity and a desire for unity had a more cultural—and less economic—expression in the work of such intellectuals as the Cuban José Martí and the Uruguayan José Enrique Rodó, who attempted to define a Latin American "spirit" distinct from that of the United States (Abellán 1972). In the 1920s, this anti-imperialist (and pro-Latin American unity) position was represented by Peruvian politician Victor Raúl de la Torre and his political party, the Alianza Popular Revolucionaria Americana (American Popular Revolutionary Alliance—APRA). Haya de la Torre formed his political party in Perú, but it had links to other political parties in Latin America. Haya de la Torre, in a representative speech in 1925, argued that

> Our campaign must be against the enemy outside and the enemy inside. One of the most important plans of the imperialists is to keep our America divided. A Latin America that was united and federated would be one of the most powerful countries in the world, and would be seen as a danger by the Yankee imperialists.
>
> (1988: 34–35)

The general thrust of Haya de la Torre's arguments about Latin America's relationship with the outside world was that without unity, the region would forever be subjected to divide and conquer policies on the part of the dominant powers in the international political economy, and particularly the United States. He argued that Latin America was dominated economically by the United States because of the complicity of local elites in this process of domination from the outside.

Brazil also developed along nationalist lines in the mid-twentieth century, represented in particular by Getúlio Vargas, who came to power in 1930. Vargas later (in 1937) assumed dictatorial powers, and the general thrust of his policies was to move Brazil in a more nationalist direction, emphasizing the need to develop the country's economy independently from the countries that had to this point dominated its economy. Burns describes the more nationalist mood as follows:

> From the outset, [Vargas] declared himself to be a nationalist. To direct the economy and to encourage industrialization and development, Vargas introduced governmental planning and participation on a large scale into the economic life of the nation . . . After 1930, it was apparent that Brazilian nationalism, like that flourishing in most of Latin America, became increasingly characterized by resentment of foreign capital and foreign personnel, suspicion of private enterprise, a growing preference for state ownership, emphasis on industrialization, encouragement of domestic production, and a desire to create or nationalize certain key industries such as oil, steel, power, and transportation.
>
> (1993: 422–23)[3]

Brazil did in fact go further than most other Latin American countries when it came to economic planning and state intervention, in part because it was a larger country and thus could be more ambitious in its ISI policies.

By the mid-twentieth century, then, integration and unity began to take on a much more economic orientation, and had an anti-imperialist or defensive orientation. Political unity was still part of the dream of integration, but as new development strategies that focused on industrialization began to take hold in the region, and as political leaders became convinced of the possibility of using public policy to further economic development, the emphasis became more economic. It is to these "developmentalist" economic efforts that I now turn.

The failure of LAFTA

Latin American nations began to address the integration issue explicitly after World War II. By this point, the main motivation of integration was not a fuzzy notion of political integration or some ideological separation from the United States or Europe; rather, political concerns had taken a back seat to economic issues. Latin America was in the midst of its ISI development strategy, and integration was viewed, at that particular point in time, as a way to push ISI forward. The basic understanding of integration in the early post-war period was as a project that would allow for Latin American industrial development. It was economically motivated, without a doubt. And politics was absent, by and large, and this absence of politics proved to be its downfall.

Economically and politically, the period between 1930 and 1980 was the age of ISI in Latin America. But after the so-called easy phase of this process, Latin American nations began to realize the limits of depending on relatively small markets for their industries.[4] Intent on continuing the industrialization drive, economists and policy makers in the region tried to figure out ways to accomplish this goal. Economic integration was an obvious option, given the circumstances.

ISI, by definition, was based on supplying domestic markets with products that had previously been imported, and quite consciously raised tariff and non-tariff barriers to imported products in hopes of stimulating domestic industry. The expectation with ISI was that these discriminatory policies could push development forward by providing incentives for the establishment of new industries, and this industrialization would help the region avoid its increasing "marginalization" in the world economy (Vacchino 1990: 120–21). The argument made by the proponents of ISI was that Latin America faced declining terms of trade for their exports, and thus needed to produce the more "valuable" products that they were importing to confront this problem (Prebisch 1959).

Alas, protectionism could only do so much to push development forward. Bottlenecks emerged, and among the smaller countries in particular (though larger economies such as Brazil and Mexico were by no means immune), it became obvious that the ISI process would be exhausted relatively quickly. Latin America's inequality also contributed to the problem of small domestic markets even in some of the larger countries; if there was great inequality (and there was, and is, in almost every Latin American country), the effective market for the new products being produced in the region was also limited.

The institution where both the strategy of ISI and the strategy of integration emerged was the Economic Commission for Latin America (Comisión Económica para América Latina – CEPAL). CEPAL was formed in 1948 as an organization within the United Nations over the objections of both the United States and the Soviet Union to promote developmentalist ideas in Latin America.[5] CEPAL cultivated an intellectual milieu that produced some of the most important economists and political leaders in the post-war period. They were committed to Latin American development, and industrial development in particular, and provided the most important intellectual justifications for an ISI development strategy.

The intellectual guiding light in CEPAL was Argentine economist Raúl Prebisch, who later became the first secretary general of the United Nations Conference on Trade and Development (UNCTAD) in 1964. Prebisch had a long-standing commitment to industrial development in the region, and also advocated Latin American economic integration when it became clear that national ISI was running into problems (Love 1980). These economists concluded, when ISI came under strain, that the best way to further this strategy of industrial development was through regional economic integration. After all, if ISI was inefficient because of the size of many Latin American markets, then it would be much more feasible if larger markets could be developed through regional integration. As Manzetti notes, "regional integration was regarded as a means of providing a market large enough to satisfy economies of scale, which in turn would deepen import substitution" (1990: 111).[6] Manzetti points out that while many economists did not support greater protection and ISI, some more liberal economists considered integration a good idea, since it could (under certain circumstances) lead to more efficient economies and a better allocation of resources.

For CEPAL and the policy makers that followed its orientation, economic integration in Latin America made sense, especially since, as Mace notes, the region was not considered "ripe" for any sort of political integration (1988: 407). If domestic markets were not large enough to support large-scale industrial expansion, surely a much larger Latin American market would do the trick. Latin American economic integration might then replicate the good fortune of the US market, which through its size stimulated economic development.

Given this analysis, economists at CEPAL pushed the idea of Latin American economic integration. This position led to the creation of LAFTA. LAFTA reflected a wide variety of objectives, as noted earlier, and no clear consensus on the direction that regional integration should take. In fact, nearly all analyses of LAFTA point to the fact that it was a compromise between competing visions of integration, and was embarked upon without a clear strategy. Various analysts refer to the agreement as a "minimal consensus," a "compromise between varying national goals," or an "integration scheme of very limited scope" (Haas and Schmitter 1964: 723; Milenky 1973: 16; Mace 1988: 410). While it is true that many integration schemes can be thought of this way—the European Community was also a compromise between varying national goals—LAFTA faced a particular vulnerability because it was occurring on the periphery of the international political economy and was begun in a context of substantial political and institutional instability in many of the contracting parties.

LAFTA was established by the Treaty of Montevideo, signed in 1960. In part inspired by the European Community's Treaty of Rome three years earlier, LAFTA aimed to create a free trade area in Latin America by 1973. The goal was ambitious, and reflected the goals of economists who saw the potential benefits to Latin American integration. These economists did not concern themselves much with the political requirements of integration; their hope was that if they moved forward with a treaty to establish Latin American integration, facts on the ground would later reinforce their ideas. Alas, this was not forthcoming. Haas points to the problems facing economic integration in Latin American when compared to Europe; in Latin America, one witnesses

> the supremacy of politics over economics in the Latin American style of decision-making. The mere fact that in Europe so many decisions could be taken on the basis of incremental bargaining among diverse units, often involving non-governmental elites, suggests the dedication to pragmatic pursuits. But society must possess groups and individuals motivated to act in this fashion before the appropriate processes develop. The intensity of demands, buttressed by passionate ideological conviction, must already have subsided. The

> slogans of socialism and capitalism, of working class and of aristocracy, of the military and the civilian, of church and state, must already be a matter of relative indifference to people. Latin America has not reached "the end of ideology."
>
> (1967: 334)

While there are some problems with this analysis—had Europe really reached the "end of ideology" either?—it is also true that Latin America at the time LAFTA was signed was beset by a degree of political instability that made real economic integration virtually impossible. In a sense, there was an imbalance between economics and politics in Latin American integration at this point: whereas the motivation was primarily economic, there was little in the way of taking politics into account in the process, and thus, politics undermined the process itself.

In the end, LAFTA failed. There were a few early successes in the two years after the Treaty of Montevideo was signed, but by and large the integration effort floundered before it had made much progress. There were some early tariff reductions in some economic sectors, but these tariff reductions were not particularly significant, and after early enthusiasm for regional integration in the first several years after the Treaty of Montevideo was signed, forward momentum halted.

Why did LAFTA fail? In some sense, failure was overdetermined—too many factors were working against success. One author, for example, lists the following reasons for its failure: 1) the fact that integration was not a priority for Latin American countries; 2) the diversity of economic policies followed by the LAFTA nations; 3) the fact that policies implemented to pursue integration did not match up with what was needed to implement integration; 4) the difference in size and economic development of the LAFTA nations; 5) the lack of infrastructure to support integration; 6) the fear of change in the region; and 7) the psychological problem of having high expectations for integration that did not yield immediate results (Vacchino 1990: 123–25). As if these factors were not enough, the 1960s was an extraordinarily tumultuous decade for Latin America. Political and economic crises led in many cases to military coups. To cite only a few examples, coups occurred in Brazil (1964), Argentina (1966), Perú (1968), and both Uruguay and Chile faced increasing crises, which led to coups in these two countries in 1973. In other words, the domestic arena was paramount for Latin American nations during this early period when integration was on the table, and international economic relations with neighboring countries received very little attention.

Indeed, LAFTA was far too ambitious, given the political context of the period. In the first place, it assumed that Latin American countries would be *willing* to limit trade barriers for the cause of a broader Latin American development effort. But by and large, most national governments were still mostly concerned with development prospects in their own countries; they did not have a region-wide development consensus. Second, the countries of the region were still far too unstable politically to coordinate economic policies to any significant degree; agreements reached by one government could easily be overturned by the next government, which made economic integration difficult. After all, one of the key elements in any integration process is trust: one must believe that one's partners will keep to agreements previously reached. Latin America, at this particular point in time, did not live up to this standard. Finally, national development strategies were not particularly amenable to influence from the outside, and there was relatively little incentive or inclination to give up sovereignty when it came to making economic policy.

By the late 1960s, it was clear that LAFTA was in deep trouble. This was implicitly recognized in 1969, when Chile, Perú, Ecuador, Colombia, and Venezuela signed an agreement to establish the Andean Group. The Andean Group was not an explicit repudiation of LAFTA, but it recognized the weaknesses in the overall framework of integration followed to that point. In addition, it pointed the way toward a much more viable alternative in Latin American integration: sub-regional integration. It also established a more modest model of Latin American integration that would be more realistic, even though the Mercosur nations would take a couple of decades to act on this model. What was clear was that regional integration on a wide scale would not work, at least at this point, because of its complexity, the weaknesses of Latin American institutions, and Latin America's position in the international economy.

A second try: ALADI and its limitations

In addition to being the year when the Andean Group was founded, 1969 was also the year when the LAFTA nations agreed to put off the achievement of a free trade area by 10 years, implying the achievement of such a goal by 1983. Indeed, LAFTA was recognized as a failure by the early 1970s, but not much was done about the failure, at least on a region-wide scale. By the late 1970s, there was a sense that something new was necessary. As Vacchino argues, there were two options: postpone the free trade area once again, or make it more "flexible" and "realistic" to deal with heterogeneity in the region (1990: 130).

To reinvigorate the integration process, another Treaty of Montevideo was signed in 1980, which created the Latin American Integration Association, or ALADI (Asociación Latinoamericana de Integración). ALADI replaced LAFTA, and was much more modest in its aims. Recognizing the previous organization's defects, the architects of ALADI focused on more concrete and achievable goals, and did not hope to establish region-wide integration implying agreements among all of the ALADI nations. Manzetti notes that it was an "umbrella organization in which member countries could engage in a variety of bilateral or multilateral integration schemes" (1990: 112). What this meant, in effect, was that ALADI could help coordinate integration, but would not have the LAFTA-like goal of making sure that all nations in the agreement came to the same conclusion.

Unfortunately for ALADI, it had impeccably bad timing. While Latin America generally enjoyed substantial growth in the late 1970s, in most cases it was fueled by increasing foreign indebtedness of Latin American countries. But just at the moment that things seemed to be looking up in the region—the signing of the ALADI agreement occurred at a particularly optimistic point—an international crisis interrupted the process when the debt crisis struck, beginning with Mexico's default in August 1982.[7] As a consequence, all Latin American countries were thrust into defensive mode, reacting to their particular balance-of-payments crises. Under such crisis conditions, it was unlikely that the nations of the region would further open their markets to one another—the primary emphasis during this point in time was *reducing* imports so as to put payments back in balance. New initiatives to open markets further, and thus put this goal at risk, were not likely. This problem was painfully obvious when looking at trade flows in the first half of the 1980s: whereas intra-ALADI imports had totaled US$12.2 billion in 1981, they had fallen to US$7.7 billion by 1986 (Vacchino 1990: 132). It was hardly an auspicious time to think about moving integration forward.

Democratization and integration: new approaches to integration in Argentina and Brazil

While ALADI cannot be considered a "success," it cannot be considered a failure, either. In fact, it was under the auspices of ALADI that subsequent integration efforts in Latin America have been undertaken. ALADI was also not the only game in town when it came to international economic and political relations in Latin America. In addition to these trade negotiations, bilateral negotiations—which were encouraged by ALADI—were taking place in the political sphere. It is in this political sphere that Latin American integration got back on track, and made Mercosur possible in the 1990s.

The key players in Latin American integration have always been Brazil, Argentina, and Mexico, because of their size and level of economic development. In South America, obviously, Brazil and Argentina have been most important. Traditionally, these countries have been military and political rivals; the independent state of Uruguay was created, in part, to act as a buffer between these two giants of South America. Brazil and Argentina, however, began moving toward a more cooperative relationship in the late 1970s, while both countries were under military governments. Ironically, in fact, it was under military regimes that the first steps toward cooperation were taken in the late 1970s. Argentina was ruled by the military from 1976 to 1983, while Brazilian generals had staged a military coup in 1964, only giving way to a civilian president in 1985. Some of their cooperation had particularly unpleasant consequences, such as when the military regimes cooperated with one another in the so-called *Operación Cóndor*, which brought these regimes' security apparatuses together in the pursuit, kidnapping, torture, murder, and disappearance of their political opponents (Mariano 1998).

The cooperation during this period between Brazil and Argentina was not wholly nefarious. Many issues were on the table, including economic cooperation, measures to share water and hydroelectric resources, measures to reduce border tensions and reorient security policies, and nuclear weapons. The first agreement involved a decision to jointly exploit the hydroelectric capacity of the Paraná River, and later Brazil and Argentina cooperated over the Malvinas war and nuclear issues.[8] None of these steps led directly to economic cooperation in the region that would later result in Mercosur. But this increased military cooperation made political and economic cooperation possible once transitions to democracy had occurred. It is unlikely, in fact, that any sort of economic cooperation would have been possible if militaries had continued to dominate politics; the militaries would have felt too insecure, and too ideologically opposed, to such cooperation. However, they laid the groundwork for democratic politicians.

It is with the new democratic governments (inaugurated in 1983 in Argentina and 1985 in Brazil) that the process of cooperation and economic integration really took off. Despite the frustrated efforts at integration in Latin America, Argentina and Brazil embarked on a new economic integration project in July 1986. Following a period of sharp contraction in trade brought on by the debt crisis—bilateral trade declined from nearly US$1.9 billion in 1980 to less than US$1 billion in 1983—the integration process marked a renewed attempt to spur growth and competitiveness by at least tentatively liberalizing foreign trade policies. This project began with a set of protocols signed by presidents José Sarney of Brazil and Raúl Alfonsín of Argentina that lowered tariff barriers in specific industries. The original agreements, the Argentine Brazilian Economic Integration Program (ABEIP), called for meetings between the presidents of both countries every six months, when they would sign additional protocols that had been negotiated by their representatives. Integration was to be negotiated on a sector-by-sector basis, with different protocols for each important economic sector.

This marked a break with previous integration efforts. The initiative for the ABEIP came from Alfonsín, who made economic integration the top priority of his administration. Both Alfonsín and Sarney saw the agreement as a way to strengthen their fledgling democracies.[9] The ABEIP mostly negotiated economic agreements, but at its base, it was essentially an integration process with overt and explicit political goals. One of the primary goals of this effort was the consolidation of democracy in two regimes that were still relatively fragile. Indeed, when the ABEIP was signed, Alfonsín made clear that any other countries that wanted to join the integration effort would have to be democratic. In so doing, Alfonsín was excluding Chile from membership at the time, since Chile was still under the authoritarian regime of Augusto Pinochet (*Senhor* 1986). In other words, it was not an accident that the ABEIP emerged when it did, right after the transitions to democracy.

How was this new integration scheme meant to consolidate democracy? First, on a rhetorical level, it was meant to emphasize the connection between new and positive political changes and new and positive economic changes. As Alfonsín and Sarney put it in their "Declaration of Iguaçú" in November 1985, "the recent successes of the two nations in their processes of democratic consolidation have created particularly propitious conditions for the betterment of their relations in diverse sectors, as well as a more intimate and close cooperation in the international scene" (América Latina precisa reforçar seu poder de negociação 1985). In addition, it was meant to build on the cooperation already begun by the militaries in both countries, in such a way as to permanently decrease tensions in the region. If there was a lower external security threat because of decreased tensions with neighbors, then the militaries themselves in the member countries would have less claim on resources and fewer reasons to be bellicose. In other words, there was an attempt to construct a "zone of peace" in the region, which would strengthen the new civilian governments.[10] Both new governments thought that if they tied themselves more closely to each other's economy, a renewal of traditional conflicts and rivalries would be less likely. One of Brazil's top diplomats, Paulo de Tarso Flecha de Lima put it this way in a speech in July 1988:

> With the economic integration program between Brazil and Argentina there is both an internal and external political strategy. . . . the political objectives are, to summarize, to substitute cooperation for competition between the two countries and thus reduce tensions in the region and eliminate any possibility of an arms race, including a nuclear arms race. There is no doubt that, given the [history of military] interference in the political systems in the region, and particularly in the Southern Cone, that the reciprocal political support between the two democratic regimes has contributed to the strengthening of each.
>
> (1988)

In this sense, democracy clearly influenced the integration process, as it gave political leaders an additional incentive to pursue the process aggressively, quite apart from any economic advantage that some sectors could enjoy.[11]

That said, it should also be noted that in the economic sphere, the ABEIP did not represent a break from previous, inward-looking development strategies. At this point in time, the worldwide trend was to turn away from such strategies, and international organizations such as the World Bank and IMF were pushing developing country governments to shed these old ideologies (Stallings 1992; Bierstecker 1995). But what would later be christened the "Washington Consensus" had not yet triumphed in most Latin American countries, and neither Argentina nor (especially) Brazil were prepared to give up the old development strategies.[12] Rather than representing a broad-based liberalization and opening up to foreign trade, ABEIP can be seen more as an attempt to continue ISI in a broader framework. In this way it did not differ substantially from the ideology behind previous Latin American integration efforts, which were all fundamentally based on an ISI logic.

This can be illustrated by considering both the general framework of the agreement and how one specific sector—capital goods—was treated. In the Act of Buenos Aires, which established the ABEIP in July of 1986, the presidents agreed that

> The Program will be equilibrated in the sense that it should not induce a specialization in either country of specific products. It should stimulate intrasectoral integration which should seek a progressive equilibrium as trade expands, both quantitatively and qualitatively in terms of large sectors of the economy as well as smaller sectors.
>
> (*La Nación* 1986a)

What this meant more precisely was seen in the protocol on capital goods, which established that there would be an increasing number of capital goods that would be traded without tariffs between the two countries. However, it was not a decrease in tariffs that was the core of the agreement. Rather, there was an explicit agreement to exchange US$2 billion worth of capital goods between the countries between 1987 and 1990, with progressive increases: US$300 million in 1987, US$400 million in 1988, US$550 million in 1989, and US$750 million in 1990 (*La Nación* 1986b). To put it somewhat simply, the ABEIP was an effort to manage trade, not open trade. There seemed to be a desire on the part of policy makers, negotiators, and business people on all sides to make sure that integration be tightly managed. It clearly represented continuity with the old regulatory way of doing things in the region.

In addition, the ABEIP initiative was clearly state-led from its inception. The private sector did not participate in the early negotiations; later, business leaders became involved only when key economic sectors were put on the agenda by trade negotiators. Manzetti argues that "the main drive behind the integration process was not so much pressure from industrial and agricultural groups as the converging political interests of the Sarney and Alfonsín administrations" (1990: xx). In fact, many in both countries were surprised by the new initiatives.[13]

The state-led nature of the integration process was evident before the July 1986 agreements when both states were negotiating the process. Brazilian Finance Minister Dilson Funaro noted that

> We are in agreement that we should advance in the integration process, with the care that is needed. But before *taking the initiative and bearing the cost of convincing our paulista [from São Paulo] businesspeople*, we need a clear definition of Argentina's [economic] policy.
>
> (*Clarín* 1986a, emphasis added)

The details of the dispute at the time are not relevant, since a bit more than a month later an agreement was signed. What is clear is that the states were taking the lead, and that they were quite concerned about how industrialists and agriculture interests would receive the news that these two economies would be more integrated.

State negotiators on both sides did have good reason to be concerned about the viability of the integration agreement because of potential opposition among national industrialists. Multinational firms were quite enthusiastic about integration, because of the potential for rationalizing production in the region (*Clarín* 1986b). But firms with majority Brazilian or Argentine control were much less likely to be automatically supportive of integration. The Argentines were nervous about integration for economic reasons, since they had a less efficient industrial sector than Brazil. For example, shortly after the first agreement on capital goods integration went into effect (at the beginning of 1987), the organization representing agriculture machinery producers in Argentina registered their "great concern" regarding what might come with integration, given the competitive advantages of Brazilian firms (*Clarín* 1987).

On the Brazilian side, because of its competitive advantages vis-à-vis Argentina, the concern was over access to policy makers, particularly since some of the previous links between business and the state had diminished at the end of military rule and during the transition to democracy (Martins 1986). So Brazilian industrialists were fundamentally concerned with *access*. This was quite evident right after Argentina and Brazil had signed the protocols that made the ABEIP operative in December 1986. Presidents Sarney and Alfonsín hosted a lunch for 600 business people from Argentina and Brazil on December 11 in Brasilia. At this luncheon, the president of the Brazilian National Confederation of Industry (Confederação Nacional de Indústria—CNI), Luís Eulálio de Bueno Vidigal was asked to speak. In the initial draft of his speech, Vidigal said that "it is important to recognize that to this point business has not been able to participate as it should in the understandings that led to the protocols in the integration process." This speech was later toned down a bit (to say that it should be recognized that business should participate in the process), but the message was clear: business felt shut out of the negotiations over integration, and was not particularly happy about this (*O Globo* 1986).

At any rate, these first attempts at bilateral integration between Argentina and Brazil were fundamentally pragmatic and piecemeal, to the point where they might even be considered overnegotiated.[14] The integration process initiated in 1986 stalled in the late 1980s, partly because of the continued economic instability in both countries. The ABEIP was begun at a propitious moment, when both Argentina and Brazil were experiencing the fleeting success of their heterodox anti-inflation plans (the Austral and Cruzado Plans, respectively).[15] However, neither Brazil nor Argentina was able to control accelerating inflation for long, and wide fluctuations in exchange rates made coherent foreign trade planning exceedingly difficult. By the late 1980s, the relatively disappointing performance of the ABEIP led many analysts to become pessimistic about integration prospects.[16] Given the economic turmoil in both Argentina and Brazil at the time, as well as the failure of some of the protocols signed under the auspices of the ABEIP, there was good reason for skepticism.

ABEIP falters

Great enthusiasm had surrounded the ABEIP initiative. Shortly after the new program had been announced, there was a significant increased in trade, as can be seen in Table 2.1. It appeared that Brazil and Argentina had solved the problem of previous integration efforts: modest proposals, specific agreements, and intense negotiation could in fact lead to greater trade in the region and improve development prospects.

But the ABEIP did not deliver on its promise. As the table shows, growth in trade was anything but consistent, and it certainly was not balanced. After initial positive results, this integration initiative, like previous efforts, foundered. Within a year there were concerns about Brazil getting more out of integration from the Argentine side, and these complaints accelerated in 1988. By July of that year, one of the principle architects of the ABEIP, Roberto Lavagna, the former Argentine Secretary of Industry and Foreign Trade, was criticizing the direction of the process, saying that it had gone from "a political agreement to grow" the two economies to a

Table 2.1 Argentine/Brazilian trade, 1980–1990 (in millions of US dollars)

Year	*Argentine exports to Brazil*	*Brazilian exports to Argentina*
1980	765	1,092
1981	595	880
1982	567	666
1983	338	655
1984	478	853
1985	496	612
1986	698	690
1987	539	819
1988	573	971
1989	1,239	772
1990	1,400	645

Sources: Manzetti (1990: 113) and Ministério de Desenvolvimento, Industria, e Comercio Exterior, *ALICEWeb*.

"commercial agreement with only one beneficiary: Brazil" (*Clarín* 1988). While the Brazilians certainly looked at the agreement differently, as Table 2.1 shows, this statement came after several years of Argentina running a trade deficit with Brazil. In addition, trade between the two countries was increasingly erratic. That said, integration was not abandoned, and at the end of 1988, Brazil and Argentina signed the Treaty of Integration, Cooperation, and Development, which promised to construct a "common economic space" within 10 years (Amorim 1994). It was not entirely clear what this meant, and there were no iron-clad commitments in the Treaty, so it was difficult to know what it was supposed to accomplish.

The problems of ABEIP also illustrated the problems associated with vulnerable integration, even before Mercosur was created. The ABEIP ran into problems for a variety of reasons. First, its progress was a victim of the continuation of ISI development strategies in the two partners. The problems that occurred were not unlike the problems that plagued previous integration efforts. When national governments were faced with the possibility of significant structural economic change, they shied away from such changes. Neither Brazil nor Argentina had embraced the "Washington Consensus" in the late 1980s. Both were still wedded—to a greater or lesser degree—to the developmentalist ideology discussed earlier, which asserted that to develop, a nation had to protect its industries. This meant high tariffs, quotas, and other non-tariff barriers. By embarking on ABEIP, Argentina and Brazil were attempting to expand this notion to encompass the markets of both countries. In this respect, ABEIP was simply a continuation of the ISI integration project proposed in LAFTA and ALADI.

Fundamentally, however, it is exceedingly difficult to have successful integration when the nation states involved in the process cling to such a strategy. If the process is fundamentally ordered by an ISI perspective, ISI politics will prevail. And ISI politics are tied to protection of national industries. What this meant, in the ABEIP context, is that thousands of details of market opening had to be negotiated. As former Brazilian Finance Minister Luiz Carlos Bresser Pereira noted,

> The only reason to carry out economic integration is to create a market between Brazil and Argentina. But if it is necessary to manage such a market so much, it will never be created. Here the problem is both with Argentines and Brazilians. Both are *protocoleros*. Perhaps the Brazilians are even more so than the Argentines. If we want to integrate, of course we have to negotiate; we cannot simply open up the market. But we must negotiate less. If we insist on negotiating everything, in such a way that no sector is driven out of the market by the other country, we are not really negotiating seriously. We are only simulating integration.
>
> (1990: 224–25)[17]

At this early stage of integration, the Argentine and Brazilian government were attempting to micromanage the process of integration. With such micromanagement, it was extraordinarily difficult to get much forward momentum on the integration process after the initial stage of enthusiasm for the integration process had passed. As two Brazilian economists noted at the time,

> [This sort of integration] is not simple. Negotiation at the product level—as opposed to establishing broader policy instruments—is complex to administer and can have the undesirable consequence of increasing bureaucratic procedures to a degree probably not foreseen by those negotiating the agreements.
>
> (Lerda and Baumann 1987)

And the more bureaucratic procedures are involved, the more likely that trade will get sidetracked along the way.

Second, ABEIP was a victim of continued economic crises in Brazil and Argentina, as neither country was able to contain rising inflation rates. High inflation made integration very uncertain, and governments were unwilling to move quickly to new agreements in this context of uncertainty. Even though they had gone through painful economic adjustments to deal with the crisis of the 1980s, neither country was able to effectively confront the challenges they faced. Despite repeated attempts to control inflation in both countries, it continued to accelerate. In Brazil, for example, annual inflation went from an already high 248 percent in 1985 to what in most countries would be a hyperinflationary rate of 2592 percent by 1990. In Argentina, the performance was even more erratic; while Brazilian inflation accelerated more or less steadily over the second half of the 1980s, Argentina's rate went from 691 percent in 1985 to 78 percent in 1986 and then way back up into hyperinflationary territory by 1989, when its inflation rate hit 3015 percent.[18] Because there was such uncertainty about future economic prospects in both Argentina and Brazil, making commitments to open markets was especially difficult.

Third, and related to the previous points, the international context during the ABEIP was particularly adverse for Argentina and Brazil. The debt crisis was still the overwhelming issue facing both countries in the external arena, and at times, the nations verged on default. Brazil, in fact, declared a moratorium on debt payments on two occasions in 1987.[19] With balance-of-payments concerns a priority, and with foreign exchange scarce because of the debt burden, it was difficult to open the economies of the region, even on a modest scale.

To put it differently, the internal economic crisis was tightly bound to an external one: the continued inability to resolve the debt crisis that Latin America faced after 1982. Both Argentina and Brazil hoped to receive external support for their "heterodox" stabilization programs of 1985 and 1986, but this foreign support was not forthcoming. Without international support, the internal stabilization programs collapsed.[20] Here I do not judge whether such support should have come, or even if such support would have helped either Brazil or Argentina maintain their stabilization programs. The point here is that such support was not forthcoming, which doomed any chance the programs might have had in stabilizing their economies. In the end, Washington—and specifically, US Treasury Secretary James Baker, whose plan for debt renegotiation was mostly ineffective—and the international financial institutions were not enamored by these stabilization programs, and continued to insist on more significant economic reforms in exchange for financial support.[21] In this sense, the international context in the mid- and late 1980s confirms a general argument of this book: that integration in emerging nations is conditioned fundamentally by the integrating nations' position in the world economy; it is at the mercy, in many ways, of decisions that are taken thousands of miles away, and even the most effective economic plan cannot work in an adverse international environment.

Finally, ABEIP was from the beginning a top-down process, and civil—and business in particular—was not quite ready to be brought along on this road to integration. In other words, states were ahead of business in this process, and if business was not willing to go along, then it would be very difficult to see integration prosper. This final point confirms another general argument of this book: without civil society support, integration is impossible. Thus, it is essential to consider domestic politics when understanding integration. It was not only the adverse conditions in the international political economy that made integration difficult with ABEIP. States led in the process, and they did not get civil societies behind them. Neither business nor labor was particularly interested in pursuing aggressive integration, and both were concerned about the consequences of such an uncertain venture, even though some elements of business favored integration in principle and saw potential advantages in it. In the end, however, changing international circumstances and the radical reorientations of domestic politics in both Argentina and Brazil made further integration possible, which I turn to next.

3 The launching of Mercosur

By the late 1980s, Argentina and Brazil both were experiencing accelerating rates of inflation and frequent changes in economic policy, which put their integration process in jeopardy. Integration optimists were in hiding, and Argentina in particular was gripped by an economic crisis that led to a political crisis—the early resignation of Argentine president Raúl Alfonsín in mid-1989. Brazil's inflation was as bad as Argentina's during this period, though the Brazilians had figured out better ways to manage the inflationary spiral. That said, neither country was even remotely able to make any credible commitments that would move integration forward late in the 1980s.

By 1991, however, integration was again on the agenda and was pursued aggressively by new presidents in both countries—Carlos Saúl Menem in Argentina and Fernando Collor de Mello in Brazil. It was a dramatically different kind of integration, and was much less managed and much more "market-friendly." The new integration process was inaugurated in March 1991, when Mercosur was formed with the signing of the Treaty of Asunción, which also incorporated Paraguay and Uruguay into the agreement.

This new, more market-friendly, approach made integration more feasible—since it reduced (though it did not eliminate) the detailed sectoral approach of previous integration. It was also more vulnerable, since it opened the Mercosur countries to more international economic forces. Indeed, Mercosur was used as a policy instrument by the governments in the region to make their economies more open, and by and large it was successful in this regard. Given the nature of the process and the situation of the Mercosur countries in the international political economy, however, integration was always at risk.

A great deal changed between 1989 and 1991. The Cold War ended. The new Presidents in Argentina and Brazil shared a neoliberal vision for their countries and were determined to move away from the old ISI strategies. And the debt crisis, at last, appeared to be over. The end of the Cold War made Latin American countries worried that they would become increasingly marginalized in the international political economy, since foreign capital would likely flow to the areas where it was suddenly much more welcome. This fear led Mexico, under Carlos Salinas de Gortari, to propose NAFTA to the first President Bush.[1] Both Menem and Collor de Mello ascribed to a neoliberal creed, even though they had hidden this from their electorates during their election campaigns. In the end, both new leaders were quite committed to changing development strategy in a dramatic way. And both of them opened their economies unilaterally.

Finally, the debt crisis, which had wracked the Latin American economies for most of the previous decade, was dissipating, particularly in reaction to the Brady Plan (Roett 1992). Foreign capital—both as foreign direct investment and portfolio investment—was at last returning to the region. This meant that quite suddenly Latin American countries would no longer have to deal with constant balance-of-payments crises that the debt crisis had engendered. Therefore, there was a greater freedom of maneuver for a number of Latin American nations, and proactive policy was possible.

And so, Brazil and Argentina, along with Uruguay and Paraguay, established Mercosur in 1991. This chapter will tell that story, from a variety of angles. The first section focuses on the changing international context facing the Mercosur countries when they embarked on integration, and how this changing context influenced the integration process. The second section considers in detail the changes in political leadership that occurred with the elections of 1989 in Argentina and Brazil. It will also delve into the different interests of state, business, and labor actors when this integration experiment first emerged, detailing their different visions and different political strategies.

The third section of this chapter outlines the main thrust of the Treaty of Asunción, which established Mercosur. Here, I will focus on the key points of agreement and disagreement and the outlines of the Treaty itself and the way in which it committed the Mercosur nations to a new process of integration. The fourth section looks at the issue that caused most consternation in the Mercosur process in its early years: the problematic nature of economic stabilization in Argentina and Brazil. Both nations had suffered, under previous regimes, from chronic high inflation, which had led to hyperinflation at certain points. Indeed, it is quite remarkable that the Mercosur nations even agreed to integrate at this particular point in time, given domestic economic and political instability. It is probably safe to say that European nations would never have agreed to integrate under the sort of instability that the Mercosur nations experienced. Nevertheless, they achieved this unlikely prospect, and this section will explain how this happened. As noted in previous chapters, there were clear limitations to this integration process, which made it quite unlikely to follow a European pattern. In part, this limitation comes out of the fact that at its beginning, it was meant to address only commercial issues. In fact, the presidents that pushed it at the outset wanted to increase trade with the entire world, and not just Mercosur's neighbors. They were skeptical of industrial policy and state intervention, and saw Mercosur as a springboard for much greater economic openness. As the integration project developed, the decisions associated with this initial impulse would cast a long shadow over what integration could become.

A new international context: neoliberalism and the end of the Cold War

The agreements between Argentina and Brazil that set the stage for Mercosur still had plenty of remnants of old development strategies in Latin America. As was discussed in the previous chapter, an ISI ideology was quite evident during this initial stage of integration. As Tomassini noted in his explanation of how Latin America's integration process had in fact disintegrated (before the onset of integration efforts between Brazil and Argentina in the 1980s), there was something of a disconnect between development and integration strategies in Latin America, and the problems with integration were "not the result of a crisis of integration but of development" (Tomassini 1985: 211). In the end, the ABEIP integration described in the previous chapter was the last stab at old-style integration, but it too was undermined by external constraints and internal crises. Particularly, the sectoral emphasis of the prior integration process was problematic, as governments and business sectors in both Brazil and Argentina were not willing to subject themselves to open competition and a more liberal economic arrangement.

This began to change in the late 1980s. In 1988, Brazil and Argentina abandoned the previous focus on sectoral agreements, focusing instead on more general tariff liberalization. This important change occurred—and laid the groundwork for Mercosur—because of a change in the international context. Since the beginning of the 1980s, a sea of change had occurred in international development circles. The elections of Margaret Thatcher in Britain in 1979 and Ronald Reagan in the United States in 1980 marked a turning point. These political soul mates pushed a common ideology towards the developing world: it was only through open markets and deregulation that economic development and growth were possible.[2] This general approach applied to their own societies and to developing countries. And they went about the process of remaking international development agencies in this ideological image.

At this time, the policies of the major international financial institutions changed as well. The most important of these institutions—the IMF and the World Bank—became much more aggressive in pushing anti-statist development strategies in the developing world. They advocated privatization and deregulation, attempting to move developing countries away from policies that were seen to promote inefficiency, inflation, and economic instability. In its *World Development Report* in 1987, for example, the World Bank laid out its full case for economic opening in developing countries, while at the same time encouraging more developed countries to maintain open markets as well. In its typical fashion, the Bank tried to avoid telling developing countries exactly what they should do, but they made their point clear:

> This report presents a study of forty-one economies which shows that outward-oriented economies tend to perform better than inward-oriented economies. Their overall output grew faster. They industrialized more smoothly, even though their explicit interventions in support of that goal were far fewer. For the economies that followed more mixed strategies, however, differences in

> average performance were small; since many factors apart from trade policy influence economic success, this is scarcely surprising. The important lesson is that the strongly inward-oriented economies did badly.
>
> (World Bank 1987: 8)

Interestingly, of course, this leaves much to be explained, and is hardly a ringing endorsement for outward-orientation; it only suggests that strong inward-orientation is problematic. In the end, though the Bank recognized a diversity of outcomes, it mostly provided a single recipe for reform.

And what emerged was what John Williamson called the "Washington Consensus." The "consensus" emerged from the international financial institutions located in Washington, and pushed a number of straightforward ideas: trade liberalization, privatization, deregulation, a realistic exchange rate, fiscal discipline, liberalization of foreign capital inflows, financial sector liberalization, secure property rights, and more "efficient" public expenditure, especially in ways that would serve to reduce inequalities (Williamson 1990).

Different countries in Latin America came to adopt this consensus at different points in time. Early adherents to the philosophy included Chile (which really preceded the Washington Consensus with its policies of deregulation, free trade, and privatization), Bolivia in 1985, and Mexico under the de la Madrid administration.[3] Other countries were much later in coming to this particular consensus, and Argentina and Brazil were among the holdouts, at least until 1989.

It was at this point that new presidents were elected in both countries. Neither of the eventual winners of these elections—Carlos Menem in Argentina and Fernando Collor de Mello in Brazil—advocated the Washington Consensus during their election campaigns, but once in office, confronted hyperinflation by advocating a significant change in development strategy. They only came to adopt these deregulatory and privatizing strategies after they had won their elections. They also received significant popular support for these new policies, at least initially.[4] The policies came to be known as "neoliberal" in Latin America, and for those who opposed the new economic strategies, "neoliberal" became an epithet. And Mercosur became a part of these new strategies; the initial impulse behind Mercosur was to help push Argentina and Brazil to significantly open their economies (Phillips 2004: Chapters 4 and 5).

One of the most interesting elements of this new integration strategy was how it was different from previous integration efforts. There was no longer an emphasis on industrial policy in the negotiations between Argentina and Brazil; now, the focus was on opening trade. Both presidents were interested in unilaterally opening up their markets, and they saw integration as an excellent opportunity to do so. As Lia Valls Pereira notes, "the change in the format of the integration process, from sectoral agreements to wide-ranging liberalization, is largely explained by national objectives."[5] These national objectives changed significantly with new presidents in power in Brazil and Argentina.

This change in development strategy in the two key countries in Mercosur was amplified by the end of the Cold War. Both Menem and Collor were elected the same year that the Berlin Wall came down, which had two important effects for the region.[6] First, the end of the Cold War suddenly discredited a state-led development model. Though no Latin American country outside of Cuba had actually tried state socialism in practice, the notion of the state leading the development process was quite popular in Latin America. While most of the left was not in favor of the Soviet model of development, many sectors of the political-ideological spectrum favored heavy state involvement in the economy, and saw intervention in the economy as positive. Suddenly, this option was discredited. This had an enormous impact on Latin America (Castañeda 1993).

The second effect of the end of the Cold War was the fear that foreign investment would now be much more difficult to attract. There was now a brand new area ripe for foreign investment, with Eastern Europe suddenly available for MNCs. As a consequence, leaders in the region looked for strategies to attract much needed foreign capital. After all, Latin America was still in the throes of the debt crisis of the 1980s, which had led to a huge outflow of foreign capital from the region (Kaufman and Stallings 1989; Roett 1992). By the late 1980s and early 1990s, foreign capital was beginning to return to the region. The fear that this capital would now be going to other areas in the international political economy led policy makers to rethink development strategies to avoid this outcome.

Mexican president Carlos Salinas de Gortari, for example, proposed NAFTA. This was quite consciously a pitch for investment in his country, as well as a mechanism to decrease persistent trade conflicts with the United States.[7] And Menem and Collor did the same, with Mercosur. Both the Menem and Collor governments came to power in the context of severe economic crises and interpreted their roles as taking bold moves to counter these crises. Because of the predicaments that both countries faced, the presidents were concerned with making changes in a wide variety of areas. Macroeconomic stabilization was at the top of the list, and the governments used a number of policies to try to achieve this. Among them was a reorientation of foreign trade policy toward greater openness. And the first step to this greater openness was regional integration, through Mercosur.

Visions of integration

Mercosur was launched on March 26, 1991 with the signing of the Treaty of Asunción. It augured a new era in Latin American integration, and was much more ambitious than previous efforts at integration in the Americas. In the preamble of the Treaty, the signatories noted that

> Whereas the increase in the size of their current domestic markets by way of integration constitutes a fundamental condition to accelerate their processes of economic development with social justice; . . .
>
> Taking into account the evolution of the international events, particularly the consolidation of large economic spaces and the need to achieve an appropriate insertion into the world economy for the member countries; . . .

> Convinced of the need to promote scientific development in the member states and to modernize their economies by increasing the availability of goods and services to improve the lives of the inhabitants [of the region];
>
> Reaffirming their political will to establish the bases for an ever closer union of the peoples [in the region], with the goal of achieving the objectives mentioned above . . .
>
> (Tratado de Assunção 1991)

This ambition went beyond what previous integration efforts had promised, and the treaty itself was quite detailed in what was to come. At the same time, the initial step was hardly viewed as a positive step at the time. For example, in Brazil, just after the signing of the treaty the most influential newsmagazine *Veja* included a report entitled "Pacto Cucaracha" (The Cockroach Agreement), and was highly critical of the new initiative (Tachinardi 1995). This skepticism came in part because the move toward a common market in the south was far ahead of the views of business or civil society. This was clearly a top-down initiative at the beginning, though as will be detailed later, civil society jumped on board quickly (Cason and Burrell 2002).

It should also be noted that the change in the regional politics of South America was altered substantially by this new integration initiative. Paulo Roberto de Almeida argued, early in the integration process, that

> Mercosur has become, above anything else, a priority in foreign policy for countries of the continent, having introduced unprecedented elements into the international relations of the entire region. The Mercosur integration project changes not only the economic geography of the region, but the geopolitics of the region as well.
>
> (1993: 95)

Almeida was speaking to a sense—and a hope—that Mercosur would transform how the large countries of South America would be treated in a post-Cold War world. He also expressed a widespread hope that Mercosur could lead to a significant change in how South American countries were viewed in the North.

When analyzing this change in political and economic orientation, one might ask why the governments involved made the leap to an ambitious economic integration program. The simplest answer would be that Mercosur emerged because of the common interests of the nations that made up the new economic grouping, and that they were embarking on this new project because they saw the future in the same way. To some degree, this interpretation is on the mark; there were many in all of the Mercosur countries that thought that integration was a good idea. Indeed, if there were not some coincidence of interests, there is no way that an agreement would have been signed. In the end, however, it is necessary to think about the interests of different actors. A first cut at these different interests divides them between states, business, and labor. Each of these groups had quite distinct visions of what Mercosur should do, how it would benefit or hurt them, and how Mercosur would transform the economies of the region.

Although integration was initially a state-led, top-down process, it is clear that integration could never have succeeded without the support of those who would actually carry it out. Most importantly, business would have to make integration concrete; without investment that would take advantage of Mercosur, it would be dead in the water. But business—and parts of business—had different notions about Mercosur. Some viewed it as an enormous opportunity, while others were frightened by the implications of increased competition in previously protected markets. So even in the business sectors, one cannot assert that integration was viewed monolithically. Some business sectors were enthusiastic about integration, while others viewed it as a serious threat.

Finally, labor matters in the integration equation as well. While labor unions were not making the strategic decisions that would lead to the success or failure of integration through investments, they could certainly help or hinder integration by their political decisions. In addition, like business, all of labor did not necessarily look at integration the same way in different sectors or in different nations. There were different ways of viewing integration, on many different levels; as Andrés Malamud notes, "People have tended to confuse what Mercosur is and what they think it should be about" (2005b: 423). This next section will explain the differing "visions" of integration held by the key players in the integration process, and how these visions affected how integration developed.

Visions of the states

As previously noted, Brazil and Argentina had been traditional rivals in South America, and as the two largest economies on the continent, they vied for influence and power. As described in the previous chapter, they eventually moved towards more accommodating positions on political and military issues in the 1970s and 1980s and increased cooperation in the region. To some degree, the signing of the Treaty of Asunción was a culmination of this process of accommodation. There is, to be sure, little risk now of hostilities among South America's two major powers.[8]

That said, the integration process that was ushered in by this treaty has not meant that these two countries saw things the same way, whether it was regarding integration or even the relationship of Latin America with the rest of the world. Argentina and Brazil still have distinct interests, and these distinct interests are not merely commercial. Brazil's foreign policy and strategic interests have been much more consistent over time than Argentina's, but even with the changes in Argentine foreign policy during the Menem administration and after, the two countries are far apart when it comes to understanding their place in the world. By and large, Brazil has been much more likely to seek an accommodation with the international system, and has done what it could to be a major player in the world. Argentina, on the other hand, has seen a much more volatile foreign policy. It has also been more frequently opposed to US policies in the region, although in the 1990s it made every effort to be a staunch ally of the United States.

In analyzing the views of the respective states, I begin with Brazil. Brazil has traditionally viewed its position in Latin America as a potential hegemon, as the leader in the region and the country that is by far most important in South America. In the post-war period, although generally it has cooperated with the United States on many foreign policy issues, it has maintained substantial independence in foreign affairs. It has contributed to the non-aligned movement, and more recently was a leader of the Group of 20 developing countries that emerged after the World Trade Organization meeting in Cancún in 2003. It has also viewed hemispheric integration with suspicion.[9]

Because of this longstanding tradition of independence in foreign and economic affairs—as well as its status as the strongest Latin American country in economic terms—the Brazilians came to view Latin American integration as a priority in the early 1990s, and they viewed it as far more important than more thorough hemispheric integration (Barbosa and César 1994). Indeed, Brazil has been somewhat hostile to hemispheric integration, fearing the possible implications thereof. As a consequence, it has been particularly active, diplomatically, in making sure that the Mercosur project goes forward, and at key moments when Mercosur was getting off the ground, it made regional integration a diplomatic and political priority.

The governmental bureaucracy that has traditionally been most interested in pushing Mercosur forward in Brazil is the Foreign Ministry, also known as Itamaraty. Itamaraty's diplomats are recognized as among the best in the region, and the foreign service in Brazil is highly professionalized. Itamaraty has long promoted an independent foreign policy for Brazil, and has provided a consistency to Brazilian foreign policy that has persisted despite government changes, and even changes in regime type (Cason and Power 2009). Although Brazilian foreign policy did undergo changes with the transition from authoritarian rule to democratic government in the 1980s, there was not a wholesale revision in approach. The professionals in Itamaraty still held sway (Lafer 2000), and their sway pushed toward integration in Latin America in the 1990s.

Argentina's foreign policy has been much more erratic than Brazil's over time. At one time, Argentina was the country most resistant to US influence in Latin America, and its nationalism is legendary (Escude 1988). But once Carlos Menem assumed power in Argentina in 1989, Argentine foreign policy did an about-face. Menem insisted on an abandonment of old anti-US positions, and Argentina became one of the most important allies of the United States in Latin America. Guido de Tella, Menem's foreign minister, spoke of Argentina's new "carnal relations" with the United States, which may have been overstating the case a bit, to be sure (Vacs 1998). But it was the case that Argentina was the only South American country to send troops to fight in the first Gulf War. There was clearly a new approach in Argentina's foreign affairs.

This sharp change in Argentine foreign policy goals had implications for the integration in Mercosur. When hemispheric integration came to the table during the George H.W. Bush administration, and NAFTA was negotiated, Argentina embraced the idea of a hemispheric free trade area. It was generally conceded that Chile would be the first Latin American country in line to join NAFTA after the negotiations were concluded, but Argentina, under Menem, hoped to be next in line.[10]

This Argentine aspiration was at cross-purposes to the Brazilian plan for Latin American integration. The Brazilians viewed a strengthening of Mercosur as a way to increase bargaining leverage with the United States (and Europe) in international trade.[11] What the Brazilians could count on was that there would certainly be a slow process of integrating other countries into NAFTA, and in the meantime, the Brazilians worked on cementing Mercosur. Argentina, under new leadership, was interested in striking a deal with Brazil, but this was a second-best option for the political leadership. Menem's government (or, more accurately, part of it) was quite interested in striking a deal with the United States, which had the potential of putting Mercosur at risk.[12] In the end, such a deal would not be possible because of economic crises that emerged during the 1990s, but Mercosur, from the beginning, was vulnerable to the siren songs of the center.

Visions of business

It is important to note that the Treaty of Asunción did not come about because of pressure from business. Above all, at least initially, Mercosur came about because of political decisions made in the executive; as Andres Malamud notes, "Mercosur . . . arose from the political will of national governments, and only thereafter generated public demand for further integration" (Malamud 2005a: 139). But because integration would fail or succeed on the basis of the investment decisions of business, we must ask a fundamental question: What did business want? There are multiple answers to this question, because different business sectors had different views on what integration would do. That said, the distribution of preferences was not random, and this section will cut and slice business along several different dimensions to identify their positions on integration.

The first cut can be made between multinational firms and internationalized firms based in Mercosur nations, on the one hand, and those firms that had concentrated largely on the domestic market and were not internationalized either through exports or links to MNCs via licensing agreements and other kinds of connections. This is a rather rough cut, and some firms in the latter category did have some international links, even if they basically concentrated on the domestic market. It is also the case that Brazilian firms were much more likely to be internationalized than their Argentine counterparts, especially when it came to trade. For example, in 1990, just before the Treaty of Asunción was signed, manufactured products accounted for nearly 52 percent of Brazilian exports, while Argentina's manufactured exports were just over 29 percent of its total exports (CEPAL 2005: 139). This difference in export structure is compounded by the much greater size of the Brazilian economy, so certainly the Brazilian economy was in some senses more "internationalized" when Mercosur was launched.

This rough cut between internationalized and domestic-oriented firms serves as a useful starting point. And, generally speaking, the MNCs and internationalized firms were much more likely to be aware of the potential costs and benefits of integration, and they were much more likely to see the integration process as beneficial. Consequently, they could be counted on by the governments of the integrating nations to support the integration process once it advanced.[13] Firms that concentrated largely on the domestic markets and had few international linkages, on the other hand, were much more likely to be wary about integration prospects, since one of the main things they would be concerned about would be increased competition from imports from other Mercosur countries. These domestically-oriented firms were much less likely to have the information that they would need to take advantage of integration, and were consequently much more hesitant about it.

A second cut would differentiate between MNCs and internationalized firms that are based in Mercosur countries. While both of these business sectors were generally favorable to integration, perceiving its potential benefits, the MNCs were much more likely to be able to take advantage of integration. First of all, they had many more potential resources at their disposal, if the local affiliates of the MNCs could convince their home offices that it was wise to put resources into the region. They had a natural advantage over even those firms in the Mercosur nations that were quite experienced internationally. These latter firms were facing adverse economic environments in both Argentina and Brazil. Because of the policies instituted by Presidents Menem and Collor, these firms were no longer able to rely on state largesse and support. At the time the Treaty of Asunción was signed, the neoliberal ideology of getting the state out of the economy had clearly taken hold. These firms had previously been able to count on state support, often tied to an industrial policy that involved subsidized credit and protection from imports.[14] To be sure, MNCs had also benefited from these policies (and MNCs, once established, were quite willing to support protectionism and state subsidies, for obvious reasons), but the MNCs were much more able to do without them and rely on other resources. The local firms faced a more precarious situation.

It should be kept in mind, in this respect, that not only were Mercosur nations opening their economies to one another, they were also simultaneously pursuing policies of unilateral liberalization vis-à-vis the rest of the world. In Argentina, the average tariff rate decreased from 45 percent in 1987 to 9.7 percent by the end of 1991. In Brazil, a similar process was at work, as average tariffs decreased from 52 percent in 1987 to 9.9 percent in 1994 (World Bank 2005: 78; López-Córdova and Moreira 2003: 7). In addition to these sweeping tariff reductions, both countries moved during this period to reduce non-tariff barriers to imports. This put enormous pressure on *all* firms in the tradable goods sector to become more competitive. The existence of Mercosur simply increased the demands on business to adjust to more competition.[15]

The implication of these twin liberalization policies for internationalized domestic firms was that they had to increase their international links in order to obtain more resources to increase their competitiveness. These increased links took a variety of forms, including selling out to MNCs, engaging in joint ventures with MNCs, or combining with fellow Mercosur firms to increase their competitiveness.

A final cut in the business sector is between tradable and non-tradable sectors, and this cut overlaps with some of the previous ones. For non-tradable sectors, their reaction to Mercosur was clearly one of indifference. After all, neither the unilateral opening nor the Mercosur opening would affect their businesses much; what mattered for them was the overall level of economic activity, and if it increased (as the presidents proclaimed it would when they signed the Treaty), then they would favor it. In the tradable goods sectors, however, the livelihood of their firms was at stake with both openings. In considering the tradable goods sectors, the previous cuts were clearly relevant.

Finally, in considering business attitudes about integration and the implications of these attitudes for integration politics, it is also important to understand the differences between Argentine and Brazilian business organizations. There is an interesting dynamic here: whereas Brazilian business is generally considered "stronger" than Argentine business—especially in the industrial sector—Argentine business is generally more "organized" than Brazilian business.[16] In the end, however, business in both countries faced a highly uncertain situation when Mercosur was launched. Both countries were in the midst of wrenching economic change. Hyperinflation had made it highly unlikely that investors would undertake risky investments; there was very little that could be counted on when it came to government policy.[17] In the end, strategic decision making was quite difficult for business, even as they saw their governments taking what were clearly profound decisions about the future direction of their economies.

On balance, what did this mean for business? It meant, generally speaking, that MNCs were most enthusiastic about integration, internationalized firms slightly less so (and probably worried more about unilateral opening than just Mercosur opening), but able to adapt, and that traditional domestic firms in the tradable sector were the least enthusiastic. It was also the case that the traditional domestic firms had the least legitimate political demands in this period of striking moves away from protectionism and toward international openness. Leaders in Argentina and Brazil consistently made the argument that much would change with the market-oriented reforms; for example, Carlos Menem warned his countrymen and women that reforms would involve "major surgery without anesthesia," and his Economy Minister (and architect of the free-market reforms), Domingo Cavallo, argued in a speech in early 1991 that

> to achieve all these goals [of greater prosperity for Argentina], our country must be equipped with a set of stable socioeconomic institutions which will jointly promote freedom and solidarity. Just as the previous government was charged with restoring our constitutionally established political institutions, history has entrusted President Menem's government with the task of rebuilding our socioeconomic institutions.[18]

Fernando Collor derided the technology in Brazilian-made cars, calling them "carroças" ("carts") (*Latin American Weekly Report* 1990). By implication, Collor was promising to open up the Brazilian market to imports of technology, which was likely to cause upheaval in the Brazilian economy. In the end, the initiation of Mercosur was one piece of this overall liberalization, and to the extent that business was concerned about overall opening, they would be concerned about Mercosur. At the beginning, at least, there was no push from business for Mercosur to happen.

Visions of the labor movement

Labor has been by far the weakest of the actors considered here. No labor movement in any country was pushing for integration when it happened; integration occurred despite labor interests. To be sure, as noted earlier, business was not pushing for integration either, at the early stages of the process. But labor was even further out of the loop. Labor had been under assault since the onset of the debt crisis, when jobs were lost because of economic contraction. It was on the defensive. And integration came about at a point in time when labor was reeling from setbacks. The onset of neoliberal reforms in both Argentina and Brazil were in many ways meant to weaken old styles of political representation of labor. Mercosur, in its initial design, was not meant to curry favor with labor.

Nevertheless, labor has not been an active opponent of integration. Indeed, as the process has gone on, labor has taken on a more active role encouraging new initiatives in the integration process, particularly when it came to encouraging some sort of social or labor code to go along with what has generally been a commercial integration process.[19]

Why didn't labor simply oppose the integration project from the beginning? After all, labor had generally opposed integration previously, out of a protective position. Labor leaders in the nations that make up Mercosur (and other Latin American countries) viewed integration as a threat. Integration had the potential of shaking up protected domestic economies, and labor had been one of the most important supporters of economic policies that increased import barriers. Populist and/or ISI development strategies had been supported by labor organizations, which viewed these strategies as the best way to protect wages and employment levels.

In addition, on a more ideological level, labor viewed integration as a way in which MNCs could become increasingly important in Latin America. It was no secret that MNCs were the most likely to benefit from integration efforts, and labor organizations in Brazil and Argentina—and in particular, Argentina—had a discourse that was frequently hostile to multinational capital. To the extent that labor movements were opposed to the spreading influence of international capital, they were opposed to economic integration schemes that would favor the interests of international capital. In addition, labor movements in the Mercosur countries were dealing with a wide variety of issues related to the reemergence of democratic politics in the region.[20]

In the end, labor did not oppose Mercosur when it came into existence. It is important to understand the context at the time, of course. On the Argentine side, Carlos Menem of the Peronist party was in power, and the Peronists had traditionally enjoyed the support of labor. And the Peronists had substantial resources at their disposal to bring labor into line, even though the Menem government was in the process of dismantling the state and the protections that labor had enjoyed since the first presidency of Juan Domingo Perón.[21] Argentine labor was going through a profound weakening of its position in the Argentina political economy, and was not in a position to oppose economic policies, as it had been during the Alfonsín administration.

Brazilian labor was not in a particularly advantageous position either. The 1989 election campaign saw the victory of a candidate supported by conservative elements in Brazilian politics, and Fernando Collor made no secret of his desire to undo the previous development model. After assuming office, Collor embarked on a (failed) economic stabilization drive that increased unemployment, opened the Brazilian economy unilaterally, and was quite opposed to labor interests. Labor was also fractured in Brazil, so united action was simply not possible, even if some elements in the labor movement were opposed to the economic opening that came with Mercosur.[22]

Finally, at the time the Treaty of Asunción was signed, Latin America was at the height of neoliberalism. Though the general movement toward freer economies continued throughout the 1990s, 1990 and 1991 were special. The Cold War was suddenly over, and with its demise, state-led development strategies were also under attack. The decade-long assault on state intervention in the economy, which had begun with the victories of Margaret Thatcher in Great Britain and Ronald Reagan in the United States, had reached maturity and was being felt throughout the developing world, and particular in Latin America. The "Washington Consensus," as noted earlier, had taken hold, and its grip was tight. Although it took longer to arrive in the Southern Cone than it had in other Latin American countries, change had arrived. Brazil and Argentina were in sync, ideologically, pushing towards a new development model in Latin America.

To put it somewhat differently, working class organizations were certainly on the defensive in both Argentina and Brazil at the time the Treaty of Asunción was signed. The world that labor had previously considered secure was being washed away, much more quickly than it could have imagined. Labor was off balance, and to the extent that labor organizations engaged in political struggle, they worked harder against general free-market reforms. Mercosur, in the end, did not provoke strong opposition.

But did labor support Mercosur? Not at the outset. Although labor came to support a particular version of Mercosur once it saw the potential advantages that might be obtained through the trade organization, when Mercosur was initiated, it neither pushed nor opposed the new arrangement. Much like business, labor was not sure about the effects of economic liberalization in the region. Since it was hard to predict what effect Mercosur would have, and since there were so many other economic policy changes underway in both Argentina and Brazil, Mercosur, initially, was not at the top of the agenda of labor. In addition, since so many economic integration efforts in Latin America had failed in the past, neither labor nor business mobilized for or against economic integration when it first came on the agenda. This would change as real integration began to take shape, and the Treaty of Asunción got integration off to a running start.

The Treaty of Asunción

On March 26, 1991, Carlos Menem, Fernando Collor de Mello, Uruguayan president Luis Alberto Lacalle, and Paraguayan president Andrés Rodriguez signed the

Treaty of Asunción, which established Mercosur. The leaders were quite aware that the Treaty took Latin American integration further than any previous regional integration agreement. Expressions of optimism and triumph are customary on such occasions, even when there is little substance to the agreements. As President Menem said, "Our concern is no longer armed warfare. Our most important concern must now be peace . . . a peace of growth, of real freedom." President Collor said that the signing of the treaty marked an important step in making "a joint effort in the common task of building more prosperous, fair societies that are deeply committed to basic freedoms and the democratic system" (*BBC Summary of World Broadcasts* 1991b). The rhetoric flowed hot and heavy, and certainly set the stage for high expectations about what Mercosur could do.

Unlike previous announcements of Latin American integration efforts, this agreement had teeth to it, and a very specific timetable for liberalizing trade among the member nations. It also suggested that member nations would engage in economic cooperation in a wide variety of areas, including dispute resolution, macroeconomic policy coordination, sectoral industrial policies, and the free flow of factors of production. But it was only in the trade area where specifics were spelled out, and as later events would show, broader economic cooperation was more difficult to come by.

In the trade area, the member states agreed to a gradual and steady elimination of tariffs on intra-Mercosur trade, beginning June 30, 1991, and concluding with the complete elimination of tariffs by December 31, 1994 (Uruguay and Paraguay were given an extra year to comply with this rule).[23] Realizing that there would be certain sectors that would have a more difficult time adjusting, countries were allowed a limited list of exceptions to this general rule. The Treaty specified the number of exceptions, ranging from 324 items in Brazil to 960 in Uruguay. The Treaty also spelled out that these lists of exceptional products would be gradually reduced over time, by a specified percent each year.[24]

This impressive specificity when it came to trade was not replicated when it came to the other key parts of the economic integration project. There were many broad goals that were placed in the Treaty, though none were as specifically laid out as was trade liberalization. The signatories committed themselves to setting up a common external tariff (i.e., a customs union) by the end of 1994. They also committed themselves to formulating a common foreign trade policy when it came to relations with other countries or blocs. Even more ambitiously, they agreed, in the Treaty, to coordinate macroeconomic, industrial, and regulatory policies in a wide variety of areas.[25] One can detect a clear ambition to be like the EU with these goals. The Treaty seemed intent on "skipping stages," as it were, to become like the EU as quickly as possible. That said, these goals were followed up, in the Treaty, by specific actions only on trade liberalization. As will become clear later, many of the other issues were quite contentious, and it was mostly in the area of negotiating a common external tariff (discussed in the next chapter), where concrete progress was made by the end of 1994. As Jacques Ginesta has put it, "the treaty [did] not constitute a Common Market, but rather [was] a commitment to create such a common market in the future" (1999: 91). In this sense, fulfilling the impressive ambition of Mercosur was put off until later.

The Treaty also created new institutions to see integration through, and these institutions confirmed the unambiguously intergovernmental approach to integration in Mercosur. It created two new organizations: the Common Market Council (CMC), and the Common Market Group (CMG). The CMC was designated as the top decision-making body in Mercosur, whose "responsibilities involve political leadership and decision making to insure the fulfillment of the objectives and terms set forth for the definite constitution of the Common Market" (Simonsen Associados 1998: 130). Its membership consisted of the Foreign Affairs and Economic ministers of the member states, and would meet as often as needed, but at least once a year in the presence of the Presidents of the member nations. The CMG was deemed the "executive" agency of the Common Market and would be coordinated by the Foreign Affairs ministries of the member states. It was charged with taking "action required for the fulfillment of the decisions made by the Council," and was also empowered to constitute working groups to address specific issues (Tratado de Assunção 1991). The working groups authorized in the Treaty included groups that would deal with 1) trade policy; 2) customs affairs; 3) technical norms; 4) fiscal and monetary policies related to trade; 5) land transportation; 6) maritime transportation; 7) industrial and technological policy; 8) agricultural policy; 9) energy policy; and 10) macroeconomic policy coordination. An eleventh working group was created later in 1991, in response to criticisms that Mercosur was too focused on just trade liberalization, which focused on labor issues and social security. While these various working groups wanted to have an influence over the integration process, it was difficult for them to push their agendas forward. In the end, again, integration remained mostly at the commercial level.

In addition, nothing substantial could be accomplished without the unanimous agreement of all the member states, which is hardly surprising, given the fact that only four countries were involved in this agreement. In general, there was little thought given to how one might make a widespread economic integration scheme work. There was political will, to be sure, but there was not much thought given to how such an ambitious scheme would be enacted in practical terms, particularly given the economic instability in the member states.

Economic stabilization and integration

The Treaty of Asunción was signed in a context of extraordinary economic instability in the Mercosur nations, which in some ways makes its signing even more remarkable. From the mid-1980s on, both Brazil and Argentina had struggled through a series of failed stabilization attempts. Uruguay and Paraguay had also experienced high inflation, but it was nothing like what was experienced in the two larger economies. Table 3.1 shows the evolution of inflation rates in Argentina and Brazil from 1985 to 1995. Given these high and varying inflation rates, it is difficult to imagine that economic integration between the two principal Mercosur countries could have ever gotten off the ground; the instability and uncertainty in both economies was immense at the time. Still, they managed to begin integration, despite their problems.

Table 3.1 Inflation in Argentina and Brazil, 1985–1995 (percent change in consumer price index)

Year	*Argentina*	*Brazil*
1985	672	226
1986	90	147
1987	131	228
1988	343	629
1989	3,080	1,431
1990	2,314	2,948
1991	172	433
1992	25	952
1993	11	1,928
1994	4	2,076
1995	3	66

Source: World Bank (n.d.).

The so-called heterodox experiments that both countries had embarked on in the mid to late 1980s had not done the trick in the two large economies. The extensive literature on these experiments blamed their failure on a variety of factors, including inconsistent policies, lack of support from international financial institutions, and distributional conflict.[26] Policy changes were occurring while Mercosur was launched: within days of the signing of the Treaty of Asunción, Argentina had embarked on its Convertibility Plan, another attempt at taming the beast of inflation. Although this plan was eventually successful at stabilization, there was no reason to think, when the Treaty was signed, that it would be. It could very well have gone into the trash heap of failed economic stabilization packages that littered the regional landscape. So there was enormous uncertainty about the evolution of the region's economies when the countries agreed to be bound by specific and programmed tariff reductions in the Treaty. In this sense, the decision to plunge into economic integration was extraordinarily risky, and was only possible because of the leadership of the presidents who signed it. Since it did not have widespread backing in any part of civil society, as noted earlier, there was no built-in base of support to sustain Mercosur when it would run into trouble. It was, in a very clear sense, a leap of faith.

Fortunately for the evolution of Mercosur, the brand new Argentine stabilization plan did work. But this created a new set of problems, because one of the key elements of the Argentine stabilization plan involved pegging the Argentine peso to the dollar at a one-to-one ratio. Because of the skepticism of economic actors, Economy Minister Domingo Cavallo took a number of steps to make sure that this ratio would not be altered. In effect, economic policy makers in Argentina had given up control over key elements of monetary policy in a last-ditch attempt to subdue hyperinflation. In addition, this peg gave Argentina an overvalued currency, which led to significant trade deficits. Table 3.2 shows the evolution of trade between the two principal partners in Mercosur as well as their broader balance of trade positions in the years surrounding the signing of the Treaty of Asunción. In general, because Brazil was still experiencing very high inflation rates, and was

Table 3.2 Trade positions of Argentina and Brazil, 1989–1995 (millions of current US dollars)

Year	*Argentina's global trade balance*	*Brazil's global trade balance*	*Argentine exports to Brazil*	*Brazilian exports to Argentina*	*Argentine trade balance with Brazil*
1989	5,109	13,327	1,239	722	517
1990	7,954	6,986	1,400	645	755
1991	2,820	6,687	1,609	1,476	133
1992	–3,952	11,897	1,732	3,040	–1,308
1993	–5,688	8,739	2,717	3,659	–942
1994	–7,915	5,515	3,662	4,136	–474
1995	–1,059	–10,652	5,591	4,041	1,550

Sources: World Bank (n.d.) and Ministério de Desenvolvimento, Industria, e Comercio Exterior, *ALICEWeb*.

Table 3.3 Real exchange rate index in Argentina and Brazil, 1987–1995 (1991=100)

	1987	*1988*	*1989*	*1990*	*1991*	*1992*	*1993*	*1994*	*1995*
Argentina	190.9	229.3	333.5	157.3	100	85.3	80	78.8	78.4
Brazil	137.4	132.5	108.1	85.2	100	109	107.2	100.5	87.4

Source: Frenkel (2004: 34–35).

continuously devaluing its currency as a response, Brazil had access to exchange rate and monetary policy instruments that were now unavailable to the Argentines. At this point in time, the Argentine currency was overvalued, and the Brazilian currency was not, as shown in Table 3.3.

There are several things that come to mind when considering this data. First, the explosion in trade among the Mercosur countries was nothing short of spectacular. After years of stagnating trade, the Mercosur nations saw an impressive increase in bilateral trade, which itself proved to be an impetus to the further development of Mercosur. At the same time, trade flows were quite erratic in the early stages of Mercosur, with Brazil's exports to Argentina more than doubling from 1991 to 1992, while Argentine exports to Brazil hardly changed. The pendulum swung back between 1994 and 1995 (at the time of Brazil's own economic stabilization program, to be discussed in the next chapter), with Argentina experiencing a more than 50 percent increase in exports to Brazil while Brazil's exports to Argentina actually declined. The relationship between real exchange rates and these trade flows was evident, as the trends in trade are closely related to changes in exchange rates. Such changes in trade quite naturally also led to trade conflicts between the main partners in Mercosur. These conflicts are also discussed in the next chapter.

In the end, the most important early problems in integration came because of the serious discrepancies in macroeconomic performance in the member countries, especially Argentina and Brazil. The Mercosur nations also had to deal with severe political crisis in Brazil, with the impeachment and resignation of President Collor after his administration's corruption came to light. Argentina had finally defeated inflation, but as a consequence its currency was seriously overvalued, which led to balance-of-payments problems, especially as the market opening with its Mercosur neighbors went forward. In other words, the political and economic environment in Brazil and Argentina was not exactly propitious for integration. The bright spots were that both countries were growing their economies quite rapidly, and foreign capital was returning voluntarily to the region, in part stimulated by the Mercosur process itself.

Indeed, the early years of Mercosur were characterized by mini-crises that were resolved through negotiations at the presidential level, keeping the integration process on track. At the same time, however, these mini-crises also meant that Mercosur did not really move much beyond the agreement to reduce intra-regional tariffs; most of the other issue areas that the Mercosur nations had agreed to tackle in the Treaty of Asunción were postponed, with one exception: the decision to move to a common external tariff. Mercosur consolidated some of the key *commercial* aspects of integration, but it was unable to go much further at this stage. Its political institutions and economic circumstances were too vulnerable to push into other areas.

The fact that integration remained only at the commercial level led to a great deal of concern, in part because Mercosur had raised such high expectations. While there were plenty of policy makers (particularly in Argentina) who wanted only commercial integration, there were many actors in civil society who expected much more. In a sense, these higher expectations came about because both Brazil and Argentina were in the midst of searching for a new development model, and were making huge changes in their economies with little certainly about where they would go. And even though many recognized that the old import-substitution industrialization policies had reached a dead end, the goals that went along with these policies—industrial development, greater social equity, whatever might be considered "modernization"—were not abandoned. For many, achieving these goals was transferred to being a responsibility of Mercosur, weighing it down with outsized expectations. The explicit comparison that many participants in integration debates made to the EU spoke to this desire to make Mercosur the cornerstone of a new development strategy for some of its advocates. This also helps to explain why Mercosur did not collapse in the early stages. But given the argument presented in this book, this hope to be like the EU was an unachievable goal.

The early stages of Mercosur integration established a number of patterns that would be repeated as integration advanced or retreated: an emphasis on presidential diplomacy in the face of recurrent crises, an unwillingness to make significant changes in institutional structures to accommodate the new reality of greater integration, and an ongoing concern with economic stabilization in the face of homegrown and international economic vulnerabilities. These patterns made integration much more fragile, even as they gave the leaders who implemented them significant flexibility, since they were less constrained than they otherwise might be by supranational institutions. It made it possible to move quickly to push integration forward, and I now turn to the short-lived glory days of Mercosur in the mid-1990s.

4 Mercosur's day in the sun

Once some of the early hurdles had been overcome and Mercosur seemed to have arrived as a going concern, there was a great deal to do to make the organization more than a temporary success. Most importantly, according to Mercosur's original goals, it was to move all the way to a free trade area by the beginning of 1995, and was meant to agree to the rules of a custom's union by the same date. This was clearly an ambitious timetable, with the goal of getting to this new state of affairs less than four years from the signing of the original treaty. Many doubted that it could be accomplished, and along the way to signing the custom's union agreement, there were widespread opinions that the date would have to be pushed back or that Mercosur would simply have to remain a free trade area.

Nevertheless, with the Protocol of Ouro Preto, the Mercosur nations did in fact agree on the framework of a customs union by the end of 1994. The customs union was hardly complete, but it did cover a large portion of the goods that are traded in the regional grouping. The period surrounding the agreement to form a customs union is in many ways the "golden age" of Mercosur; it was at this point that trade was growing at breakneck speed, foreign investment was increasing at a rapid pace, and Brazil had finally matched Argentina by embarking on its own successful stabilization policy. The stars seemed to be aligned, and there was a great deal of optimism about what Mercosur could be.

Nevertheless, Mercosur demonstrated a continuing weakness in a number of areas. First, the member nations—Brazil in particular—continued to resist any sort of supranational institutions that might help sustain Mercosur. The countries were also buffeted by international economic shocks, the first of which—the Mexican peso crisis—was taking place even as the final touches were being placed on the Ouro Preto protocol. And finally, the demands for civil society participation increased during this period, clearly stressing the (limited) institutional infrastructure of the integration organization. These weaknesses proved nearly fatal at the end of the 1990s, when economic instability returned to the region.

This chapter discusses this (relative) golden age of Mercosur in several steps. First, I discuss the problems that preceded that actual signing of the Ouro Preto protocol. Following this I turn to a discussion of how changes in the political and economic environments in Argentina and Brazil affected the particulars of the negotiations between the two main Mercosur partners. I then return to a discussion of the "visions" of the different actors in Mercosur—states, business, and labor—and consider how each of these visions fared as Mercosur advanced. Finally, I turn to the specific deal that was struck at the end of 1994, which laid the groundwork for the attempted consolidation of Mercosur. The general argument here is that the Protocol of Ouro Preto set the outer boundary for what was possible in economic cooperation in South America, given the vulnerabilities of the nations of the region. It marked the point when there was the greatest "reach" for the Mercosur countries, and was only accomplished because of the rapid economic growth in the nations of the region. The signing of the deal also occurred just prior to turbulence in the international political economy that would hit developing countries in particular in the second half the 1990s, making their vulnerabilities quite clear. The difficulties that the Mercosur countries had in making the reach in the first place—in a quite forgiving international political economy—makes it clear how difficult it is for developing countries to deepen integration in the first place.

Bumps in the road

The conflicts revolving around Mercosur began after it was clear that the Argentine stabilization program was working. Key sectors suffered as a consequence of their suddenly uncompetitive position vis-à-vis Brazil, as Argentina was met by a flood of imports. Because of Argentina's overvalued currency, its external accounts took a quick turn for the worse in 1992, as noted in the previous chapter.

Even in the midst of this increasingly serious imbalance among Mercosur nations, they were making some big strides in reaffirming that they would move ahead with integration. The most important early event occurred in June 1992, when the Mercosur presidents—all four original signatories—met in the Argentine ski resort of Las Leñas. At this meeting, they reaffirmed the goal of achieving complete free trade by the end of 1994, along with the establishment of a common external tariff (CET). As Argentine President Menem put it at the summit, there was

> a need to integrate our economies, [to] create a bloc through which we can have access to some markets and improve our bargaining power in a world in which powerful blocs have emerged . . . Our time is now. We cannot waste another minute on insignificant issues.
>
> (*Latin American Regional Report—Southern Cone* 1992a)

The emphasis on trade issues here is significant; at the Las Leñas summit, the only concrete agreements were related to trade. A broader social, regulatory, or institutional agenda was not a key part of the summit.

There was also a recognition at this stage that some sort of mutual reassurance was needed, given the political and economic turmoil taking place in the Mercosur nations. In addition to the wide swings in trade flows noted in the previous chapter, Brazil in particular was experiencing the unfolding of a corruption scandal at this point that would eventually bring down the presidency of Fernando Collor de Mello in December (Flynn 1993). This scandal, combined with continued instability and inflation in the Brazilian economy, led one financial sector analyst to assert that Brazil was "still a basket case. Until Brazil gets its fiscal side in order, it is difficult to see Mercosur as much more than a regional free-trade zone among the countries" (Nash 1992). The Argentine government was facing increasing pressure from industrialists to increase trade barriers in response to the flood of imports that followed economic stabilization and its undervalued peso. At first, the Argentine authorities tried to resist the pressure to take measures against the increase in exports—Economy Minister Domingo Cavallo said on July 14, shortly after the Las Leñas summit, that the government "will not subsidise the rich or the entrepreneurs who have mismanaged their businesses" (*BBC Summary of World Broadcasts* 1992).

Those were fighting words, but in the end, Cavallo and Menem could not resist the pressure forever. Instead of devaluing the Argentine peso—which would have been tantamount to abandoning the stabilization plan in the eyes of its architects—the Argentines decided to increase its "statistical tax" on imports. They raised the tax from 3 percent to 10 percent. The major target of this new levy was Brazilian exports that were flooding the Argentine market (*Inter Press Service* 1992; *Business Latin America* 1993). The Brazilians initially threatened retaliation—and Brazilian industrialists encouraged such retaliation by suggesting that Brazil slow down the rate of tariff reductions agreed to in the Treaty of Asunción (*Latin American Regional Report—Brazil* 1992)—but cooler (and strategic) heads prevailed. To encourage Argentina to moderate its protectionist behavior, the Brazilians agreed to address the trade imbalance with Argentina by purchasing more Argentine wheat and oil (Manzetti 1993: 124). Consequently, the Argentines agreed to phase out the import levy. The crisis passed, and set a pattern for subsequent conflicts in the region: countries would react to short-term economic crises or difficulties by imposing certain costs on their neighbors, and then the leadership in the various countries would get together to iron out a compromise. There was nothing unusual or extraordinary in this behavior, to be sure.

And these early conflicts were a precursor to subsequent controversies; both Argentina and Brazil would face balance-of-payments problems throughout Mercosur's early development, and both took unilateral measures against the other. Remarkably, however, there was no significant move backward, though there was plenty of worry that the integration effort would not advance (*Inter Press Service* 1993; *Latin American Regional Report—Brazil* 1993). In this regard, political leadership was essential, especially since there was little in the way of supranational institutions to rely on to provide a more stable base of support for the integration process. One of the most important reasons that integration continued to advance in this period was the fact that both Brazil and Argentina were growing, finally, after the "lost decade" of the 1980s. In addition, trade was expanding rapidly, so neither country was interested in putting a brake on the process. With increasing trade, there were many more actors interested in maintaining it, which began to build a base of support for Mercosur.

This increase in trade also led to more actors putting pressure on their governments, and civil society began to get up to speed in trying to influence the shape of integration. This meant that Mercosur still faced occasional crises, largely because of the profoundly different macroeconomic conditions in Argentina and Brazil. Europe certainly faced difficulties in coordinating macroeconomic policies, with differences between strong currency countries such as Germany and weak currency countries such as Italy. But it never faced a situation where inflation in one of the member countries was at 11 percent while the other had an inflation rate of nearly 2,000 percent, which was the situation in 1993. To think of the problem somewhat differently, the change in the relationship between the Argentine and Brazilian currency between 1989 and 1992 was nothing short of breathtaking: when looking at the exchange rate indices presented in Table 3.3, one can see that in this short time frame, the Argentine peso nearly quadrupled its value in relationship to the Brazilian cruzeiro. It is hard to imagine any economic integration project going through such a dramatic change in relative exchange rates without major problems.

After the Argentine import tax conflict, there was continuing concern—from both Argentina and Brazil—that economic integration would be jeopardized by continued economic instability in Brazil. Cavallo suggested that integration "cannot come about through the approximation of healthy or better-managed economies with those with greater problems" (*Latin American Regional Report—Southern Cone* 1992b). There was no mystery about what he was referring to. In addition, since Mercosur integration was happening so rapidly, and trade was increasing so quickly, those left out from the discussion began to push their own agendas. At the end of 1992, trade unions in the four member countries had requested that their governments give greater attention to the social aspects of integration, and there was little response forthcoming, which led the Uruguayan labor confederation, the PIT-CNT, to begin a publicity campaign in April 1993 to slow down the tariff reduction plan contained in the Mercosur treaty (*Latin American Weekly Report* 1993). There was clearly concern about the disruptions that economic integration—particularly in the context of economic instability—would provide.

Despite these conflicts and concerns, over the course of 1993 and 1994, times were good for most of Latin America, which made it possible to advance in negotiations to establish a tighter integration project. Table 4.1 considers the major indicators in the Mercosur countries, and illustrates that growth and exports were increasing rapidly in most countries. Such rapid increases in growth and exports decreased the number of losers in the integration project, making it more feasible to make commitments to further integrate the economies in the region. As this integration gained momentum, and growth accelerated as well, it was not too large a leap to associate the two, and if more integration led to more growth, then the best move would be to leap forward in the integration process. The one outlier here is Brazil, which was still struggling in the early 1990s with trying to come up with a lasting stabilization plan. However, since Brazil was the country most interested in pursuing integration for geopolitical reasons—and since it was enjoying large trade surpluses with Argentina—it was not interested in slowing integration down. This became clear when the CET was negotiated, and I now turn to the particulars behind the negotiations that led to the Protocol of Ouro Preto.

Table 4.1 Economic indicators in Mercosur countries, 1982–1995 (growth rates, percent per year)

	Argentina		*Brazil*		*Paraguay*		*Uruguay*	
	Growth	*Exports*	*Growth*	*Exports*	*Growth*	*Exports*	*Growth*	*Exports*
1982–89 avg	–0.7	4.0	3.1	7.6	2.1	13.0	0.0	3.4
1990–95 avg	5.2	9.2	1.9	4.7	3.2	14.3	3.4	7.9
1990	–2.4	18.0	–4.3	–4.9	3.1	19.6	0.3	13.7
1991	12.7	–3.6	1.3	6.6	2.5	7.4	3.5	2.7
1992	11.9	–1.0	–0.5	10.4	1.8	–4.1	7.9	9.1
1993	5.9	4.0	4.9	10.2	4.1	39.6	2.7	8.6
1994	5.8	15.3	5.9	7.7	3.1	6.5	7.3	15.1
1995	–2.8	22.5	4.2	–1.4	4.7	16.9	–1.4	–1.9

Source: World Bank (n.d.).

Attempting to deepen integration: the politics behind Ouro Preto

Signing the Treaty of Asunción was just a first step in the integration process. It did go further than any previous Latin American integration attempt, since it locked in tariff reductions among the member countries. But given previous Latin American integration efforts, there was no guarantee that the integration process would go further. Nor was there a guarantee that this process would not be reversed; since there were no significant supranational institutions set up as part of Mercosur, and thus no mechanisms that could do much if some member countries violated the agreements, it was still a relatively tenuous process.

The Mercosur countries, had, however, committed themselves on paper to establishing a CET when they negotiated the Treaty of Asunción. If nothing else, it was evident that there was significant "political will" behind the decision to integrate. As one Argentine Central Bank official noted several years after the Treaty of Asunción had been agreed upon, "the decision to integrate the Mercosur countries [within four years] was crazy. But we *técnicos* had to figure out how to make the political decision work. And now it is irreversible" (Author interview, August 4, 1995). It was not going to be easy to pull off this accelerated integration process, particularly when it came to establishing the CET.

Nevertheless, the Mercosur nations succeeded, more or less. They did not arrive at a complete CET—there were many exceptions to the common tariff—but they did come up with an "imperfect customs union." When the CET was being negotiated, at times it appeared that negotiations would break down and that Mercosur would remain a free trade area. Nevertheless, most of the obstacles were overcome, and when they could not be overcome, the difficult decisions were put off until later. Mercosur nations adopted a strategy typical of international negotiations: they would figure out what they could agree on, and when it became impossible to go beyond certain agreements, they would agree to put the more difficult decisions off until later. Generally, though, the momentum was towards increasing integration and figuring out, on an ad hoc basis, how to finesse the difficult decisions.

Despite the commitment on the part of the presidents who signed the Mercosur agreement to follow through with the formation of a customs union, there were no details in the Treaty of Asunción that spelled out how a customs union would be accomplished. It is important to note here that setting up a customs union is far more complicated than general free trade. In the latter, all the participant countries have to agree to is to remove barriers for imports from the other countries in their regional grouping. While this can often be a painful process, and may meet plenty of political resistance, it does not require as much international cooperation as a customs union. When forming a customs union, nations must agree to share at least part of their foreign economic policy with their partners. Accomplishing such cooperation is extraordinarily difficult, which explains why there are relatively few customs unions in the world.[1]

The Mercosur nations managed to get to an imperfect customs union through difficult negotiations. They managed to agree on the customs union sooner than most analysts had expected, and perhaps sooner than even key policy makers in the region had expected. The timing of the negotiations was fortuitous, since Brazil's economic stabilization program (the Real Plan) had posted good results, and thus Brazil felt confident enough in its economic future to accept more long-lasting commitments.

New contexts and new political leadership

When the Protocol of Ouro Preto was negotiated during the course of 1994, the Mercosur nations were pushing their integration process forward at astounding speed. Very few observers thought it would be possible to agree on a CET by the agreed-upon date, but a combination of international political and economic forces and domestic changes in Brazil, in particular, made it possible. This section explores the factors that made the agreement possible.

First of all, overall trade had exploded in the early 1990s in the Mercosur region, as noted earlier. This made the Mercosur process a clear positive-sum game for the nations involved. Economic growth also picked up in all nations of the region, so there were no serious crises to confront, rather unusual for Latin America, which had experienced the chaos associated with the debt crisis of the 1980s. This positive-sum game made it much less likely that key players would object to integration, since they were witnessing clear benefits from the process. In other words, a constituency for continued economic integration had emerged.

Another key contextual variable that made further integration possible was the fact that finally, after years of trying, both Argentina and Brazil had finally stabilized their economies. Argentine stabilization was a bit more established and secure than Brazilian stabilization, but in both countries there was a great deal of optimism that they had finally conquered the demon of inflation. Stabilization had one overriding effect: it reduced uncertainty. As noted earlier, in Chapter 2, one of the main problems associated with previous Latin American integration efforts—including the initial Argentine-Brazilian agreements of the mid- and late 1980s—was the uncertainty over macroeconomic tendencies. When firms do no not know what the inflation level will be over the following few months, let alone years, it is rather difficult for them to agree to the risks associated with economic integration. Integration is, after all, an inherently risky process.

In addition, and associated with the stabilization plans, the currencies of both Argentina and Brazil were overvalued. While this caused problems on the external front for both countries, it meant that within Mercosur, the key nations were operating on more or less equal footing, finally, with a commitment to use exchange-rate policy to continue their stabilization. This commitment was more absolute in Argentina than in Brazil, since Argentina had tied the peso to the dollar, but it was a key element of Brazilian stabilization as well.[2] Overvaluation might not have been a wise policy in the long run—and it ended up causing serious problems several years down the road—but it worked to make agreement on a CET possible.

The external context was also favorable for Mercosur. Foreign investment was pouring into the region, also helping to stabilize the Mercosur economies. One of the major problems associated with the failed stabilization programs of the 1980s was the fact that foreign investors were unwilling to commit their capital to the unstable economies (García Munhoz 2003). But by the early 1990s, this capital returned, as foreign investors became enamored with the economic potential of "emerging countries." And Mercosur was seen as one of the most promising regions. Table 4.2 shows the rapid increase in capital inflows into Argentina and Brazil. In part because of the economic integration efforts, foreign investors saw many growth possibilities, and between 1990 and 1994, US$23.5 billion in foreign direct investment flowed into Argentina and Brazil. This compared to a total of US$10.5 billion in the five years prior to 1990. In addition, after 1994, the direct investment accelerated even more rapidly, helped along by privatization in both countries. Foreign capital inflows helped to make Mercosur a reality. As noted in the previous chapter, this is precisely what leaders had hoped for when they embarked on the integration process in the first place.

Table 4.2 Net foreign direct investment inflows, Argentina and Brazil, 1985–1997 (in millions of current US dollars and as percentage of GDP)

Year	*Argentina Amount*	*% of GDP*	*Brazil Amount*	*% of GDP*
1985	919	1.05	1,441	0.65
1986	574	0.52	345	0.13
1987	–19	–0.02	1,169	0.40
1988	1,147	0.91	2,804	0.85
1989	1,028	1.34	1,131	0.24
1990	1,836	1.30	989	0.21
1991	2,439	1.29	1,103	0.27
1992	4,431	1.94	2,061	0.53
1993	2,793	1.18	1,292	0.29
1994	3,635	1.41	3,072	0.56
1995	5,609	2.17	4,859	0.69
1996	6,949	2.55	11,200	1.45
1997	9,159	3.13	19,650	2.43

Source: World Bank (n.d.).

Political changes in the Mercosur countries also provided added impetus for the integration effort. Whereas Presidents Collor and Menem had established their timetable for rapid integration to ensure that it would be completed by the time they had both finished their first terms, the negotiation for the CET occurred under quite different circumstances. President Collor was impeached in late 1992 and resigned the presidency. On the other hand, Carlos Menem had achieved constitutional changes that allowed him to run for a second term, and all indications were that he would win a second term in the 1995 elections.[3]

Nevertheless, though Brazil's political situation was somewhat more unstable, it was also in the midst of a profound transition under the leadership of Finance Minister (and later president) Fernando Henrique Cardoso. Cardoso was the architect of the Brazilian stabilization program during his stint as Finance Minister under the President who replaced Collor after his resignation, Itamar Franco.[4] Franco gave Cardoso a great deal of latitude to formulate a plan to halt inflation, and as the Real Plan developed, it gathered support. This was in itself remarkable, since Brazil had had so many failed stabilization plans over the course of the previous decade. But there was a widespread sense that something had changed with this stabilization program. As Cardoso himself put, the success of the Real Plan depended in part

> on the exhaustion of the population . . . This led to a desire for some sort of pathway of hope. The popular support [the stabilization plan received] led to high hopes that it was possible to improve the country, even if the pathway wasn't exactly clear. This diffuse feeling turned into more concrete action on the part of the media and business, which both played an important part in the acceptance of the program. Almost because it was "saturated," the old order gave an opening for the transition to a new state of affairs
>
> (2006a: 205)

It was Cardoso's good fortune that the timing of Real Plan, and its success, happened on the cusp of the presidential election campaign. Cardoso won the 1994 election in the first round of balloting, and assumed the presidency at the beginning of 1995.

As Cardoso was winning his presidential campaign and preparing to assume office, Mercosur was at a critical stage. Itamar Franco was clearly committed to the pursuit of integration in Mercosur, and importantly, his vision of what integration should mean was significantly different from that of his predecessor. While Fernando Collor was clearly committed to neoliberalism and opening Brazil's market unilaterally, Franco was much more of an old-style politician who was interested in preserving protectionist policies. He did continue Collor's market liberalization, however, and Mercosur remained a priority. It was also during the Franco government that Brazil proposed a South American Free Trade Area, which was certainly a priority of some within Itamaraty (Batista 1994). A South American Free Trade Area would have a hard time coming into existence, to be sure, but the fact that Brazil has encouraged this idea from time to time makes its own overall strategic preferences clear: Brazil wanted to avoid greater integration with the United States, and wanted to diversify its trading relationships as much as possible.

In Argentina, the perspective was somewhat different, given the continued sway of Domingo Cavallo in Argentine economic policy. The goal of the Menem government in Argentina was to open the region to outsiders, reduce trade barriers, and hold out the potential for hemispheric integration. This helps to explain the degree to which Argentina still entertained a NAFTA option up until very late in the CET negotiations, until it became evident that such an outcome was not viable (Teubal 1998).

The specifics of the negotiations that led up to the Protocol of Ouro Preto revolved around several issues. One concerned the overall average level of tariffs that Mercosur nations would impose on imports. Generally speaking, Brazil was on the higher end of the scale, and Argentina was on the lower. Second, negotiators were concerned with exceptions to the CET; there was, implicit in the negotiations, an understanding that not everything that the Mercosur countries imported would have a harmonized tariff, and the number of exceptions was a sticking point. Third, there was significant disagreement about dispute settlement procedures, since such disputes would likely become more frequent as Mercosur increased integration. Finally, there were special areas—automobiles and sugar, to name the two most important—where there were fundamental disagreements about how to regulate the region's commerce with the rest of the world (*Latin American Weekly Report* 1994). Reaching an agreement on how to proceed in Mercosur was complicated, and in the end, required political will. This meant that negotiations would have to be authorized and pushed from the highest levels in Mercosur nations, so presidents had to become involved.

Indeed, presidents had always been essential for the negotiation of Mercosur and the agreements that led up to it. The process had been top down, by and large, and initially, as noted earlier, many actors in civil society were taken by surprise when presidents announced new initiatives in the process. Fundamentally, integration would have never occurred without the leadership from the top.

This presidentialist dynamic has thus been present throughout integration in Mercosur (Malamud 2005a). This has become particularly evident whenever a crisis erupts in Mercosur; when these crises come to the fore, there is a great deal of hand-wringing and complaining, and in the end, presidents have had to step in to make things right. In effect, presidential diplomacy substituted for supranational institutions in the early development of Mercosur. Because there was little willingness (particularly on the part of Brazil) to create new institutions as part of the integration process, something had to take their place. It might have been possible for presidents to delegate the key work to the most important ministers in the Foreign Relations and Economic ministries, and indeed, this happened to a significant degree. But when push came to shove, presidents had to intervene to get the integration process back on track. So, not only was Mercosur a supremely *intergovernmental* affair—this aspect of the European integration project is by far more relevant in the integration process than is neofunctionalism—it was also primarily a *presidentialist* integration project.

This tendency towards presidentialism in Mercosur reflected long-standing Latin American political traditions. Institutions had always been up for grabs in Latin America, with the expectation that the rules of the game could be changed at any moment, in what Douglas Chalmers (1977) famously referred to as the "politicized state." Leaders have traditionally been unwilling to lock themselves in via institutional ties and commitments, and economic integration has been no exception in this regard. The previous Latin American integration experiences made this clear, as no nation signing on to LAFTA or ALADI was willing to give up sovereignty to pursue the cause of integration.

That said, Mercosur did illustrate one way in which presidents were willing to give up control, to at least a small degree. With the Treaty of Asunción, they decided to commit themselves to tariff reductions as integration proceeded. Even this, though, can be seen through the prism of the politicized state: it was no coincidence that when Carlos Menem and Fernando Collor agreed on the timetable for integration that this tariff reduction program would be completed by the time both of them finished their first terms in office. At the time, no one knew that Menem would be able to win a second term in office, or that Collor would be ousted through impeachment. Both presidents were attempting to preserve and guarantee the continued existence of Mercosur through specific treaty agreements. And both presidents had clear (and different) goals that they were pursuing as Mercosur developed in the early stages. Before turning to specifics related to the negotiation of the Protocol of Ouro Preto, I consider how the visions and goals in the states, business, and labor evolved in the early years of Mercosur's existence.

Changing context, changing visions

Because Mercosur jumped the initial hurdles and surprised the skeptics who thought that it would end up like so many other Latin American integration projects, it rapidly changed the views of many of the key actors in the integration process. Starting with a relatively limited constituency, it quickly built a more substantial one, and after its initial success, many more actors had an interest in seeing the integration process go forward. Numerous publications also sprung up to deal with Mercosur, a clear signal that Mercosur had captured the imagination of the business community. And labor unions began to take the process seriously, publishing their own analyses of the project, with proposals on how to include issues of importance to labor unions in the negotiations. As in the previous chapter, here I consider, in turn, the changing views of states, business, and labor as they confronted an increasingly vibrant Mercosur.

Visions of the states

As noted in the previous chapter, visions of the Argentine and Brazilian states on integration were different when the Treaty of Asunción was negotiated. Brazil was mostly focused on a geopolitical strategy, one of using Mercosur to strengthen the region vis-à-vis outside powers, while Argentina was more interested in using

Mercosur to force its firms to become more competitive in international markets, which would be a first step toward hemispheric integration. That said, Brazil also had, to some degree, a "neoliberal" vision of integration in the early stages, as President Collor was quite committed to a unilateral opening of the Brazilian economy, come what may. In the early years of the integration process, however, the positions of the main partners moved further apart: after Collor's impeachment, the pace of unilateral reform slowed a bit, and there was increased uncertainty about the direction of economic policy in Brazil. In Argentina, on the other hand, there was a deepened commitment to using Mercosur as only a first step toward broader market opening.[5]

Brazil's move towards a more pragmatic application of neoliberal principles began shortly after the Treaty of Asunción was signed. Brazil was one of the last countries in the region to embrace free markets, and even when it did move in a more neoliberal direction, it moved there in a tentative way. This is not to say that Brazil has not continued along a road to liberalization, privatization, and market-opening; it has. But in contrast to many other Latin American countries, Brazil has strong constituencies both in and out of government who have reflexively protectionist points of view. Successive governments have defended market opening and liberalization, and many efforts have been made in this regard. But Brazil is not at all shy about raising tariffs when it needs to, or imposing non-tariff barriers when the balance-of-payments is in bad shape. And there is political support for such steps.

Within government, the strongest forces to put a break on unilaterally opening markets were to be found in the Development Ministry, the National Development Bank (BNDES), and the Foreign Ministry (Itamaraty). In addition, in Itamaraty, there is a long tradition of supporting an "independent" foreign policy, as noted previously, and in particular there is a strong desire to maintain some degree of independence from the United States.[6] Whereas the Development Ministry largely opposed rapid opening of the economy because of its ties to industry and the preferences of industry to be protected from intense foreign competition, Itamaraty opposed an especially rapid opening on more ideological grounds. Itamaraty was mostly opposed to a hemispheric free trade area, and was unwilling to move quickly toward greater integration. Indeed, this can be seen as a very consistent part of Brazilian foreign policy during Mercosur's heyday: it maintained a cautious reluctance to move forward with hemispheric integration.[7]

Argentina under President Carlos Menem, on the other hand, was moving in the opposite direction. It had already demonstrated its newfound commitment to cooperation with the United States when it sent troops to fight in the Gulf War in 1990–1991. The Argentine government did everything it could to convince more developed countries that it had made a drastic change in the way it related to the rest of the world, and among the goals that the new government had were joining the North Atlantic Treaty Organization (NATO), despite the geographical contradiction, and joining the United States on a regular basis in its votes in the United Nations (Bernal-Meza 2002). There was a clear move away from a more independent foreign policy on the part of Argentina, even as Brazil maintained its relative distance from the United States. Carlos Menem himself made the case for the change in Argentina's orientation:

> Argentina was a country that aligned itself with so-called Third World . . . but for me, there's no reason for this world to exist. We decided to align ourselves with the world that exists. On this point, we all know that there is one country that is a leader in the United Nations, and that's the United States.
>
> (Onuki 2004: 4)

Beyond this strong desire to be a diplomatic ally of the United States, Argentina was quite interested in NAFTA; after it was passed in 1993, the Argentine government expressed its hope to follow Chile into NAFTA, in relatively short order. Domingo Cavallo said in early 1994 that if Mercosur was restricted to the "more realistic goal of just a free trade area, given the complications involved with achieving a customs union" that Argentina would be quite willing to aim for a free trade agreement with the United States (Mello 2002: 39). In other words, Argentina still saw Mercosur as a first step to hemispheric integration, which was clearly at odds with the Brazilian position.

One should not exaggerate Argentina's lack of interest in Mercosur, however. After all, the Brazilian market—even with Argentina's overvalued exchange rate—was proving to be a bonanza for Argentine exporters, and there was certainly no guarantee that a deal with the United States would work out (as later became obvious). In the end, when a NAFTA option was eventually closed off to Argentina, the most attractive game in the neighborhood was Mercosur, and they moved in this direction.

In sum, the positions of the Argentine and Brazilian governments moved apart to some degree during the early stages of Mercosur. Brazil was increasingly committed to using Mercosur as a vehicle to resist hemispheric integration (and strengthen its position vis-à-vis other regions), while Argentina was committed to using Mercosur to *promote* hemispheric integration. As the negotiations toward the Protocol of Ouro Preto advanced, these different positions were reflected in the negotiating positions of each side, as will become apparent later. These differences did not make an agreement to deepen impossible, but they did shape how the agreement would conclude, and it set the stage for greater conflict in subsequent years.

Visions of business

By the time the Protocol of Ouro Preto was being negotiated, Mercosur was clearly a success in commercial terms. Trade had increased dramatically, as can be seen in Figure 4.1. For both Argentina and Brazil, Mercosur was becoming a much more important market, and this increase in trade increased the number of stakeholders in the integration process. Because of this increase in trade—and because of the broader economic openings taking place in both countries—there was much more interest and political activity by social actors. As Lima and Santos point out in the Brazilian case, "with economic liberalization, it became rational for domestic entrepreneurs and unions to participate in international negotiations" (1998: 20). That is to say, when protection was firmly in place, international negotiations were not of much interest to economic actors, since they would not have much effect on the material circumstances of these actors. But with freer trade, this calculus changed. Many multinational firms and internationalized business sectors in both Argentina and Brazil were reaping large benefits from the integration process, and generally speaking, the large economies of the region were booming. Mercosur could not take all the credit for this boom, but it was seen as an important contributing factor to growth in many of the sectors.

But would business be interested in deepening integration, moving beyond a free trade area to a customs union? In principle, there is no a priori reason to assume that it would. In some cases, a CET could make some imported inputs more expensive for firms if tariffs were raised, thus hurting competitiveness. Then again, if the tariff were raised for a firm's final product, that would presumably give it a competitive edge against imports. The same logic applies if the CET were to be lowered: for those who would use the inputs of these cheaper products in their production, it would help them competitively, while those whose final product saw the import tariff lowered, it could increase competition and reduce profit margins and/or sales. Indeed, individual firms might face cross-cutting pressures in this regard, favoring increases or decreases in tariffs in different product areas.

So, there is no way to generalize about business. Just as there were different visions within the business community when Mercosur was launched, there were different visions at this stage of the integration process. The dynamics were somewhat different, however, for a number of reasons. First, changes in hemispheric

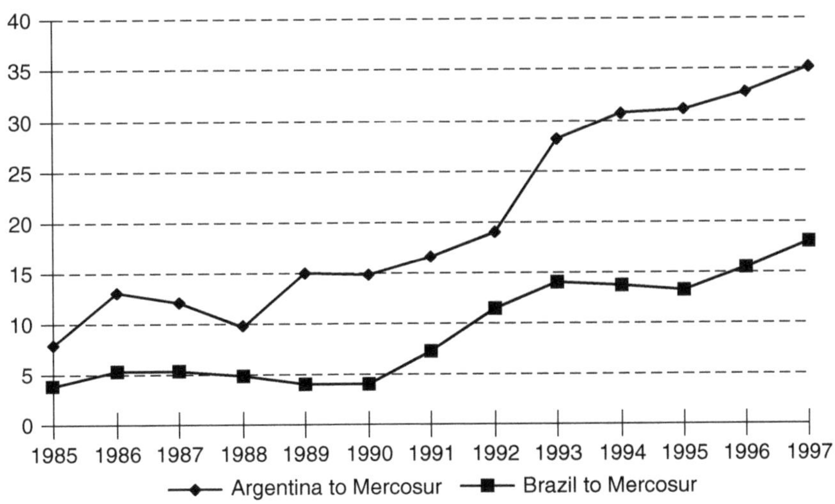

Figure 4.1 Argentine and Brazilian exports to Mercosur, 1985–1997 (as a percentage of total exports)

Source: International Monetary Fund (1992: 82–84: 111–13; 1998: 102–04; 136–38).

dynamics—with the passage of NAFTA and its possible extension to other countries in Latin America—made integration with North America a viable option. Second, as noted earlier, political conditions in Brazil had changed since the impeachment of Fernando Collor, and Brazil showed tendencies of reverting to its more traditionally protectionist instincts under new President Itamar Franco. Third, tariffs in Brazil were generally higher than tariffs in the other Mercosur countries, which meant that any move towards a CET would largely mean lowering Brazilian tariffs and increasing tariffs in the other countries. Finally, the experience of Mercosur had made it clear who the winners and losers were in the process so far, and constituencies had emerged in the business sector for integration, while others viewed themselves as losers in the process.

Though it is impossible to generalize about business in Mercosur, it is possible to divide business segments as coalescing around particular positions on further integration (Hirst 1996b). The divisions cut both between and within nations, as was the case with the earlier disaggregation. First and foremost, multinational firms were very interested in seeing the integration process deepened. They might be for higher or lower tariffs in their particular sectors, but a solidification of the integration process was largely in their interests. Since they were more able to move production between the nations making up Mercosur, they would prefer a political and economic environment that guaranteed access to the entire region, and moving toward a CET would do this. In the case of some industries—auto, for example—firms had already moved integration forward at a rapid rate. Other sectors that took quick action to take advantage of a more integrated market were in the agroindustrial and petrochemical sectors.[8] In addition, multinationals looked kindly on a more integrated market since it would lead to competition between the nations in Mercosur for their investments, which could lead to better tax and other incentives for their investments. That said, it is also the case that multinationals who were already installed in the Mercosur countries were forced to reevaluate their investment and production strategies as a result of integration, since they would no longer be able to count on the protection that they had grown up with. In the end, integration—and broader economic liberalization in the Mercosur countries—led to a very large increase in foreign direct investment in the region.[9]

Internationalized domestic firms also sometimes saw opportunities in further integration—they had seen what integration could do for them so far, and tighter integration would make more cross-border investments feasible and less risky. They could take advantage of partnerships with both multinationals and firms in other countries to expand market share and grow, and increasing numbers of internationalized Argentine and Brazilian firms struck deals with one another.[10] In the end, much would depend on their competitive position, and they, like MNCs, were forced to reevaluate their strategies in the face of Mercosur and broader economic liberalization (Kingstone 1999). Some sectors were more competitive than others as they faced this new reality, but many sectors had resources that they could use, making these firms more likely to support further integration in Mercosur.

Less internationalized domestic firms in the tradable goods sector were somewhat more ambivalent. If they were uncompetitive in relation to their Mercosur neighbors, then they would have already paid the price of integration and would have taken steps to cope with this new reality. If they were more competitive, they would have reaped the benefits of integration. In either case, whether they supported moving towards a CET or not would depend on whether or not that CET would increase or decrease the tariffs in their particular industrial sector. In principle, then, since Brazil generally had to decrease tariffs, and Argentina generally had to increase them, more Brazilian firms and sectors in this particular slice of the economy would oppose a CET, at least if it was set very low. Indeed, as the automatic tariff reductions contained in the Treaty of Asunción took effect, business—of all kinds—complained about the drops in tariffs among the Mercosur nations, and petitioned the government to slow down liberalization.[11] The complaints often followed exchange rate swings: Argentine business was especially vocal after the convertibility plan (and the overvalued exchange rate) achieved stability in Argentina; Brazilian business was likewise upset with increased imports from Mercosur (and outside Mercosur) after the Real Plan actually worked.

In the end, as Mercosur showed real success, more and more business sectors came to support it. In part this was due to the fact that Mercosur was simply becoming a reality, and integration was unlikely to be reversed. Business understood that the rules had changed. It was also due to the fact that there was such impressive growth in the early years of Mercosur; something seemed to be going right in the economy, and there was money to be made in investments that focused on the region. Finally, once some businesses adopted "Mercosur strategies," others felt compelled to follow suit for competitive reasons. There was a concern among many businesses that failing to invest in the new regional economy could leave them at a competitive disadvantage, so they made decisions that made Mercosur more likely to become a reality.

Visions of the labor movement

There was a similar dynamic unfolding among labor unions as Mercosur became a reality. As noted in the previous chapter, labor did not oppose Mercosur when it was first proposed, as might have been expected. And as Mercosur advanced, most labor unions also realized that there were few benefits in trying to resist the process; Mercosur was part and parcel of the new economic reality. And it was the part of the new economic reality that was conceivably most amenable to achieving at least some of labor's goals.

It was also the case that labor was the weakest player when Mercosur was first introduced. And in the early 1990s, labor's power decreased, as neoliberal reforms weakened labor's influence, even if it was not weakened as much as reformers would have preferred (Cook 2002; Castro 1996). As is evident in Figure 4.2, labor in the Mercosur countries faced an unfavorable environment as the Mercosur process advanced, with unemployment increasing, for the most part. The increases in unemployment came for different reasons in each country, but were certainly related to some degree to the increased economic opening that all countries experienced, leading to greater competition and increased unemployment in the industrial

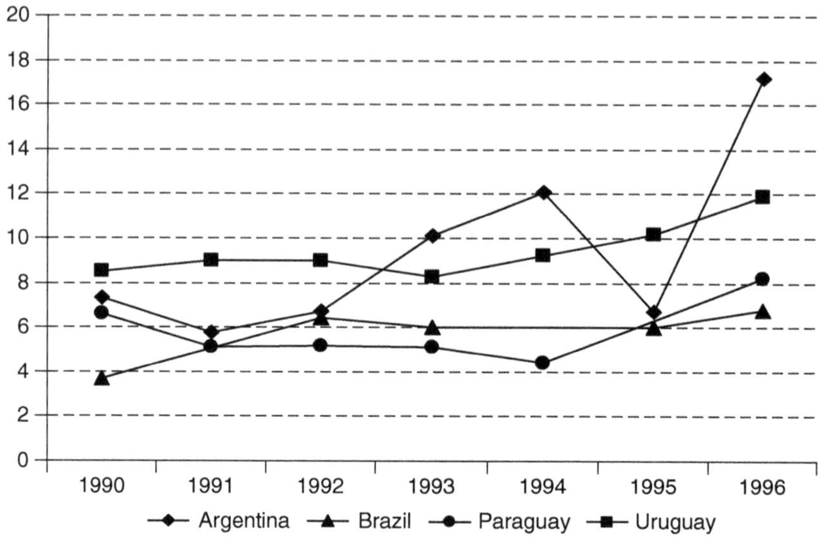

Figure 4.2 Unemployment rate in Mercosur countries, 1990–1996 (as a percentage of total labor force; official figures)

Source: World Development Bank: *World Development Indicators.*

sector in particular. For example, Argentina saw the share of its workforce in industry decline from 32.7 percent in 1991 to 24.9 in 1996. In Uruguay, the share of its workforce in industry declined from 33 percent in 1991 to 26.7 percent in 1995. Even Brazil, which was still interested in protecting its industrial base in this period, saw a drop in the share of its workforce engaged in industry, from 22.7 percent in 1990 to 19.9 percent in 1996.[12] Clearly labor—and particularly industrial labor—was not faring well with the economic opening in this period.

Nevertheless, and somewhat counterintuitively, labor became one of the strongest supporters of deepening the integration process. Instead of its somewhat cautious position when Mercosur was initially launched, labor became an active proponent of integration, particularly in Brazil. It favored a particular version of integration that is yet to be realized, but it was a strong supporter from early on in the process (Vigevani and Veiga 1996).

How to explain this enthusiasm for integration? Fundamentally, it comes down to two factors: first, labor unions were weak, and thus had few alternatives when it came to advocating different development strategies. Second, the labor movement realized that it could use Mercosur to push a whole host of demands, ranging from policies to improve labor standards in the region to pushing social pacts on the regional level that were difficult to achieve on the domestic level. As noted earlier, labor could have been a disruptive force in the integration process, but it was not. In supporting integration, labor unions put numerous issues on the table, hoping that they would eventually be negotiated in a deeper Mercosur.

It was able to put new issues on the table because of the agreement among the Mercosur negotiators to include labor issues in Mercosur discussions after the Treaty of Asunción was signed. This was something of an afterthought: the working groups that were established in the Treaty did not specify labor issues. The main Brazilian labor federation, the Central Única dos Trabalhadores (the Unified Workers' Central—CUT) approved a specific set of demands relating to Mercosur at its fourth National Congress just six months after the Treaty of Asunción was signed, and it made quite specific (and reasonable) demands of Mercosur, consistent with international norms of labor rights (Alimonda 2000: 34). Indeed, the demands were framed in such a way as to make them quite compatible with democratic capitalist development; they were hardly radical. At the end of 1991, in response to pressure from labor organizations to put labor issues on the agenda, an eleventh working group was established to focus on labor issues.

Understanding the position of labor regarding integration is somewhat simpler than disaggregating the position of business. In part this is because labor unions in the Mercosur countries have not traditionally developed extensive expertise—until recently—on international trade issues. It is also the case that labor unions have been much less able to influence state decision making more informally, quite distinct from business. Therefore, labor is likely to push a broader set of positions that focus on the rules of the game, whereas business is more likely to push for particularistic advantages. Finally, labor unions in the Mercosur countries are much more likely to present their demands as a social class rather than as representing a particular industry.

There were several goals that labor unions had as they confronted Mercosur. First and foremost was a desire to increase labor rights and protections in the regions. Labor had generally been successful in the transitions to democracy in increasing labor rights, at least formally (Cook 2002). Though labor codes differed throughout the region, in no nation in the early 1990s were labor rights strong, with the possible exception of Uruguay.[13] In addition, unions wanted to be involved in decision making in the Mercosur negotiations themselves; they wanted to have a place at the table. Finally, labor unions wanted to protect their members against the costs that would be associated with a transition to more open economies (Alimonda 2000). They were not making extraordinary demands, but the demands were not what the original trade liberalizers had in mind.

Although the Mercosur process did have the effect of increasing this intraregional cooperation, it is important to emphasize that unions in the different Mercosur nations were responding to quite different circumstances. In the case of Argentina, unions there were in the most difficult position, because of their general support for the Menem government. These unions did not know what they were in for when they supported their Peronist candidate. After his election, Menem took immediate steps to reduce union power in politics—in this sense, he executed a "Nixon in China" policy; only a Peronist could limit the power of Peronist unions.[14] The labor movement split as a result of these reforms, with a new labor federation, the Confederación de Trabajadores Argentinas (Argentine Workers Confederation—CTA) emerging in 1992. The CTA came about in response to the

traditional (and Peronist) labor federation, the Confederación General de Trabajadores (General Workers Confederation—CGT), which supported the Menem government's reforms (Ranis 1998). This split made it much more difficult for the Argentine labor movement to offer an articulate and united position when it came to Mercosur integration.

While not necessarily united, Brazilian labor was much more involved than Argentine labor in the early stages of Mercosur integration. It was not thrown off balance in the same way as Argentine labor was, and it was especially active when it came to studying the integration process. It proposed new plans that would include labor initiatives on the agenda, and put pressure on negotiators to include labor issues in integration discussions (Riethof 2004). The Brazilian labor movement was divided as well, but not as divided as Argentina's was. The most important labor federation, the CUT, which was connected to the Worker's Party (PT), held sway over labor politics in general.[15] In general, the attitude of Brazilian labor was one of engagement, though there was also concern that regional integration would in fact only involve commercial issues and would leave matters of importance to labor off the agenda.

In the end, as noted earlier, labor did not oppose integration. In this sense, labor—like business—reacted to a changed international and domestic environment. Labor endeavored to put issues on the table that negotiators would rather not deal with. But put those issues on the table they did, and states and business could not always ignore them, try as they might. At the same time, the weak position of labor underlines an important part of the vulnerable integration model: whereas the preferences of labor, and labor organizations, had been an important part of the European integration process, in Mercosur labor stayed on the margins when it came to the actual decisions that were made. Because of the weakness of this particular sector of civil society, integration continued to have a mostly commercial character, one of the key elements that I have identified as part of a process of vulnerable integration.

Negotiating a common external tariff

In the end, these changing visions toward what integration should be had a strong effect on the development of Mercosur after the Treaty of Asunción was signed. And the fact that states, business, and labor all had different reasons for wanting Mercosur to go forward led to the important next step: the signing of the Protocol of Ouro Preto, which established the outlines for a CET. Although the Mercosur nations had agreed to establish such a tariff in the original treaty, they had also agreed to do many other things that never came to pass. Mercosur was no nearer to establishing macroeconomic coordination or establishing a dispute settlement mechanism with teeth than they were when the Treaty was initially signed. In this sense, the Mercosur process was much like the European integration process: there were many things that nations agreed that they would do at a later date, putting off difficult decisions that were never made, or were made only *much* later. The CET could have faced a similar fate, but it did not.

Signing the Protocol of Ouro Preto marked the high point of Mercosur, in several ways. First, it demonstrated an extraordinary degree of cooperation among the member states, and moved far beyond anything that had been accomplished in Latin America to date. Second, negotiating a customs union is something that normally would take much more time than the Mercosur nations took; the speed of negotiations was impressive. Third, since trade was expanding at such a rapid rate in the region, there was much more interest on the part of all parties to sign an agreement that would further integration. Finally, since the major economies of the region had experienced such economic instability in the very recent past, the fact that they were able to come to an agreement promising much greater cooperation was striking.

The Protocol itself did a number of things to push integration forward (Protocolo de Ouro Preto 1994). Most fundamentally, it fulfilled the promise of the Treaty of Asunción to form a customs union. While many of the other promises of the Treaty were not fulfilled, this one was. The customs union itself was "imperfect," as the participating nations agreed: quite a number of products were left off the final list of goods where a CET could be agreed upon, but it was agreed that more than 80 percent of all products would have a common import tariff in the region. In addition, trade in most of these products would be free of duty within the region. There were exceptions to these general rules—Uruguay and Paraguay had more exceptions than Argentina and Brazil—but this was still an enormous step for all the Mercosur countries (*BBC Summary of World Broadcasts* 1994).

With Ouro Preto, Mercosur also became an international legal entity; i.e., it gained status as a grouping that could negotiate international agreements and could be seen by the rest of the world as having some legitimacy as an organization. While to some degree this enhanced status was symbolic, it went beyond this. From this point on, Mercosur nations would begin to coordinate foreign economic policies. This was particularly important in negotiations with the United States and other countries in the Americas over a Free Trade Area of the Americas (FTAA), as well as negotiations with the EU over free trade. At this point in time, the Mercosur nations hoped to use their agreement to enhance negotiating leverage with both the United States and Europe.

Finally, the Ouro Preto agreement established some new institutional parameters for Mercosur. It maintained the structure of the Common Market Council as the top decision-making group, as well as the Common Market Group as the principle executive body within Mercosur. In addition, the Protocol established several other groups with specific responsibilities within Mercosur, though none (except the Mercosur Trade Commission) would have any decision-making authority. The new organs that came into being with the Protocol (without decision-making authority) were a Joint Parliamentary Commission, the Mercosur Secretariat, and the Consultative Forum on Economic and Social issues. It is important to note here that the Mercosur nations were quite deliberate in their avoidance of any supranational institution that might impinge on the sovereignty of any of the member nations.

Getting to this agreement—despite its limits—was something few would have predicted a few years before, even after the Treaty of Asunción was signed. There

were several factors that helped to make it possible. The international context was crucial in pushing Mercosur nations toward agreement. To begin with, as noted earlier, the early 1990s were good years for Latin America's broad economic prospects. International capital was finally returning to the region after a decade of having avoided Latin America. This capital came from investors interested in purchasing stocks in the region, investors willing to buy government securities, and MNCs willing to pour money into new productive investments in the region (Griffith-Jones 2000). In an important sense, the initial success of Mercosur ended up reinforcing further success: the initial plan was designed to attract more foreign capital to region, and this is exactly what it did.

Therefore, international conditions—principally, the willingness of foreign investors to put money into the region—encouraged greater integration. Since the leaders in the Mercosur countries saw that their integration efforts had quite concrete economic benefits in this regard, they had strong incentives to push integration forward to continue these inflows of foreign capital. Mercosur had accomplished one of its principle goals: to avoid marginalization in the international political economy after the end of the Cold War.

Political developments in the United States also had an impact on the acceleration of integration in the region. As noted earlier, the successful negotiation and passage of NAFTA put hemispheric integration on the table. This had a particularly significant effect on the Brazilian attitude towards Mercosur, since the Brazilians were not especially interested in hemispheric integration. As a consequence, Brazil was the driving force behind the negotiation of the CET. Brazil was more willing to make concessions to make a CET happen—though not in the area of supranational institutions—which made coming to a robust agreement possible (Mello 2002).

Although agreeing to a (qualified) CET at Ouro Preto was a triumph for Mercosur nations, the agreement still left a great deal to be resolved. Mercosur was far from achieving its goal of a common market. In particular, it is useful to consider what Mercosur did *not* do when Ouro Preto was negotiated. Primarily, it established new policies and rules of the game in the commercial arena, but virtually nowhere else. This particular characteristic of Mercosur integration came under increasing attack from many quarters in the latter half of the 1990s, as will become clear in the following chapter. Here I lay out the main areas where Mercosur did not make progress, and consider the implications of this lack of progress. Three issue areas in particular stand out: social and labor rights, dispute resolution, and macroeconomic coordination.

In the social and labor area, labor's vision of what integration could do was mostly frustrated. As noted earlier, a working group on social and labor issues had only been added to the other major groups after the Treaty of Asunción had been signed, as an afterthought and in response to criticism from labor unions and others. Labor and social issues were treated similarly in the negotiations over the Ouro Preto Protocol. Those pushing these issues were given something of a table scrap, when the Consultative Forum on Social and Economic issues was formed. The Forum had no decision-making authority; it could debate these issues and provide

recommendations, but these could be ignored by governments, and in fact they were ignored regularly (Bustamante 2005).

The frustration of those hoping to put social issues on the agenda was obvious, but it is not surprising in a case of vulnerable integration. Given the weak situation of labor and other relatively powerless groups in emerging countries, it would be extraordinarily difficult for them to get leaders to move on this front. Here, the contrast with Europe is striking and illustrative. Whereas the EU did agree on certain social and labor protections over the course of their integration, they did this at a relatively late stage, and even when they did, the approach adopted (and the only politically feasible solution) was to establish standards that reflected an approach that was flexible and could establish certain minimum standards (Trubek and Mosher 2003). In contrast, those pushing social and labor standards in Mercosur were attempting to establish standards that were *better* than legislation existing in any of the member countries. Their task was much more difficult as a consequence. No nation in Mercosur had the sort of standards that labor unions and non-governmental organizations hoped to achieve by putting these issues on the agenda. In other words, the vulnerability of weak actors in civil society made their task much more difficult, if not impossible.

On the question of dispute resolution, Mercosur also made little progress. The Treaty of Asunción had promised the formation of such mechanisms, and though negotiators did create an arbitration tribunal at Ouro Preto, this fell far short of a more robust court that might issue binding decisions which member nations would have to abide by (*Latin American Weekly Report* 1994d). This tribunal had no teeth to enforce any of its decisions. Therefore, any significant dispute that came up in the process of integration had to be resolved through direct government-to-government negotiations.

This lack of agreement on how to resolve conflicts is also not surprising, given the hegemony of Brazil within Mercosur. As I have already mentioned, Brazil was particularly wary of supranational institutions that might constrain its behavior. An independent dispute-resolution mechanism in Mercosur would have benefited its partners far more than it would have benefited Brazil, and it resisted calls for such mechanisms at every turn. This was one area where Brazil was quite unwilling to compromise. In addition, there was no strong push from Argentina for such dispute-resolution mechanisms, in any event. As Diana Tussie and her colleagues point out,

> Perhaps the dispute-resolution mechanism agreed to in Mercosur does nothing more than reflect the power of domestic actors who favor protection, and who from different areas pressure their governments not to commit themselves to measures that would restrict their maneuvering room to use protectionist measures.
>
> (2001: 215)

To put it somewhat differently, it would appear that few economic actors are willing to relinquish control over policy instruments that might *restrict* trade.

Finally, when it came to macroeconomic coordination, no progress was made, largely because the Mercosur nations were still far apart when it came to making domestic economic policy. While it is true that by the time the Ouro Preto Protocol was negotiated Brazil had finally stabilized its economy, it had done so quite differently from Argentina. Both countries had overvalued exchange rates, but they had gotten to this point through very different policies: Argentina had tied the peso to the dollar in a non-negotiable form, while Brazil continued to admit to gradual devaluation of the real, and maintained certain monetary policy instruments that the Argentines had given up on. And Brazil was not about to put itself in the exchange-rate straight-jacket that Argentina had donned. Consequently, there was no serious effort made to coordinate macroeconomic policies with the Ouro Preto agreement.

Again, this should not be surprising, given the vulnerable nature of integration. Each of the economies in the region was vulnerable for its own reasons. And each of these countries had adopted policies to confront this vulnerability. They remained far apart on how they managed their external and internal vulnerabilities, and negotiations about a CET were not about to make them more willing to cooperate on a wide variety of issues.

In sum, Mercosur took a huge leap forward with the Ouro Preto Protocol, but there were clear structural limits to deeper integration, even at this moment of optimism. When a region's economic prospects are heavily influenced by its overall relationship with the outside world, the region has less room to maneuver, particularly when it is interested in attracting foreign capital. Since the Mercosur nations were in the throes of turning themselves into good citizens in the eyes of the international financial community, it is not surprising that their integration focused mainly on commercial integration. Leaders may have been interested in an agenda that pushed industrial or social policy, but they did not make either industrial or social policy a part of their integration strategies. They stuck to trade integration. The following chapter will show how integration in the Mercosur countries ran into a wall when international and domestic environments became less favorable for integration.

5 Mercosur in slow-motion crisis

The extraordinary speed at which the Mercosur process progressed surprised most observers of the region. Most of the mistakes of previous integration failures had been avoided. And crucially, there was high-level political commitment to see the integration move forward quickly, and these political efforts were backed up by investments and trade relationships by key business actors. Important as well in the rapid expansion of integration was the fact that there were no major international or regional economic crises between the signing of the Treaty of Asunción in 1991 and the conclusion of the Protocol of Ouro Preto at the end of 1994. A lack of international turbulence and a return of foreign capital to the region gave the integration process important breathing space, which leaders used to consolidate the process.

The years after the signing of the Protocol of Ouro Preto, however, were not so kind. In fact, precisely at the time the final details of the Protocol were being negotiated, Mexico went through a frightening devaluation that sent financial shock waves throughout Latin America. Several years later, the Asian financial crisis began in Thailand, moved to many other countries in Asia, arrived in Russia, and culminated with a devaluation in Brazil. This turbulence in international financial markets wreaked havoc on the economies of the region, and as a whole, the second half of the 1990s saw slower (and more volatile) economic growth throughout Latin America, which also had an effect on integration.[1] This volatility put Mercosur at risk, and above all made it virtually impossible to contemplate a further deepening of the integration process. Finally, after years of building crisis, Argentina's economy imploded in late 2001, leaving Mercosur facing the most severe crisis in its short history. Both the volatility of the international political economy in the second half of the 1990s and the Argentine meltdown illustrate the two sides of vulnerability in Mercosur. On the one hand, international shocks have an outsized impact on developing countries, making cooperation difficult to achieve, while on the other, weak institutions domestically (in the case of Argentina) make it difficult to sustain a consistent economic policy.

This chapter analyzes the period following the signing of the Ouro Preto Protocol by focusing on the international arena and the domestic and regional responses to it. The first section looks at the two major financial crises in the second half of the 1990s and considers their impact on Mercosur. Interestingly, the Mexican peso crisis and the Asian financial crisis had very different effects on integration in Mercosur: the Mexican peso crisis in fact strengthened Mercosur because of its impact on US politics. After this crisis, it became apparent that there was little chance that more Latin American nations would be invited to join NAFTA because of US Congressional politics. As a consequence, Mercosur became the only game in town, and hemispheric integration was a long way off.

The Asian financial crisis had a very different effect: it made the weaknesses and limitations of the Mercosur process clear. It eventually forced a devaluation in Brazil, and since Argentina at the time refused to devalue its currency because of its convertibility plan, the Mercosur nations went into full-scale crisis mode. Conflict between the Mercosur nations replaced cooperation, and integration itself was at risk. Although there were some suggestions after this crisis that Mercosur should be "relaunched" with stronger supranational institutions and greater coordination of macroeconomic policies, a great deal of damage was done. This does not mean that Mercosur could not be "relaunched," but it did make the weaknesses of the integration process clear, and showed how difficult it would be to engage in greater deepening of the process itself.

The second section goes into some detail about the conflicts that arose in the second half of the 1990s. Whereas the previous two chapters considered important decisions that moved integration forward, this chapter looks at how the integrating partners managed their closer economic relationship and increased ties. I consider the first important conflict after Ouro Preto: the automobile industry conflict that unfolded a mere six months after the signing of Ouro Preto. The auto industry is crucial in both Brazil and Argentina, and it took years of negotiation and conflict to come up with an agreement that both sides could live with, at least provisionally. This also clarifies the key role that MNCs played in the Mercosur project. It is no accident that the most bitter conflicts in Mercosur came in an industry dominated by MNCs. Both Argentina and Brazil wanted to secure the investments of these MNCs, and the stakes were high. Since auto trade is among the most important industrial sectors involved in integration, taking a close look at the conflicts in the auto sector is revealing.

This section also considers other conflicts that emerged, which largely focused on the persistence of non-tariff barriers in an ostensibly free trade area and its imperfect customs union. On numerous occasions, both Brazil and Argentina took steps to limit imports from their Mercosur partners, in response to both balance-of-payments pressures and lobbying from domestic businesses who were hurt in the integration process.

The third section considers the two wrenching events that threatened to undo Mercosur even before it was a decade old: the Brazilian devaluation of 1999 and the Argentine meltdown of 2001. Both of these events wreaked havoc on the integration process and led many commentators to conclude that integration was dead. I conclude that it was not dead, necessarily, but crucially limited in how far it could advance.

The final section returns to the changing interests of states, business, and labor as integration stagnated during the first decade of the twenty-first century, discussing briefly how interests changed substantially once crisis began to infect the Mercosur process. Both states reevaluated what they could do in a context that was becoming increasingly unfriendly, and one in which domestic political dynamics overcame any foreign policy desire to deepen integration. Business became even more involved in negotiations, achieving greater influence over the process. Business involvement increased to such a degree that instead of waiting for the state to act, industrial sectors started to negotiate agreements on their own, with relatively little interference from the state. In some sense, the integration process itself showed signs of "privatization." Finally, labor continued to push for a "social Mercosur," largely without success. Nevertheless, they continued to support integration, even though they were increasingly critical and frustrated at how integration developed.

The international arena: instability in the global economy

Mercosur was launched under auspicious international conditions. As the Treaty of Asunción was being signed, the United States was beginning to emerge from its brief recession and was poised to begin the longest economic expansion of its economy in the post-war period. It also appeared that the debt crisis of the 1980s had run its course. International capital was beginning to move back to Latin America voluntarily (as noted in the previous chapter) for the first time in quite a while.[2] The region in general seemed to finally be back on a growth path after years of pain. The pie was growing again.

That said, in developing regions, foreign capital is likely to rush in or out with changing circumstances, particularly in this age of globalized and liberalized financial markets. This was the case for Latin America before the current wave of globalization occurred; as Stallings notes in her historical study of foreign portfolio investment in Latin America, the region suffered as soon as investors lost confidence in the 1920s/1930s and the 1980s. Foreign investors tend to behave with a certain herd mentality, rushing in when the getting is good and pulling out just as quickly when news makes them wary of a region (Stallings 1987). This is not to say that this phenomenon does not occur in more developed regions of the world economy; it does. But more developed regions have the advantage of being home to many of the investors making these moves, which often means that they will take their money home when crisis occurs. And, importantly—and this is particularly true of the United States—investors view more developed country markets as a safer place to park their money.

Thus, while the US economy was experiencing an unprecedented boom during the 1990s, Mercosur and Latin America were struck by two momentous events in the international economy that had profound effects on Mercosur's integration and Latin American economic growth. The first was the Mexican peso crisis, which spawned the so-called "tequila effect" in much of Latin America, leading investors to take their capital out of the region and bringing on fears that the bad old 1980s were coming back. The second was the Asian financial crisis that was ignited in Thailand in the summer of 1997, and eventually had profound effects in Latin America and Brazil in particular, which was forced to devalue and float its currency in January 1999.

The Mexican peso crisis

Instability in the global economy—and its effects—is not a new phenomenon in Latin America. As policy makers in all the nations of the region would be able to recount, they are profoundly influenced by happenings in the international political economy. After all, the debt crisis was not a homegrown Latin American crisis: it came about as a consequence of changes in monetary policy in the United States, oil price changes, commodity price changes, and global recession. Latin American countries are used to being affected by international economic shocks.

And while these shocks have normally come from outside the region, the most important challenge (and opportunity) for Mercosur originated in Latin America. In December 1994, Mexico, after spending some time and foreign reserves defending its currency, concluded that devaluing was inevitable.[3] This set off alarm bells around Latin America, because the Mexican peso was not the only currency in the region that was overvalued. After the crisis struck Mexico, foreign investors rapidly pulled some of their money out of other Latin American countries. Both Argentina and Brazil were affected by this change in mood among international investors.[4]

Mercosur was thus faced with an international crisis, its first large-scale crisis at that. Both Argentina and Brazil were hard hit, as foreign investors suddenly grew concerned about the possibility of a repeat of the financial debacle of the 1980s debt crisis. Figure 5.1 gives one measure of financial flows from abroad, showing portfolio investment flows to Argentina and Brazil in the 1990s. For a short period of time there was a concern that this currency crisis in Mexico might drive Latin America back into deep depression. After all, it was Mexico that had set off the debt

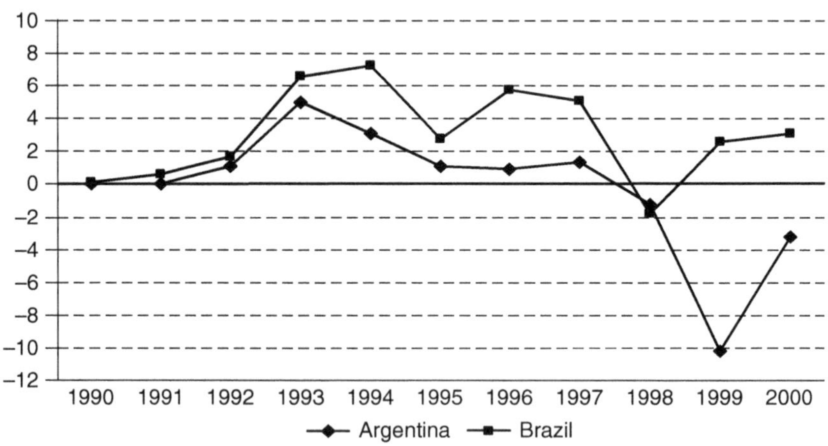

Figure 5.1 Net portfolio investment flows, Argentina and Brazil, 1990–2000 (in billions of current US dollars)

Source: World Bank: *World Development Indicators*.

crisis in August 1982 when it announced that it could no longer pay its foreign debts; some were worried that history would repeat itself (Espana 1995).

This time, however, Mexico's crisis did not set off a general Latin American crisis. Most countries recovered relatively rapidly quickly from the so-called "tequila effect," and since the United States was particularly interested in making sure that Mexico did not collapse (because of the recent passage of NAFTA), Mexico received enough support from international financial institutions and from the United States to adjust to the crisis without catastrophic consequences for the region (Wiarda 1995). In addition, the Mexican peso crisis did not derail the integration process of Mercosur.

In fact, one could make a reasonable case that the Mexican peso crisis *helped* Mercosur, in unintended ways. Before the crisis hit, many in Argentina were still hopeful that NAFTA might be extended to South America, and that after Chile (the first obvious candidate), Argentina would be next. But the Mexican crisis shut the door on the rest of Latin America. There had already been a great deal of conflict over passing NAFTA in the US Congress, and it only made its way through after extensive pressure from the Clinton administration. In particular, what became more difficult was achieving "fast-track" authority from the US Congress. Fast-track authority (since renamed "trade promotion authority" by the second Bush administration) allows the president to negotiate foreign trade deals with foreign countries without allowing Congress to offer amendments to any deal that is reached, offering only an up or down vote.[5] Such authority is essential for the United States to reach any significant trade agreement; without it, the countries that negotiate with the United States cannot possibly take its proposals seriously, since they know that whatever they agree to could be altered by the US Congress.

In this context, the Mexican peso crisis meant further accession to NAFTA for other Latin American countries was highly unlikely in the short to medium term. This had effects on both Argentina and Chile. Argentine policy makers and business leaders who hoped for a tighter economic relationship with the United States could no longer expect that this would be forthcoming. And Chile, which had planned on being the next NAFTA country, saw its possibilities for this outcome reduced substantially (Cason and Burrell 2002). In both cases, this disappointment meant that Mercosur would be stronger, at least in the short run.

Quite simply, the US Congress was not about to give the Clinton administration the permission to expand integration in the Americas after the Mexican peso crisis. Although President Clinton had committed to trade liberalization in the Americas at the Summit of the Americas in 1994 in Miami, the peso crisis made it difficult to make more positive moves towards trade liberalization, especially in advance of Clinton's reelection campaign in 1996. When the Clinton administration put trade liberalization back on the agenda in 1997, it failed miserably (Domínguez 1997–98). There was no chance that Congress would approve fast-track authority, and before it could suffer a defeat in Congress, the Clinton administration withdrew its request for that authority. The administration had many other foreign policy goals, and free trade in the Americas was not one that the Clinton administration deemed essential. Even if it had decided it was essential, there was no guarantee that it could have achieved its goals in the US Congress (Bardwell 2000).

Therefore, the Mexican peso crisis gave Mercosur a unique breathing space to foster integration. While the Brazilians had never been particularly interested in integration with the United States, Argentina was much more likely to have moved in that direction if the United States had provided appropriate signals, at least during the Menem administration. Therefore, the US reluctance to consider American integration solidified the Mercosur process.

Here, then, one can note a strength in weakness, if we can consider the advancement of Mercosur as a sign of strength. Mercosur would not be as strong as it is now if it were not for the Mexican peso crisis and its consequences on US political dynamics and debates. In effect—and following some historical patterns—Latin American was neglected by the United States. But unlike in other periods, the Mercosur nations (and Brazil in particular) took advantage of this circumstance to push forward a Latin American agenda on hemispheric relations. At the same time, this neglect from the United States could only push Mercosur forward so far, and the effort remained vulnerable to other international shocks, as the effects of the Asian financial crisis made clear.

The Asian financial crisis

The second major international event that affected the consolidation of Mercosur was the Asian financial crisis that began in Thailand in July 1997, spreading quickly to other Asian nations including Indonesia and South Korea, and then infecting other emerging economies. The causes of the Asian financial crisis have been debated extensively, but there is little doubt that the crisis (and its contagion) was facilitated by liberalization of capital flows in developing countries.[6] Since many developing countries had liberalized their capital accounts in the 1980s and 1990s, more money flowed in and out of these markets. Investor tendency towards a herd mentality means that loss of confidence in a particular country tends to be magnified and become self-reinforcing.[7] This happened in a spectacular way in East Asia, and international financial institutions (particularly the IMF) responded in such a way that exacerbated the crisis (Woo 2000). As a result, the Asian financial crisis was not contained to Asia, and spread around the world.

Most spectacular was the effect on Russia, which in August 1998 was forced to devalue the ruble sharply and saw its stock market drop precipitously over the course of 1998. In addition, the government defaulted on much of its foreign debt.[8] It was the Russian meltdown in particular that led to problems for Mercosur: less than five months after the Russian crisis, the Brazilian government was forced to let its currency float, leading to a massive devaluation. In the end there was nothing the Brazilians could do to avoid this devaluation, though their crisis was quite mild compared to what happened in Russia. Once Russia experienced its crisis in August 1998, the drain on Brazil's foreign exchange reserves increased dramatically. It tried for months to head the devaluation off, particularly because the Cardoso government was in the midst of a reelection campaign, and the Cardoso government considered (quite rightly) that a devaluation before the elections would put reelection in doubt. The IMF assisted the Cardoso government in its efforts, coming up with a program that pledged US$41 billion in October 1998 (Bulmer-Thomas 1999). This temporarily stemmed the hemorrhage of foreign exchange reserves, and in late 1998 it appeared that there was some chance that the worst of the crisis was over. On January 6, 1999, however, any chance of fending off financial speculators was torpedoed: former president Itamar Franco, by then the governor of the state of Minas Gerais, said that he would no longer pay his state's debt to the federal government. The Brazilian currency was eventually devalued by around 40 percent, and a new floating exchange rate regime was adopted.[9]

The devaluation demonstrated how vulnerable developing or emerging countries were in the international political economy. These countries were pressured to open up capital accounts and deregulate financial flows by the more developed countries, and one of the primary results of this deregulation was a much greater vulnerability to decisions made by international investors interested only in earning a high return in a very short period of time. A loss of confidence in a particular country can lead to a massive exodus of foreign capital, even when fundamental economic conditions do not warrant a run on the banks.[10] For an integration project such as Mercosur, the Asian financial crisis was a clear warning sign, and both Brazil and Argentina eventually found themselves victims of their greater financial openness.

Conflicts in Mercosur and the gradual unraveling of the promise of integration

Economic and political pressures from outside Mercosur had a profound impact on the integration process. Nevertheless, these international factors did not usually control the particulars of the integration process. The conflicts that emerged as integration advanced (or regressed) were often related to domestic pressures that the Mercosur nations faced. While these pressures often came about because of the relationship of the Mercosur countries with the international political economy, they also came about because of the domestic political and economic institutions in each country. Generally speaking, these institutions made it difficult for Mercosur to go beyond simply commercial integration, despite the best intentions and hopes of many of the actors involved in the process.

This section will illustrate this general argument by focusing on four defining incidents during Mercosur's consolidation process: conflicts over the definition of Mercosur's automobile regime, the establishment of non-tariff barriers to slow the integration process, the Brazilian devaluation of January 1999, and the Argentine collapse of late 2001 and early 2002. The evidence will illustrate the contradictory processes underway in a case of vulnerable integration, and will show how events in the international political economy interact with domestic political and economic factors to place significant limits on what integration can do. These incidents do not spell doom for integration among emerging economies, but they should make it clear how such integration faces inherent limitations.

The automobile industry: a source of regular conflict[11]

Perhaps the longest-running conflict for Mercosur has focused on the automobile industry. This is hardly surprising, since automobiles are one of the most important industrial sectors in an economy that has such an industry, and in the case of Mercosur, Brazil, Argentina, and Uruguay all produced automobiles. Brazil and Argentina in particular had a long experience and tradition in the auto sector, and with its many backward and forward linkages, it was a key sector to protect and support in both countries.[12] In addition, the auto sector accounted for around a third of all intra-regional trade in Mercosur; clearly, it was by far the most important industrial sector in integration (O'Keefe and Haar 2001).

Autos emerged as a key issue during the negotiation of the Ouro Preto Protocol, as noted earlier. Neither Brazil nor Argentina wanted to give up its auto industry with deeper integration for obvious reasons. In addition, since it was becoming clear that the Mercosur region would receive many new investments in the auto sector, both nations were interested in an agreement that would guarantee these new investments.

In the end, at Ouro Preto there was a decision to put off a permanent resolution of automobile trade to the future. The Brazilians and the Argentines agreed on a temporary solution bilaterally, which was somewhat complicated, and made some progress towards freeing trade between the two countries. For example, the Argentines agreed to allow Brazilian autoparts to be seen as "national" Argentine autoparts as long as Argentina was able to export its own autoparts in a specified proportion to its imports. And Brazil agreed to allow Argentine cars that were produced in line with its "popular car" segment (vehicles with a engine displacement of 1000 cubic centimeters or lower) to be sold in Brazil as if they were Brazilian cars. Both sides, however, reserved the right to continue with some of their own policies in the automotive sector (Organization of American States 1994). In practical terms, this meant that both countries were putting some limits on the liberalization of trade, and they were putting off a final agreement on the status of the automotive sector until later, with the goal of completely freeing trade by the beginning of 2000.

This limited agreement to have free trade in completed vehicles between the two countries did not last long. On June 13, 1995, Brazil, facing a mounting trade deficit associated with its economic stabilization plan, announced that it would limit imports of automobiles in the second half of the year to 50 percent of the total of imports in the first half of the year. To the shock and dismay of the Argentines, the decree that announced this decision made no exception for Argentine auto exports to Brazil (*TELAM Noticias* 1995a). Some felt that the Mercosur itself was in danger because of this unilateral decision by the Brazilians. Argentine president Carlos Menem threatened to boycott a summit meeting of the Mercosur presidents scheduled for later that week in São Paulo, declaring that

> I don't understand Brazil's position and I don't think it would be suitable for me to travel. If we are going to erase agreements we have just signed, I don't think it suitable for me to go to that meeting.
>
> (*Reuters* 1995a)

That the Brazilians decided to limit auto imports *in general* came as no surprise to observers of Brazil's trade policy and trade balance. The decision to lower import duties on automobiles to 20 percent the previous year had led to an explosion of imports during a period in which Brazil was experiencing an economic boom and an overvalued currency.[13] In April Brazil had increased import duties to 35 percent in an attempt to stem the tide of imports. There was an expectation that further steps would be taken, both for balance-of-payments reasons (Brazil was experiencing trade deficits for the first time in many years) and because of pressure from local MNC affiliates who were seeing their market share slip to imports from producers who did not have affiliates in Brazil. This pressure from MNCs was hardly surprising, even though they may have sometimes used the rhetoric of free markets when applying political pressure on the state. As one former minister put it, "the auto firms *love* quotas."[14]

What was unexpected, however, was that the Brazilians did not exempt the Argentines from their policy, at least initially. As noted earlier, President Menem threatened to boycott the São Paulo Mercosur summit. He eventually agreed to come once Brazilian president Cardoso committed the Brazilians to a negotiated settlement of the auto dispute, and Cardoso suspended application of the quotas to Mercosur partners for 30 days (*TELAM Noticias* 1995b). Negotiations proceeded apace and resulted in a two-part agreement: Brazil would not apply the quotas to Argentina for the remainder of 1995, and the Brazilians and Argentines would embark on negotiations to establish a definitive common automobile regime that would last until the year 2000 (which was later postponed), when the common external tariff would become effective in the auto sector and trade between the two countries in the sector would be completely free.

This resolution was not surprising. After all, it could hardly be argued that Argentine exports of cars to Brazil were undermining the Brazilian balance-of-payments position; Argentine exports made up less than 5 percent of total Brazilian auto purchases (*Reuters* 1995a). What was really at issue was the joint auto regime, which the Brazilians saw as increasingly threatening as multinationals began to make decisions on their investments in the Mercosur region. Many Argentine and Brazilian analysts agree that Argentina had been favored by the agreement at Ouro Preto. In this accord the Brazilians agreed to allow the Argentines to continue to have an auto regime that demanded carmakers export as much as they imported, which acted as a non-tariff barrier in the auto industry (*Inter Press Service* 1994). While Argentina was allowed this beneficial arrangement, Brazil opened its market to Argentine car imports unilaterally in the "popular" car segment.

This became a concern for the Brazilians once the pace of investments picked up. The concern was clear both for the Brazilian state—which hoped to increase overall investment in the economy—and for the automakers who were threatened by investments of their competitors in Argentina. If Argentina could promise automakers free access to the Brazilian market of 160 million, Brazilian policy makers worried more investments would go to Argentina. In short, Brazilian state officials began to fear that they were going to allow their auto industry to shrink, while firms already established in Brazil were concerned that rival firms would gain a competitive edge by taking advantage of Argentina's attractive regime.

It became quite clear when the dispute surfaced that it was really about who would get investments shortly after Brazil announced its new quota policy. Argentine Industry Secretary Carlos Magariños noted two days after the Brazilian policy was announced that "the real dispute is over investments" (*Reuters* 1995b). This was obvious for several reasons, most notably the fact that the Brazilians reduced tariffs on non-Mercosur autoparts imports to 2 percent, from a previous rate of 18 percent (*Reuters* 1995c). The Brazilian strategy was apparent to many observers, one of whom put it bluntly: "The only people who are surprised at what happened are those who don't understand the traditional policies of Brazil, which have been, if not imperialistic, at least overwhelming" (*TELAM Noticias* 1995c). The comment was made by Oscar Salvi, the director of Toyota Argentina. Toyota had a substantial factory in Argentina, from which it exported to Brazil, and at that time it only had a relatively insignificant operation in Brazil, one that produced light trucks. Indeed, subsequent to this auto industry conflict, Toyota committed to producing passenger cars in Brazil.

As it turned out, the negotiations over a joint auto regime ended up resolving most of the contentious issues, at least temporarily. On January 22, 1996, Brazil and Argentina announced that a deal had been struck over the auto regime that would be in place until 2000, with negotiations on a subsequent auto regime put off until later (which was put off again, and again). Many observers considered that the agreement leveled the playing field between the two countries, as the interim agreement established some basic rules to encourage auto TNCs to invest in Mercosur. In Brazil, auto firms that export were able to import as much as they exported paying half the 70 percent duty normally levied on finished vehicles. In Argentina, the previous policy of requiring firms to export as much as they import was maintained. In addition, to strengthen the local parts industry and avoid investments that would be based only on assembly, duty-free intra-Mercosur trade in automobiles required that they have at least 50 percent of their components made in the country that was doing the exporting. In addition, Brazil continued to levy only a 2 percent duty on extra-regional autopart imports, while Argentina counted the purchase of capital goods for the auto industry as an investment for purposes of tax breaks (*International Trade Reporter* 1996).

Financial Times noted that

> Critics suggest the agreement will do little to open up the region's highly protected motor industry. By blocking most imports from outside the region, they argue, Argentina and Brazil are effectively blackmailing multinational vehicle makers into setting up local plants.
>
> (*Financial Times* 1996)

Then again, that is precisely the point, and both the Argentines and the Brazilians hope that the auto industry can contribute to economic dynamism in the region. This point was reinforced by subsequent negotiations over the auto regime. In late

1998, a new temporary agreement established a four-year transition period, from the beginning of 2000 to the beginning of 2004, for a complete free market in the auto sector in Mercosur. The agreement that was concluded had a *much* higher tariff than the average Mercosur tariff—35 percent for finished vehicles. The agreement also established a common 14–18 percent tariff on autoparts, and increased the minimum Mercosur content of vehicles (if they were to be considered Mercosur vehicles) to 60 percent) (*Inter Press Service* 1998). All in all, this arrangement was quite protectionist, and in this sense reflected Brazilian goals in the region. It also involved a highly regulated trade, quite different from what one would expect among nations that professed to want to integrate their economies (*Folha de São Paulo* 1998).

It is also important to note that Argentina and Brazil continued to find it difficult to come to a definitive conclusion on their auto trade, and still have not managed to come to an agreement on free trade, almost two decades after the signing of the Treaty of Asunción. While they promised to reach an agreement by the beginning of 2000, they were unable to do so. At the end of 1999, there was still no definitive agreement on what the auto regime should be, so both parties agreed to a temporary agreement, which would preserve the managed aspects of auto trade in the region. Among other things, this managed trade required a relative balance in auto trade between the two main Mercosur countries, and so the temporary agreement that was reached at the end of 1999 was thought of as a "transition to a transition" (*Folha de São Paulo* 1999a). In the end, it wasn't even that.

It was, rather, part of an attempt to make Mercosur right again, when it was becoming more and more difficult to sustain forward momentum. In March 2000, Argentina and Brazil did come to another agreement about automobile trade, and this time they put off the final agreement on free trade in automobiles until 2006. At the time, Brazil wanted to speed up the timetable to free trade, and Argentina wanted to slow it down (*Clarín* 2000). There was a sense, as well—on the Brazilian side—that Argentina was in increasingly desperate shape economically, and the Brazilians were willing to accommodate the needs of the Argentines to keep Mercosur from collapsing. As chief Brazilian Mercosur negotiator José Botafogo Gonçalves said after the March 2000 auto accord was reached, "We [Brazilians] don't have any interest in gambling everything here . . . if we pull the carpet from under them now, Argentine industry will die" (*Folha de São Paulo* 2000). In the end, the "temporary" auto regime that the Brazilians and Argentines agreed upon simply continued the then-prevailing practice of assuring that trade in the auto sector would be more or less balanced between the two countries. It stipulated that the balance could become gradually more unbalanced over time, to the point where each country could import 2.6 times as much as it exported free of duty. In 2006, trade was supposed to be completely free in the sector. Not surprisingly, when 2006 came around, there was still no definitive agreement in the auto sector (*Folha de São Paulo* 2006a).

The fact that it was so difficult to reach a definitive agreement in the auto sector makes several forceful points about the vulnerability of integration in Mercosur. First, both countries are aware that what is at stake is the decision about where multinational corporations will put their investments, thus making them reluctant to relinquish control over trade flows. This concern itself makes deeper integration more difficult to accomplish. Second, the ups and downs of the auto sector in each country have reflected the macroeconomic and exchange-rate problems that each country faced over the lifespan of Mercosur. These macroeconomic and exchange-rate swings led to massive moves in trade flows, and both countries have taken turns finding themselves facing enormous import surges, putting pressure on the balance of payments. Finally, the fact that over a nearly 20-year period it remained difficult, if not impossible, to completely liberalize trade in one of the most important industrial sectors in the two key partners in the integration process demonstrates the limitations inherent in the integration process itself.

New arenas of conflict: non-tariff barriers

Since Mercosur had handled many tariff-related issues at the time the Protocol of Ouro Preto was signed, most trade disputes in the region were waged over non-tariff barriers in the second half of the 1990s. And these conflicts were not over small issues, as the previous discussion of the auto industry makes clear. In addition, because there were no supranational institutions to mediate conflict between the trading partners, and relatively little consultation between the governments before they took unilateral measures, these disputes often spun out of control quite quickly. In other words, Mercosur, through its lack of institutionalization, proved less than adept in resolving disputes, another sign of its overall vulnerability.

Two representative conflicts of the late 1990s illustrate the problems that Mercosur had in consolidating its integration process and which made the deepening of that process particularly difficult. The first originated with a unilateral measure adopted by Brazil to limit financing for its imports in 1997; the second initiated with unilateral measures taken by Argentina to place quantitative limits on imports in 1999, after the Brazilian real was devalued. Whereas the previous story discussing the automobile industry focused on a particularly sensitive industrial sector, these two disputes (and the conflicts that the Brazilian devaluation unleashed) discussed here point to broader limitations on integration in Mercosur.

The import-financing conflict

On March 25, 1997, the Brazilian government issued *Medida Provisória* 1569, which initiated a firestorm of protest from its Mercosur partners. The decision, taken in large part because of an increasingly threatening balance-of-payments deficit, required importers in Brazil to pay cash for most imports. This was meant to counteract the common practice of using low interest rate credits (in dollars) to purchase imports, which would be followed by sale of the imports. Since the loans did not have to be repaid immediately, importers would then invest the proceeds at higher interest rates in Brazil, thus gaining a profit on the differential between domestic Brazilian interest rates and the international rates at which the importers had borrowed the money. The only exceptions to paying cash for imports were on shipments of less than US$10,000, oil and petroleum by-product imports, and financing that exceeded 360 days. In all, the requirement to pay cash for imports was meant to affect 65 percent of all Brazilian imports, including those from Mercosur.

As expected, Brazil's Mercosur partners were up in arms, complaining that this was yet another example of Brazilian arrogance and hegemony in the block; as a spokesman for Uruguay's exporters association put it, this was just another way in which Brazil was "marking the rhythm to which the rest of us dance" (*Inter Press Service* 1997a). And again, the alarmist voices prevailed for a few days: in the words of Alberto Alvarez Gaiani, a vice president of the Argentine Industrial Union, "With these measures, we become less than serious as markets, and if there is not a solution found [to the conflict] in the short term, the continuation of Mercosur is in danger" (*La Nación* 1997a).

As expected, the Brazilians were willing to negotiate with their Mercosur partners, leading to at least a temporary solution. The resolution led to an exemption for Mercosur partners in which shipments of less than US$40,000 would not need to be paid for in cash; instead, these (relatively small) shipments could be paid for in credits of up to 89 days (*Inter Press Service* 1997b). This exception lasted until July 31, 1997.

Given the rather paltry concessions that the Brazilians made, Argentine business sectors were still not happy with the resolution. In the process of negotiating after it had adopted a unilateral measure, the Brazilians still got most of what they wanted. As Gaiani put it,

> We are accustomed to this type of behavior from Brazil. We know they will back down in the end, although not to their original position. But what we cannot accept is having to deal with a new conflict each month as a result of the unilateral decisions taken by this country.
>
> (*Inter Press Service* 1997c)

Nevertheless, what the Argentines and the other Mercosur partners certainly did realize was that Brazil is large enough to do precisely this. The Brazilians frustrated their trading partners, but since key Brazilian economic policy makers—in this case both the Central Bank and the economic team in Brazil—backed the import-financing restrictions because of a desire to avoid a balance-of-payments crisis, it was a foregone conclusion that the Brazilians would get most of what they wanted. It should also be noted that Brazilian Finance Minister Pedro Malan pointed to devaluation as an alternative, noting that such an outcome would have a much more negative effect on the integration process than the financing restrictions (*Inter Press Service* 1997d). Ultimately, this set of measures by Brazil only postponed the need to devalue.

This import-financing conflict demonstrated how conflicts among Mercosur were resolved when times were relatively good. Argentina was not about to precipitate a debilitating crisis; if they were to do so, they would only be shooting themselves in the foot. In addition, after the crisis passed through its early tumultuous phase with recriminations on all sides, the Argentines began to downplay the crisis itself, recognizing that Brazil was really forced to do something about its balance-of-payments position. If Brazil's problems were to lead to a Mexico-like financial crisis, Argentina would suffer enormously (*La Nación* 1997b). Needless to say, the eventual crisis that hit both Brazil and Argentina was far worse than what happened in the wake of the Mexican crisis.

In the end, Argentine exports were not greatly affected by these import-financing restrictions in any case; total Brazilian imports actually increased after the new import-financing restrictions were enacted, from US$4.84 billion in March 1997 to US$6.05 billion in July 1997 (Secretaria de Comércio Exterior [Brasil] 1997). One Argentine businessperson noted that exporters had figured out ways to get around the restrictions, either through breaking down shipments so that they were small enough to avoid the restrictions or through getting financing for longer time periods.[15]

It seemed, at least for a short time (until Brazil's 1999 devaluation) that there was a growing understanding that conflict is normal in an integration process; as Brazilian president Cardoso's spokesman, Sergio Amaral, put it in an interview in an Argentine newspaper: "This 'noise' is part of the game; there is no such thing as a process [like Mercosur]—that is so intimate and so large—where there is no conflict of interests" (*La Nación* 1997c). Of course, these words came from a Brazilian spokesman, and Brazil continued to view recurrent conflicts with somewhat less alarm, since they were often the instigators of the conflicts, and gained advantages when they sprung up. Argentines were much less happy about the outcomes, to be sure. But it certainly was accurate to note that integration inevitably produces conflicts, and the need to resolve them.

This particular conflict also illustrates one of the Mercosur-specific weaknesses of integration: the overwhelming weight of Brazil in the integration process. Because Brazil accounts for more than three-fourths of the GDP of Mercosur, it knows that it can call the shots when it comes to integration. And because Brazil's government has also been the most consistently interested in integration in South America, it is not interested in upsetting the process itself. However, when balance-of-payments crises occur, the Brazilian government does not hesitate to take unilateral actions. And it is not constrained by any supranational institution or a powerful partner. Consequently, integration itself is limited. When Argentina tried to pull off a similar unilateral action in response to balance-of-payments problems, the overall situation became much more complicated, as the next section demonstrates.

The Brazilian devaluation and the Argentine reaction

The conflicts that occurred after Ouro Preto were substantial, but did not compare to the crisis that came in January 1999, when Brazil, after months of fighting off speculation that its currency would be devalued, finally gave in to these pressures and let the real float freely. This sent shock waves throughout Mercosur, as it suddenly upset the balance of the stabilization plans that had been in place in the

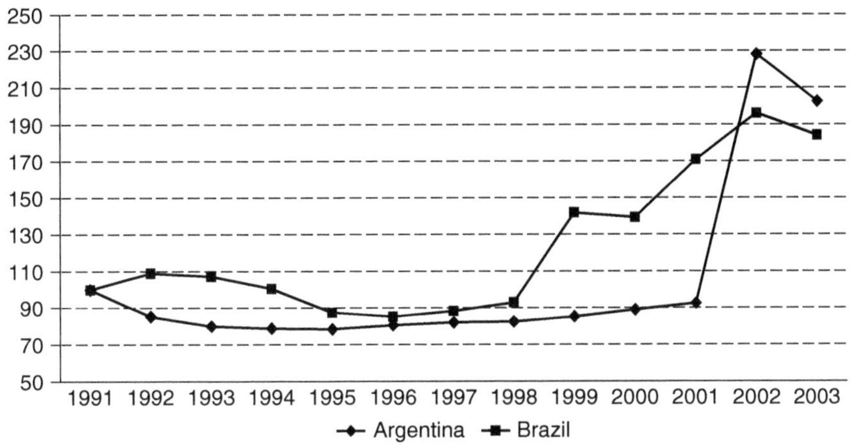

Figure 5.2 Exchange rate index in Argentina and Brazil, 1991–2003 (1991=100. Value above 100 indicates devaluation)

Source: Frenkel (2004: 34–35).

Mercosur countries. After all, when most Mercosur currencies were overvalued relative to the dollar, they could still trade amongst themselves without great concern. But the Brazilian devaluation brought a new element into the integration process: the most important members of Mercosur saw a massive alteration in exchange rates, making exports from Brazil to Argentina far cheaper, and Argentine exports to Brazil far more expensive. Figure 5.2 details this impressive change.

This figure only begins to tell the story. Even when both Argentina and Brazil had relatively overvalued exchange rates, Brazil was generally more competitive in many industrial sectors. And when its more competitive economy got a boost from a devaluation, while Argentina continued to stick to its convertibility plan, it was hard to fathom how Argentina could survive this blow. Specifically, the real went from 1.21 per dollar at the beginning of January to 1.98 per dollar by the end of the month, reaching a peak in early March of 2.16 reais per dollar.[16] The reaction to the floating of the real was exaggerated, to be sure, and eventually the real settled down (Bulmer-Thomas 1999). By the end of 1999 the real was trading at 1.79 per dollar. Thus, with the devaluation, Brazilian exports were around 40 percent less expensive for their trading partners, and these countries found the price of their exports to Brazil increased by a similar amount. Even the most robust trading organization would have a hard time digesting this kind of economic shock, and the news immediately following the Brazilian devaluation was mostly about how *this time*, Mercosur was indeed in deep trouble. At least while both the Argentine and Brazilian currencies were overvalued, this overvaluation could be overlooked in Mercosur. The Brazilian float changed all that.

Many investors (both Brazilian and international) had concluded after the Russian financial crisis in August 1998 that Brazil was next on the list of countries that would be attacked. Many took their money out of Brazil, investing in safer environs (Goldfajn 2000). In addition, Brazil's internal political situation, with weak parties making the passage of reform difficult and its federal system making central control difficult, exacerbated the challenges facing the Cardoso government when it was fighting off currency speculators.[17] Indeed, it was the action of one state governor, former president Itamar Franco, which triggered the final decision to float the currency. Franco, governor of the state of Minas Gerais, threatened not to pay his state's debt to the federal government, which led to enormous pressure on the real. With billions of dollars leaving every day after Franco's threat, policy makers saw they had little choice but to devalue. Here, the interaction between forces in the international political economy, combined with Brazil's domestic politics, brought on this latest existential crisis in Mercosur, once again highlighting the vulnerable nature of the integration process.

The crisis facing Mercosur with the Brazilian devaluation was made particularly difficult to handle because Argentina simply had no policy instruments available to change its own exchange-rate regime. Its stabilization, based on the convertibility plan introduced in 1991, made the peso's one-to-one link with the dollar an essential pillar of its economic policy. In effect, the state consciously gave up the use of most monetary policy instruments when it stabilized the Argentine economy. It was thought that this was the only way to ensure credibility on the part of the state to fight inflation.[18] Thus, while Brazil was able to adjust its exchange-rate regime in the face of pressure on its currency, Argentine policy makers' hands were tied.

The particulars of the Brazilian devaluation underline one of the main arguments of this book: weak institutions in the Mercosur nations made the integration process more precarious. The decision of one governor was able to trigger a series of events that forced Brazil to devalue. It does not particularly matter, in this regard, whether Brazil *should* have devalued; it probably should have, and it recovered relatively quickly from this crisis, giving some credence to the notion that a devaluation was good for the Brazilian economy. But the fact that its institutional weakness forced this change, and put the Mercosur process in peril, points to a key element of vulnerable integration.

What was the impact of the Brazilian devaluation on Mercosur? In terms of trade, the impact was immediate. As Table 5.1 indicates, intra-Mercosur trade, which had been growing at an impressive rate during the early and mid-1990s, began to decline, and this decline accelerated over several years. This was especially painful for Argentina, which had been running consistent surpluses with Brazil in the mid-1990s; in effect, Brazil was keeping Argentina from running into even deeper trouble, given its overvalued exchange rate.

The data in this table are remarkable for several reasons. First, both Argentina and Brazil saw their exports to their key integration partner stagnate or decline from 1998 on and Argentina, in particular, saw a steep drop in its exports to Brazil in the several years after 1998, when the effects of the Brazilian devaluation were felt.

Table 5.1 Argentine/Brazilian trade, 1996–2005
(in billions of current US dollars)

Year	*Argentine exports to Brazil*	*Brazilian exports to Argentina*
1996	6.81	5.17
1997	7.94	6.77
1998	8.02	6.75
1999	5.81	5.36
2000	6.84	6.23
2001	6.21	5.00
2002	4.74	2.34
2003	4.67	4.56
2004	5.57	7.37
2005	6.24	9.92

Source: Ministério de Desenvolvimento, Industria, e Comercio Internacional, *ALICEWeb*.

Second, Argentina's exports to Brazil were actually lower in 2005 than they were a decade earlier, even in current dollars. Clearly, the integration process had been thrown off track.

Even more disturbing from the point of view of progress in integration is the degree to which the main integrating nations are trading less with one another, in relative terms, than they were a decade ago. Figure 5.3 shows the proportion of Brazilian and Argentine exports that went to one another from 1991 through to 2005. The drop in mutual trade dependence from its peak is quite striking, and

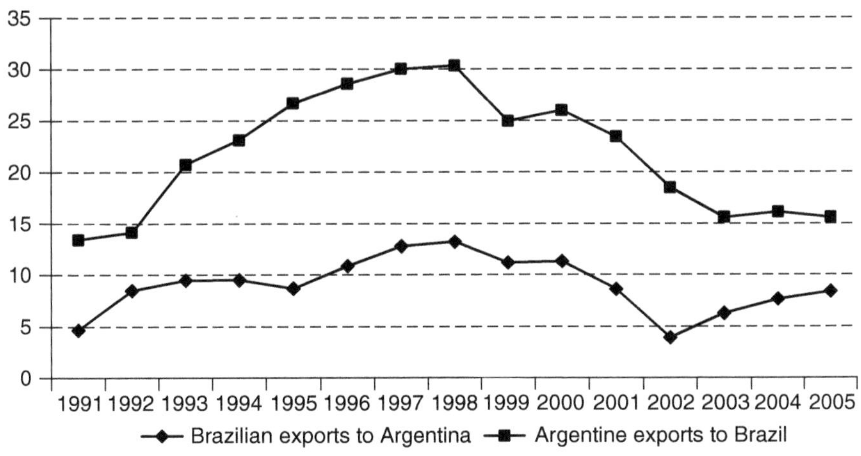

Figure 5.3 Argentine and Brazilian exports to Principal Mercosur partner (as a percentage of each country's total export)

Sources: Ministério de Desenvolvimento, Industria, e Comércio Internacional (Brasil), *ALICEweb* and Instituto Nacional de Estadística y Censos de la República Argentina.

shows how the turmoil in Argentina and Brazil did lasting damage to the integration process. Enthusiasm for integration declined substantially, and policy makers in both large Mercosur countries concluded that they should not place a large bet on integration, either. Given its more diversified trade profile, this was not such a blow to Brazil. For Argentina, however, the drop in exports to Brazil that came with the 1999 devaluation was jarring, given its greater trade dependence on Mercosur.

These economic effects of macroeconomic turbulence translated into political effects. Within months of Brazil's devaluation, Argentine industrialists were pushing their government to adopt protectionist measures against Brazil. The first such measure was announced in late July 1999, when Argentina decided to protect its textile sector through import safeguards that would impose quotas on Brazilian exports. Brazil immediately protested, arguing that there were no such safeguard provisions in the Mercosur agreements, and that Argentina was prohibited from adopting such policies (*Folha de São Paulo* 1999b). The pressure from the Brazilians against these Argentine measures was intense, and in the end, Argentina agreed not to impose the safeguard quotas on Brazil, after Argentine President Menem visited Brazilian President Cardoso in Brasilia at the end of July (*Agence France Presse* 1999; *La Nación* 1999a). Brazil clearly did not like getting a taste of its own medicine of taking unilateral actions in the face of balance-of-payments crises, and managed to force Argentina to back down. Despite this resolution, it did not resolve the underlying problem: Brazil's devaluation was a huge blow to Argentina's foreign trade prospects, and there was little that could be done to change the economic imbalance, other than an Argentine devaluation.

The political tension in Mercosur was further complicated by the fact that 1999 was an election year in Argentina, and Carlos Menem was not able to run for a third term, try as he might.[19] Whereas Menem had earlier exercised impressive leadership on behalf of Mercosur, he had relatively little incentive to do so when he was a lame duck president in the last year of his term. Instead, thinking about his political future (and a potential comeback for another term after the upcoming election) he engaged in populist rhetoric and advocated populist positions, which were not necessarily favorable to Mercosur. After all, Argentina was in serious economic straits after the Brazilian devaluation, and both firms and workers were suffering because of it. And there was little incentive to compromise, since any agreements could be negated by Menem's successor.

In the end, 1999 was a year of increasing conflict in the Mercosur bloc, and led all actors involved in the process to consider the possibility that Mercosur might cease to exist (*Clarín* 1999). The bloc was not in serious danger of dissolving—no important actor was interested in seeing it fail—but the fact that there was an "existential" concern was troubling for the future of the bloc. Both Brazil and Argentina were headed into more turbulent economic times, which made it more difficult to commit to anything new. The integration process proved to be vulnerable indeed.

The Argentine implosion and its effects on Mercosur

As if the Brazilian devaluation crisis were not bad enough for Mercosur, the Argentine economy entered into a tailspin of epic proportions in late 2001. Argentina's economy was already in dire straits for several years before it imploded in late 2001, and unlike Brazil, Argentina had relatively little help from international financial institutions. Rather, it was left to fend for itself. Its currency was certainly overvalued (as was Brazil's), but Argentina was unwilling to admit to its problem until it became impossible to ignore; several years of recession took their toll (Pastor and Wise 2001; Kiguel 2002). Argentina was in a multi-year recession and finally reached the breaking point in December 2001, with disastrous results.

The causes of the Argentine crisis were many, and there is no need to discuss them in detail here, as the story has been laid out elsewhere (Corrales 2002; Schamis 2002). The short version is this: by late 2001, Argentina had been in recession for more than three years, its currency was massively overvalued, fiscal discipline had disappeared, and the international financial community had lost any faith that Argentina would put its house in order without a default and a devaluation. Expectations were self-fulfilling, and the final crisis was intense and painful: the peso went from the one to one parity with the dollar to being worth just 25 cents (the exchange rate later stabilized at around 3 pesos per dollar), political chaos ensued (with 3 interim presidents), and the Argentine economy declined by nearly 11 percent in 2002, after having fallen by nearly 10 percent over the previous 3-year period. Once again, as in decades past, Argentina had experienced a massive crisis in its economy.

A crisis of this magnitude obviously had a large impact on Mercosur. The decline in economic activity in Argentina as well as the peso devaluation dramatically reduced Argentine demand for Brazilian exports—Brazilian exports to Argentina declined by more than 50 percent from 2001 to 2002, to a level not seen since the early 1990s. In effect, the Argentine devaluation—like the Brazilian devaluation three years earlier—became, in practice, a barrier against imports. Brazil did not react angrily, however; the distress in Argentina was obvious for everyone to see, and Brazil knew that there was nothing to accomplish with more aggressive policies. In fact, the Brazilians and other Mercosur nations did what they could to assist Argentina in the period immediately following the crisis. Mercosur held an extraordinary summit in late February 2002 in Buenos Aires, at which the Mercosur nations issued a joint communiqué requesting help from international financial institutions for Argentina's recovery plan, and Brazilian president Fernando Henrique Cardoso offered to intercede on behalf of Argentina with French and British leadership. In addition, Brazil's Development Minister at the time, Sérgio Amaral, announced that Brazil would do away with all its barriers to Argentine exports, saying that "our objective is to open the borders to Argentina" (see *Clarín* 2002a; see also *Folha de São Paulo* 2002; *Clarín* 2002b). While this was certainly an exaggerated offer, it did reflect Brazil's willingness to do what it could to help Argentina during this severe crisis. It also reflected Brazil's ability to make a crisis into an opportunity: as Brazil had always been skeptical of the Free Trade Area of the Americas (FTAA), and Argentina had been more tempted to come to an accommodation with the United States, Brazil could now show Argentina who its real friends were.

Argentina eventually pulled itself out of the catastrophe, in part because of the devaluation. The economy grew at nearly 9 percent in both 2003 and 2004; coming after years of economic decline, this was not surprising, and repeated patterns of previous Argentine recoveries. But Brazil's solidarity with Argentina did not last that long: in 2002 Brazil was in the midst of its own election campaign, and saw another sharp decline in its currency. The real, which was trading at around 2.3 per dollar at the beginning of 2002, got above 4 per dollar in the run-up to the election, as financial markets worried about what would happen with a left-leaning government in Brazil. Argentina also saw its exchange-rate advantage diminish over the course of the year with what was, in effect, a second devaluation in Brazil.[20]

Despite this turbulence, Mercosur became much more important in Brazil in the political arena when Luis Inacio Lula da Silva was elected president in 2002. Lula's party—the Partido dos Trabalhadores (Workers Party—PT) had long emphasized the importance of regional integration in its platform, as a way of encouraging a South-South solidarity, in opposition to close alliances with wealthier countries.[21] And so when Lula was inaugurated on January 1, 2003, he announced that Mercosur would be of utmost importance, stating in his inaugural address that

> The main priority in foreign policy during my government will be the construction of a South America that is politically stable, prosperous, and united, based on democratic ideas and social justice. To accomplish this, it is essential that there be a strong move to revitalize Mercosur, which has been weakened by crises in each member state and by visions of integration that are narrow and selfish.
>
> Above all, Mercosur, as well as South American integration in general, is a political project. But this project rests on an economic and commercial foundation that urgently needs to be restored and strengthened.
>
> We will also focus on the social, cultural, and scientific and technical aspects of the integration process. We will stimulate joint projects and support a lively intellectual and artistic exchange among South American countries. We will support the necessary institutional arrangements so that true Mercosur and South American identity can flourish. Several of our neighbors are now going through difficult situations. We will contribute—when asked and to the best of our abilities—to help find peaceful solutions for these crises, based on dialogue and the democratic and constitutional norms of each country.
>
> (*Agencia Brasil* 2003)

There is no doubt that the new Lula government was ideologically predisposed towards pushing for deeper integration in Mercosur, and in Latin America more broadly. In general, the Lula government inaugurated a new rhetorical era, and the president himself went out of his way to encourage cooperation. But when it came to practical ways to pursue this goal, Lula's government ran into problems.

Regional or anti-imperialist solidarity worked well rhetorically, but it did not go far in the real world, especially when there were many conflicts between the two principal Mercosur partners.

In the late 1990s and the first decade of the twenty-first century, many have talked about the need to "relaunch" Mercosur once again, but much damage was done by the turbulence in the Brazilian and Argentine economies in these years.[22] Those arguing on behalf of Mercosur have emphasized how well Mercosur had advanced trade in the mid-1990s, and how it had contributed to growth in the region. How much it contributed to growth is surely debatable, but there is little question that integration provided some degree of dynamism to all the Mercosur economies.

Despite this dynamism—and perhaps because of it, to some degree—conflicts in Mercosur continued after the Argentine collapse. In part, these conflicts emerged because of the sharp exchange rate swings that the region experienced. In the end, however, the problems came about because of old-fashioned trade politics, and the issues that were involved in these disputes would occur in any integration project.

These conflicts, themselves, illustrated the weaknesses of Mercosur. To make Mercosur work, given its instability, there was a need for some kind of dispute resolution mechanism to handle such conflicts. The Mercosur nations had agreed on an interim solution to resolving disputes during the Ouro Preto negotiations, which ratified the temporary dispute-settlement mechanism established by the Brasilia Protocol of 1991. However, as Nicola Phillips notes,

> Throughout its first decade dispute resolution in the Mercosur was conducted entirely on an *ad hoc* basis and was limited to direct consultation between the affected parties, the presentation of claims to the CCM [Mercosur Trade Commission] or *non-binding* third party arbitration under the provisions of the Brasilia Protocol.
>
> (2004: 99, emphasis in original)

The fact that the Mercosur nations could not come to an agreement about how to resolve disputes was hardly shocking; to come up with a binding dispute resolution system would require a substantial surrender of sovereignty, and the conditions were not favorable for this in Mercosur. First and most obviously, Brazil, by far the largest country in the bloc, had no interest in seeing its hands tied by any mechanism that would limit its freedom to do what it wanted in trade policy. Second, even though the smaller countries in the region might have had a greater interest in tying Brazil's hands, they also faced unstable macroeconomic environments at different times during the Mercosur process, and were reluctant to really tie their hands. So there was never, in the Mercosur process, a serious discussion about how to resolve disputes in a binding way. Rather, disputes were always dealt with ad hoc.

That Brazil and Argentina could not come up with a satisfactory way to resolve disputes led them to start restricting trade when hard times came. The huge deficits that Argentina began to run in its bilateral trade with Brazil when Argentine finally began to grow again after its four-plus years of recession led Mercosur to come up with new institutional mechanisms to *limit* trade. Through 2004 and 2005, one of the major stumbling blocks to progress in Mercosur was Argentina's demand that Brazil agree to a safeguards regime that would protect sectors of the economy when other countries in the economic bloc were threatened by a large surge in imports (*Folha de São Paulo* 2004a; *Clarín* 2004a; *The Associated Press* 2004). The reason that safeguards came on the agenda is because of the macroeconomic instability in Mercosur. Since exchange rates have varied so widely in Mercosur, and since there are only two countries with a heavy economic footprint in Mercosur, the emergence of restrictive measures of this kind are not surprising. This is especially true for Argentina, since a larger portion of its trade occurs with Brazil (Pereira 2004). In a sense, the eventual emergence of safeguards protection can be seen as a consequence of the relative success of Mercosur. If the Mercosur countries had not opened up their economies to one another, trade would have continued to be limited and controlled. But since they did open trade with one another, changes in demand and exchange rates could have very significant effects on trade flows. As Argentina saw its trade balance deteriorate with its economic recovery—and business began to complain about Brazilian imports, which increased suddenly and rapidly—it began to demand more managed trade in Mercosur.

Brazil resisted safeguards provisions in Mercosur for a long time, but in the end, came to an agreement. They tried to buy off the Argentine demands, by, for example, offering to help finance infrastructure projects in Argentina through the Brazilian National Development Bank (BNDES) (*Folha de São Paulo* 2004b). This was an ineffective offer, and the strains in the bilateral relationship intensified in 2004 and 2005.

In the end, Brazil did agree to accept a safeguards regime, much to the dismay of the Brazilian business community. In large part, they accepted it because there was no other way to make sure that Argentina would continue to make Mercosur a priority in its foreign policy, which would harm Brazil's pretensions as a regional leader (discussed in the next section). The final agreement that was signed, in early February 2006, established that any industry that considered itself threatened by a flood of imports could start a process that might lead to either an imposition of a quota or an additional tariff in their sector. Argentine industrialists, who had just begun to recover from their long-lasting recession, were delighted with the conclusion to these negotiations; Brazilians were not amused (*La Nación* 2006; *Folha de São Paulo* 2006b; *Inter Press Service* 2006). The overall problem, however, was that any new agreements or understandings in recent years have tended to slow integration down rather than speed it up. Despite rhetoric to the contrary, there are no important actors in the Mercosur countries who are aggressively pushing Mercosur.

Furthermore, one of the reasons for encouraging greater integration in Mercosur was to increase the weight and negotiating power of the region in negotiations with other countries and blocs. While there were ongoing negotiations with many countries—most notably with the United States over an FTAA and with the EU[23]—the Mercosur countries also discovered the limitations of banding together in a world economy that was not stacked in their favor. The main sticking points in their negotiations with both the United States and the EU related to agricultural trade and trade in labor-intensive manufactures. What the Mercosur negotiators came to realize was that in fact, neither of these developed country blocs were about to make serious concessions to Mercosur in bloc-to-bloc negotiations; concessions in such areas were part of a much larger game that continued to be played out in the context of the World Trade Organization, not in regional negotiations. Simply put, there was not much that could be accomplished in these negotiations with richer and more powerful countries; the most that could be done was to *avoid* an agreement on less favorable terms. And while such agreements continue to be avoided, not much has occurred to demonstrate the weight of Mercosur.

New visions of integration?

Clearly, the ground shifted under the integration process around the turn of the century. In previous chapters I discussed the changing visions of different actors as they confronted integration. Here I do not engage in a detailed analysis of each of the key actors, but I do provide an update on how important actors viewed their own interests, and how they changed over time.

Indeed, it would be normal to expect interests to change as integration consolidates and matures. This is especially likely with vulnerable integration processes, since the nations engaging in the integration process are buffeted by rapidly changing internal and external political and economic trends. While it is the case that European preferences changed over time as the EU developed (Moravcsik 1998a: 24–50), vulnerable integration presents actors with more external shocks to the system. Certainly there was no shortage of such shocks over the first 20 years of Mercosur's life.

That said, some preferences have remained remarkably consistent, while in others, actors have changed their approach to integration as they have responded to a changing international and domestic context. The most stable interests are generally to be found in the internationalized business sector: MNCs have remained consistent supporters of integration, even though they do not necessarily express much support for a "deeper" integration project. Business based in Mercosur countries (both internationalized and domestic-based) became somewhat more ambivalent over time, particularly in Argentina after Brazil's January 1999 devaluation. They did not come out to oppose integration, but they were much less supportive than previously. When in mid-2004 the Argentines imposed restrictions on imports from Brazil of a variety of products, industrialists, who had supported the move, were quite pleased (*Clarín* 2004b). With the government of Nestor Kirchner (elected in the wake of the Argentine collapse, in 2003), business also had a receptive ear in the executive when it came to protecting local industry (Muchnik 2006).

Labor continued to support integration, and emerged as perhaps the strongest supporter, which is something of an irony given its pre-Mercosur opposition to integration. That said, it was still unhappy with the course of integration, and continued to place hope in the possibility of making integration more "socially conscious." Though it has yet to succeed in pushing its agenda, it hoped that with the election of Lula in 2002 its luck might change. As it turned out, however, labor is still waiting for a change.

It is among state actors that opinions and negotiating positions have changed the most. Argentina had been hedging its bets about Mercosur in the early stages of integration, hoping that it might get a chance in NAFTA or hemispheric integration. But with the changed international context that made hemispheric integration a somewhat distant dream, the Argentines were the most aggressive in pushing for deepening Mercosur institutions, since such institutions could constrain Brazilian behavior. And the Brazilian state had the opposite reaction: although they still had a strong desire to avoid hemispheric integration, they no longer had to worry as much about it happening. As a consequence, the Brazilians did everything they could to dampen expectations regarding the possibility of creating new supranational institutions that would limit their room for maneuver. Consequently, the Brazilians went about negotiating with non-Mercosur countries in South America on a bilateral basis, largely excluding the other Mercosur nations from this process.

Because of both changes in international and domestic contexts, the visions of the key states—Argentina and Brazil—changed as well as they confronted a tumultuous international environment. Since there were no supranational institutions of any importance created in Mercosur, moving forward depended to a large degree on what the states decided to do. And since Mercosur has been a process led by presidents, this is where any new initiatives would arise. Of course each president was influenced by ministries with policy-making responsibilities in the foreign trade area, but presidents made the key decisions. Just as Fernando Collor and Carlos Menem wanted to use Mercosur to open up their economies as part of a wide-ranging and largely unilateral opening to the rest of the world, the most recent presidents in the region—Lula, and Néstor and Cristina Kirchner—put their own stamps on the integration process.

When Lula and Néstor Kirchner came to power, they did so after the experience of economic turbulence in the international political economy of recent years, and they saw how Mercosur suffered in the face of these external shocks. They began their presidencies with the full understanding of the vulnerability of the integration process itself. They also came with very different perspectives on Mercosur. In Lula's case, he was interested in making Mercosur and South American integration the centerpiece of his foreign policy; in a sense, he was establishing his leftist credentials in foreign policy. Like Mexican governments under the rule of the Institutional Revolutionary Party (PRI), Lula was compensating for a more conservative domestic economic policy by promoting progressive policies abroad. In the case of Néstor Kirchner, he came to power in the wake of the tremendous economic dislocation caused by the crash of the convertibility plan. He was also elected on a platform of defending Argentine industry and workers, in a more old-style Peronist fashion. This meant, in effect, that he was going to take a much more cautious view of Mercosur. This did not mean Argentina was going to abandon the regional bloc, but it did mean that Argentina was going to want to protect its industry more. And so when these new presidents came to power in 2003, they were pushing in very different directions. And since integration only moves at the pace of the most reluctant partner, this meant that while Brazil was still the dominant economic power in the bloc, Argentina's willingness (or lack thereof) to integrate controlled the pace of integration. And this pace was going backwards.

Other issues intruded on the integration process. With Lula, Brazil embarked on a more activist foreign policy (Cason and Power 2009). While there was a substantial degree of continuity between the Cardoso government and Lula in foreign policy, the tone and posture changed in important ways. Lula put the emphasis in his foreign policy on South-South cooperation on a global scale, and also became interested in relaunching the idea of a South American bloc. Through its proposal for a South American Community of Nations, it was attempting to provide regional leadership, much to the irritation of the Argentines. This Brazilian initiative—which also competed with Hugo Chavez's own vision of South American integration—coincided with Brazil's more proactive push for a permanent seat on the United Nations Security Council, among other global goals. Brazil wanted support for these projects from other Mercosur nations, but Argentina was in no mood to provide such support.

In Argentina's case, the concerns became much more internal. Given the traumatic collapse of the convertibility plan, and the associated decline in economic activity in Argentina, this was only natural. There was a need to put its house in order, and this meant much greater protection and nurturing of business, and a rapprochement with labor. Argentina was interested in a greater "institutionalization" of Mercosur, but this interest was mostly focused on finding ways to *limit* Brazilian exports to Argentina, as discussed earlier. To a certain degree, one can view the Kirchner administration as being one that took a much more "nationalist" view towards Mercosur, and was more aggressive in its dealings with Brazil. And this had the effect of slowing down integration.

In the end, the late 1990s and early twenty-first century saw Mercosur come up against what can be viewed as its natural limits. It found itself buffeted by international financial crises, domestic financial crises, and weak political institutions. Combined with a lack of supranational institutions, this meant that Mercosur had little to rely on to push it forward, and there was little that constrained the behavior of the member states. The vulnerability of the integration process led many to question the future of Mercosur. These questions, however, are mostly related to unrealistic expectations of the regional bloc. It was never going to be like the EU, whatever the hopes of the proponents of the project. It faced inherent limits, and this period made these limits obvious.

6 The future of Mercosur and the challenges of economic integration in the developing world

Mercosur still exists. Despite the challenges it has faced, it still stands as the most significant economic integration program carried out in Latin American history. In addition, we can recognize that all integration efforts stumble from time to time, as the European experience has demonstrated repeatedly. Important decisions, taken by visionary leaders in particular countries or within transnational bureaucracies, move the process forward, often in times of crisis or flux. And as societies and governments deal with the consequences of the leaps forward, there is frequently a reaction either from the losers in the process, or as an intended or unintended consequence of freer trade and integration. Forward momentum is counteracted by reaction almost without fail. A generalization about this process would be this: moves toward greater economic and/or political integration are followed by reactions that slow integration's momentum. In a sense, these reactions are the reverse of spillover: there are times when integration itself leads not to pressures for greater integration, but for a halt or reversal of integration.

It is also the case that most integration processes do not succeed. The EU, the European Free Trade Area (EFTA), NAFTA, and Mercosur stand out as the most important successes in the post-war period. Many other efforts at integration, in Latin America, Africa, and Asia, have failed. And given the track record of integration in the developing world, Mercosur should not have succeeded, but it did, relatively speaking. Despite its problems and challenges, Mercosur has not collapsed. Trade, despite its recent volatility, is still greater—both in absolute terms and as a percentage of total trade—among the Mercosur countries than before the integration project began.

But Mercosur has stagnated for years. One might reasonably ask: Can Mercosur advance further? Will there be new decisions taken by national leaders, on the scale of the Treaty of Asunción or the Protocol of Ouro Preto, that will give a new impetus to the integration process? Or has Mercosur reached the limits of its potential development, and will it simply refine its status as a customs union, with no real move toward a common market that would allow for the free circulation of workers, for example? Has Mercosur achieved the limits of what is possible in developing countries?

These questions cannot be answered definitively, of course; social sciences are not especially adept at prediction, particularly with complicated phenomena like regional integration. In addition, the general characterization of Mercosur as a process of vulnerable integration makes prediction particularly difficult. After all, one of the consistent arguments in this book is that Mercosur has seen its fortunes largely determined by events in the international political economy, which have often taken the regional grouping by surprise. There is no way to know ahead of time what international events might affect Mercosur in a profound way. Comparing the future of Mercosur to the future of the EU is illustrative in this regard. European integration occurs in a more constrained range of possibilities than Mercosur: we can state with reasonable certainty that the EU might move forward or backward, but it will not collapse or be superseded by another economic grouping in the near, or probably distant, future. The Mercosur process is much more unstable in this regard. While it is unlikely that Mercosur will simply collapse—after all, economic facts on the ground have made it difficult to abandon the integration effort—it could, given certain international conditions, be superseded if it expands geographically. It could also lose its status as a place that is attractive to international investment, making it increasingly irrelevant in the international political economy. Assuming no catastrophic breakdown in the international political economy occurs, this simply could not happen to the EU.

This concluding chapter addresses the future of Mercosur, by focusing on some recent events in the region and some of the key challenges that will determine its evolution. The main section considers some of these challenges facing Mercosur, looking both within the bloc and at the bloc's relationship with the rest of the world. The final section considers some of the lessons of Mercosur for other emerging country regions.

Challenges facing the integration process

As should be clear from the preceding chapters, Mercosur's integration has not been easy. Conflicts have been more or less permanent as integration has gone forward, and actors have repeatedly said that the process itself was in grave danger each time a new crisis appeared on the horizon. Those pronouncements were exaggerations, made for domestic political consumption or to compel partners to come to the bargaining table, and were not usually representative of what key actors really thought about integration. The economies of the region were increasingly interdependent, even if this interdependence was asymmetrical, in Brazil's favor.

In this section I consider three main challenges facing integration in Mercosur. Two of them are inherent in any integration process, while one is specific to the Mercosur case. The two general issues are, first, the natural conflict between broadening and deepening an integration process, and second, the challenge of macroeconomic coordination. The Mercosur-specific challenge is that of Brazilian hegemony in the region, on the one hand, and the potential for hemispheric integration led by the United States, on the other. Each of these challenges is significant, and on balance, makes it difficult to conclude whether Mercosur can advance much beyond its present phase.

Broadening versus deepening

As Felix Peña (1999) points out, Mercosur, like any regional integration project, faces the tension between broadening and deepening. Broadening involves including additional countries in a regional integration scheme. Deepening involves increasing the degree to which countries integrate their economies and their economic and foreign policy. Generally speaking, a deeper process implies more commitments on the part of member countries. Deepening reduces sovereignty, while broadening expands the coverage of the regional agreement. These two processes are not necessarily mutually exclusive, and they can proceed simultaneously. But usually, an integration project will place emphasis on one or the other at a particular point in time, and it may alternate between the two processes. Achieving both at the same time, however, is difficult, for a simple reason: broadening, usually understood as bringing more countries into an arrangement, implies the imposition of discipline on the new member countries as they adapt to the rules of the regional grouping. Deepening implies new rules constraining all of the member countries. Therefore, imposing *new* rules on *new* countries is difficult. Presumably the new countries will already have to be making some sacrifices—in exchange for expected, but as yet unrealized, benefits—by joining the new organization. Deepening integration while trying to broaden it at the same time implies that these sacrifices will likely be greater, making new countries more reluctant to join.

There is thus tension in these two processes, and as Peña notes, "achieving a dynamic equilibrium between broadening and deepening may be fundamental for maintaining the framework of mutual benefit that holds together the bonds of association" (1999: 50). Mercosur faces this dilemma, and it is a far different dilemma than the one facing the EU, largely because of its vulnerability. Whereas Europe considered potential expansion to the East from a position of strength, with the potential new entrants lining up at its door, Mercosur is not in such a position. Eastern European countries wanted to be associated with one of the main centers of international economic power, and expected substantial benefits from this association.[1]

The potential broadening of Mercosur faces competing pressures. On the one hand, there is the draw for other Latin American countries of associating with the largest economy in the world, the United States, through bilateral agreements that a number of countries have signed (Hornbeck 2009). While Mercosur can offer benefits to other Latin American countries, the main benefit in this regard is the Brazilian market. And the Brazilian market pales in comparison to its US counterpart. Integration with the United States might also entail higher costs for some countries, but the point to be made is simple: broadening means convincing countries that their best bet is with Mercosur, which is not necessarily an easy sell (Vaillant 2005). The EU does not face this dilemma with its neighbors to the east.

There are also ways in which a broadening dynamic could weaken the current members of Mercosur, thus giving them second thoughts, and here we can return to the problems associated with vulnerable integration. As noted in prior chapters, a major raison d'être of Mercosur was its desire to attract foreign investment; it was meant to be the key magnet for the investments of MNCs in South America. However, if Mercosur expanded substantially, to what extent would international investments come to those countries that originally formed the economic grouping, and which would go elsewhere? EU countries also have to consider this possibility, but since they would be one of the major *sources* of this investment, the logic is somewhat different. In the case of Mercosur, most of these investments will continue to come from outside the region, thus making it riskier to broaden.

In addition, in the particular case of Mercosur, broadening—as currently practiced—brings with it some serious political implications. The one country that has agreed to join Mercosur, and has been (almost) accepted by the member countries, is Venezuela. Though its inclusion in Mercosur was approved in 2006, the ratification process has been slow and at the time of writing had not been completed. Brazil's Senate only ratified Venezuela's inclusion in December 2009, and not without serious debate and concerns (Guerreiro 2009).[2] The concern that many have had is that including Hugo Chávez in the grouping will greatly increase the politicization surrounding integration and move it away from its primarily commercial nature (Klonsky and Hanson 2009). Broadening is not so simple if a new member is not especially well behaved.

When it comes to deepening, the main issue revolves around the question of whether the member countries will be willing to give up sovereignty in Mercosur and invest power in supranational institutions. Outside of Brazil, there might be some support for this (de la Balze 2002). And certainly, Uruguay would be ready to host such institutions, given its location, diplomatic proclivities, and small size. Brazil, on the other hand, continues to prefer ad hoc resolution of disputes, and its major tendency is to shoot first and ask questions later (Cason 2000a; Rozemberg 2002). There is no push to deepen integration in Mercosur, in the end. Early in the integration process, there were those who insisted that a greater institutionalization—and in particular establishing supranational institutions—was necessary, but those voices are hardly heard anymore. Any thoughts about deepening the integration process in Mercosur have been sidelined by the demands to deal with trade imbalances; no one has proposed a serious supranational body that would regulate Mercosur's relations.

Indeed, some recent events, coming on the heels of the monumental financial crisis of 2008–2009, have illustrated the near impossibility of forming supranational institutions in Mercosur. Figures 6.1 and 6.2 illustrate the precipitous decline in trade that occurred with the financial crisis. They illustrate both the large drop in trade experienced in 2009 and the relative stability, in Brazil, of the relative share of its trade with Mercosur. As the politics played out, shortly after the crisis hit, Argentina reacted first, by imposing unilateral restrictions on imports, including those coming from Brazil (*La Nación* 2008). Brazil did not react strongly at first, realizing that Argentina was in dire straits. But as time wore on, and as Argentina took additional measures over the course of 2009, mutual threats increased, with ever greater acrimony (Rebossio 2009). By the time of the Mercosur summit in December 2009 in Montevideo, Argentine president Cristina Fernández de Kirchner announced to her counterparts that the financial crisis had "made clear

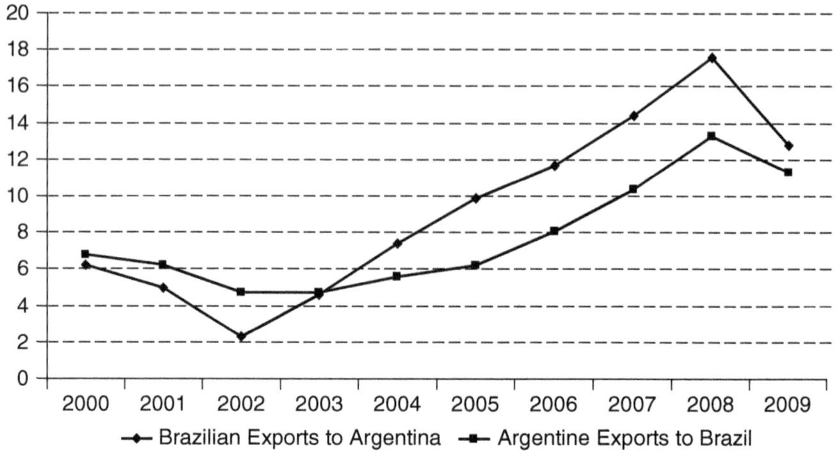

Figure 6.1 Brazil/Argentina trade, 2000–2009 (in billions of current US dollars)

Source: Secretaria de Comercio Exterior (Brasil n.d.).

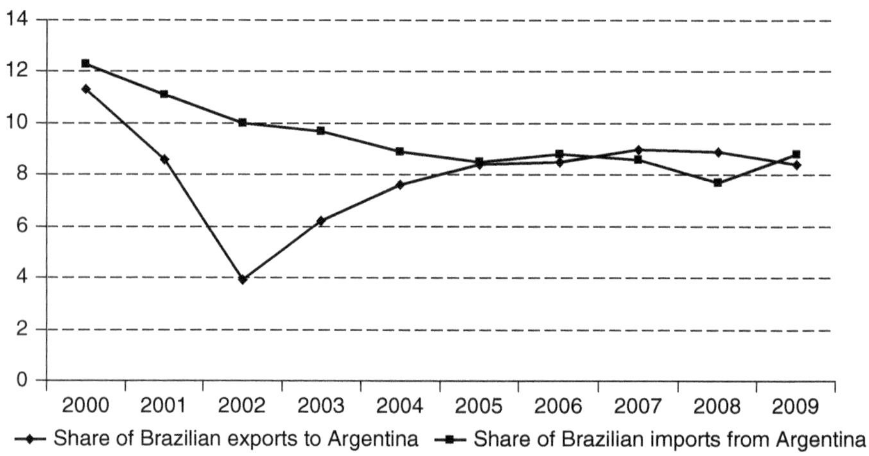

Figure 6.2 Share of Brazilian exports to and imports from Argentina, 2000–2009 (as percentage of total exports and imports)

Source: Secretaria de Comercio Exterior (Brasil n.d.).

everything that Mercosur could not achieve or construct. Today, all we have is a commercial sphere" (*Clarín* 2009). President Lula, while not responding directly, simply left the summit meeting without having lunch with his colleagues.

This is by now a familiar story, and only serves to remind us of the virtual impossibility of deepening integration in Mercosur. In a sense, the path that Mercosur went down—purely intergovernmental integration, dominated by the agendas of the executive—has become solidified, and it is difficult to see how Mercosur could jump to a more institutionalized integration. As Gómez-Mera (2008) has noted, the "new" regionalism—as exemplified by Mercosur—retains many of the characteristics of the "old" regionalism. In this regard, Mercosur's focus on interstate interactions stands out.

Policy coordination

Another area that has received a great deal of attention—if not concrete action—is policy coordination across a wide variety of areas. In a region known for its instability, such coordination has proven especially challenging, and also points to the limitation of the Mercosur project.

Macroeconomic instability has been the bane of Mercosur. From early on in the integration process, fundamental macroeconomic policies of the main partners, Argentina and Brazil, were worlds apart. As noted earlier, at the birth of Mercosur, Argentina had embarked on a radical plan to stabilize its economy by removing major monetary policy instruments from the hands of policy makers to tackle hyperinflation and give its stabilization plan credibility. Brazil, on the other hand, continued to muddle through on the anti-inflation front until mid-1994, when it adopted policies that were somewhat similar to Argentina's, in that they also relied on an exchange-rate anchor to stop inflation. As a consequence, both countries had overvalued exchange rates, which helped to encourage greater integration, and contributed to the landmark signing of the Protocol of Ouro Preto.

But the similarities in these plans were only superficial. Brazil was unwilling to tie the real definitively to the dollar, and instead relied on a tried and true policy of gradual devaluation of the currency. This policy had its roots in the late 1960s, and this mini-devaluation policy had allowed Brazil to cope with persistent inflation over the previous three decades (Ferrari Filho 2003; Veiga and Iglesias 2003). Even though Brazil was using an exchange rate anchor with its stabilization policy, it was not tying its currency as tightly to the dollar as Argentina was. Brazilian state officials were not about to give up monetary policy instruments as Argentina had. In part, this is a reflection of Brazil's long-standing tradition of greater intervention in its economy, which has not gone away despite its liberalization attempts. In the end, policy makers in Brazil simply wanted to preserve flexibility when it came to making economic policy, and if they tied the real to the dollar at a fixed level, they would lose that flexibility.

The divergence in strategies became obvious when Brazil was forced to devalue in 1999; in a sense, the vulnerability of the entire integration project was laid bare when the devaluation occurred. The imbalance and *lack* of coordination in Mercosur was abundantly clear (Andrade 2003). More importantly, it revealed that there could not be any serious macroeconomic coordination in Mercosur; neither of the primary Mercosur countries had enough control over their own macroeconomies to make such coordination possible.

To overcome this fundamental problem, a number of solutions have been proposed, including greater consultation among economic policy makers in the region or a common currency.[3] With the former, policy makers would have to decide what they wanted to accomplish with such consultation, and would need to decide that these consultations could on some occasions lead to changes in their own policies. When it comes to a common currency, it is difficult to envision it happening for at least several decades, if ever. Mercosur nations are certainly not ready for such a giant step. Indeed, the arguments laid out in this book regarding the vulnerability of integration in the region suggest that it would be virtually impossible to have such coordination.

Greater consultation among economic policy makers is a fine idea, and of course does need to happen for integration to advance. After all, if there were greater consultation, countries would not be taken by surprise when one of its neighbors gave advance warning about policy changes, and they could prepare for it. But by itself such consultation accomplishes little; without rules that would restrict the decisions made by any individual country, it is relatively meaningless (Fanelli 2001). Such consultation is even less relevant in a region like Latin America that is vulnerable to international shocks. After all, the most important changes in macroeconomic policy in Argentina and Brazil in recent years have come about because of pressure from the international political economy. Whatever consultation might have occurred would not have prevented the shocks from happening. And it would not have altered, to a significant degree, the behavior of policy makers.

The creation of a common currency has been proposed multiple times over the life of Mercosur, but it has never been discussed seriously by policy makers. Before the Brazilian devaluation, since both the peso and real were tied to the dollar, one could have plausibly argued that a common currency tied to the dollar made sense. It made much less sense after the Brazilian devaluation, even though Argentina tried to deny this reality: during the Brazilian devaluation crisis, Argentine president Menem went as far as to suggest that Mercosur adopt the dollar as the Mercosur currency, and that all of Latin America should adopt the dollar as its currency (*La Nación* 1999b; *Gazeta Mercantil* 1999). This, of course, reflected the fact that Argentina continued to tie its peso to the dollar at a one-to-one basis, and was its response to what it knew would be its own problems with a devalued *real*. But Brazil was as likely to adopt the dollar as its currency as it was to send a man or woman to Mars by 2015. Nationalism, a preference for intervention, and the practical difficulties of instituting real dollarization rendered this proposal dead on arrival.

In addition, despite Menem's suggestion that Mercosur adopt the dollar as its currency, Argentina's recent experience with its own peso makes monetary union unimaginable. It speaks to Mercosur's EU-envy that the issue even comes up, given the objective conditions that would argue against a common currency for the region. When Europe decided to establish a common currency, it came after a very long period of monetary cooperation.[4] Mercosur comes nowhere near the relative monetary stability that was necessary in Europe before a common currency could be contemplated. Indeed, Argentina and Brazil have been an advertisement against monetary union in recent years, given their instability. In particular, given the fact that there are no supranational institutions in Mercosur that have any political weight, discussing monetary union is fantasy. Unless countries in the region are willing to give up at least some sovereignty on less important issues, it is hard to imagine them being willing to give up sovereignty on monetary policy.

Alternatively, one could picture policy coordination in industrial policy. In some ways, Mercosur was born through such coordination in the 1980s with its predecessor, ABEIP. On the other hand, in the 1980s industrial policy was much more legitimate as a policy tool than it is today. Even so, both Argentina and Brazil continue to use policy tools to support distinct economic sectors (if not always successfully), and it is possible to imagine coordination happening in this area. If there were any place where that might be sensible, it would be the auto sector, where much effort has gone into managing trade. Still, after two decades of trying, common policy in the auto sector is as elusive as ever. Some continue to suggest that Mercosur keep trying (Arza and López 2008). But it is difficult to picture how this will happen, for several reasons. First, the most consequential decisions in the sector are made by transnational firms, which have global strategies that are only partly affected by regional auto regimes, and have many options for investment. Second, as noted earlier, the major reason that Argentina and Brazil feuded over the auto regime in the first place was their competition over investments, and that competition has not gone away. Finally, there is nothing approaching a consensus in the two major Mercosur partners over what the auto regime *should* be.

In the end, then, policy coordination is limited, and there are few mechanisms to support making it happen. Some incremental progress may be made from time to time when it comes to policy making, and certainly some sectors in each country have gotten to know one another better because of integration (which has led to cross-border investment and collaboration in the private sector). But there are not sufficient structures in place to oblige policy makers to coordinate in key areas, especially in times of crisis.

Brazilian hegemony

A recurrent theme throughout this book is how Brazil's economic and political weight has driven the integration process. This is not to say that Brazil has consistently *controlled* the process; another key theme in this book is that the integration has often been swayed and shocked by economic forces from outside the region. Indeed, many of the unilateral actions of the Brazilians were a direct result of shocks coming from the outside world. Argentina also responded in a unilateral way when circumstances made it necessary. Brazil's weight is still much greater, and the asymmetry in the integration process makes greater progress difficult (Terra 2008).

At the same time, because Mercosur was a priority for Brazilian policy makers, they were not reacting without regard to the effects that their actions would have on their Mercosur partners. Each time they took a unilateral action that angered their partners, they were willing to negotiate, even though they often got most of what they wanted with the eventual bargains that were struck. Brazilian policy makers continued to insist that Mercosur was a priority in Brazil, and indeed it was. Since Brazil viewed itself as having a leadership role in "representing" South America, it wanted its economic allies to be seen as partners, even if these partners might resent Brazil's sometimes heavy-handed approach. Both Brazil's ambition and the resentments of other Mercosur countries have made for turbulent Mercosur relations.[5] What has made the entire process more difficult is the fact that Brazil has often changed tactics as it pursues its strategic goals.

One of the problems with vulnerable integration such as that experienced by Mercosur is that strategic decisions do not necessarily translate into a consistent policy direction. To put it differently, Brazil's overall goal to be a leader in Latin America saw frequent changes in tactics, much to the irritation of Brazil's Mercosur partners. Brazilian policy makers certainly wanted to see Mercosur consolidated as a solid bloc that would be recognized internationally as an important player. They wanted to use it to challenge the US vision of what a Free Trade Area of the Americas (FTAA) should look like. They wanted to use it to attract foreign capital to the region. They wanted to use Mercosur to increase the Brazilian profile on the global stage. It is much more doubtful that they really believed in a "common market" goal, even though they expressed a preference for this in public statements. Consolidating a free trade area and an imperfect customs union among the Mercosur members is really all they would need to accomplish their general goals; a common market would put many more restrictions on Brazilian behavior, and they were much less interested in this. Although some argue that Brazil needs to exercise more leadership and behave as a responsible hegemon should, this is not likely to occur. One such call for greater Brazilian leadership argues that "more favoured countries—like Brazil—should adopt a magnanimous attitude that would correspond to its standing as a leader . . . [and] less favoured countries, such as Argentina, Paraguay, and Uruguay, should show more understanding regarding the exercise of Brazilian leadership" (Medeiros 2002: 45). While President Lula was somewhat more magnanimous than his predecessor, it was mostly along the lines of being more tolerant in the face of unilateral actions taken by Argentina. It most certainly was not proactive in terms of institution building. Being more proactive would certainly make Mercosur more robust, but there are no indications either that Brazil is willing to take on this responsibility or that the other Mercosur nations would accept Brazil acting as a more "responsible" hegemon.

Indeed, Brazil's recent actions in South America make this case. Instead of placing emphasis on strengthening or institutionalizing Mercosur, it has considered seeking broader South American cooperation outside a Mercosur framework.[6] This would seem to imply that Brazil is interested in *neither* deepening *nor* broadening the Mercosur process, and may in fact consider that Mercosur has advanced as far as it can. Brazil has consistently resisted moves toward deepening, to be sure, and prefers to conduct its own foreign policy, rather than engage in joint policy making with other Mercosur countries. After all, if Brazil were to negotiate in a strongly collective way with other Mercosur countries as a bloc, it is likely that it would have to eventually accept some supranational institutions that would constrain its behavior, and Brazil does not want to do this (Phillips 2004: 100–102). Brazil, as a sensible regional hegemon, is not especially interested in seeing its freedom of action constrained by the preferences of its neighbors.

Given Brazilian goals, therefore, there is only one scenario under which it is likely that it would move in the direction of either broadening or deepening Mercosur: renewed interest in the United States for hemispheric integration. Obviously, this renewed interest would have to be backed up by political resources and will in the United States, which in the current context is highly unlikely. During the 1990s, the Clinton administration repeatedly said that it was interested in the FTAA, but it did relatively little to move the integration process forward, particularly after the Mexican peso crisis. And while the Bush administration did receive fast-track authority (renamed Trade Promotion Authority) in 2002, there was little demonstrated interest in pushing free trade with Latin America, especially after 9/11 (Roett 2003; Prevost and Weber 2003). The Obama administration has taken no concrete steps to try to relaunch hemispheric integration, and would likely fail if it tried. But in the unlikely event that the United States did push hemispheric trade more aggressively, there is a chance that Brazil would react by trying to strengthen Mercosur.

This general point can be understood by turning the clock back to the early days of Mercosur. For at least the first decade and a half of its existence Mercosur integration took place in the shadow of broader hemispheric integration. In many ways, the Mercosur project emerged in response to these hemispheric integration possibilities, and has evolved as it has because of the prospects, or lack of prospects, for an FTAA. It was after the first President Bush announced his Enterprise for the Americas initiative in 1990 that the Mercosur nations, and particularly Brazil, put regional integration *within* Latin America at the top of the agenda. When Bush proposed, at this summit, free trade in the Americas, it was something of a surprise for Latin American nations, who had become accustomed, over the course of the 1980s, to a US policy that focused on security, democratization, and the debt crisis. Aside from the Caribbean Basin Initiative during the Reagan Administration, and trade conflicts with some Latin American countries (particularly Brazil),[7] commercial policy had largely been absent from US policy toward the region. In a sense, this was the most important *region-wide* policy initiative for Latin America since President Kennedy's Alliance for Progress, which came about as a response to the Cuban Revolution.[8] And as such, it required a response.

The response did not take long to emerge in Latin America, and it was somewhat surprising: many Latin American nations were interested in more trade with the United States, particularly if this could grant them more stable access to the US market; indeed, as some have pointed out, much of the initiative for free trade came from Latin America itself, which was at the time liberalizing rapidly.[9] This was a profound shift from previous Latin American reactions to free trade with the United States; it signaled a new era in trade relations in the Americas, as well as a restructuring of hemispheric relations more generally (Phillips 2003). The embrace of free trade in the Americas was not universal, however, and Brazil was among the most skeptical about such economic opening (Wise 1999;Veiga 2000; Machado and

Ferraz 2005). The response from Brazil was particularly active because the Brazilians felt that they had the most to lose from an FTAA, notwithstanding the neoliberal changes underway in Brazil at the time.

Thus, Mercosur was reactive to the potential of hemispheric integration, but at the same time proactive, since it created a new Latin American organization to confront the possibility of integration in the Americas. In the initial stages, Brazil was clearly the leading force in this integration effort, whereas Argentina tilted much more in the direction of hemispheric integration, as noted in earlier chapters. But as time went on, and it became more difficult to envision how a hemisphere-wide integration deal could be done, Brazil was content to have Mercosur be a part of its normal foreign policy priorities, with greater or lesser emphasis accorded to it, depending on circumstances.

Therefore, unless there is a sudden resurgence of interest in hemispheric integration on the part of the United States, it is difficult to conclude that Brazil would be interested in deepening integration. It is hard to picture Brazil being willing to move toward things such as a common currency, free movement of labor, and supranational institutions that would actually have some teeth. Brazil is content to see integration proceed along the lines of what has happened so far; there is no desire from Brazil to see any sort of great leap forward in Mercosur. And since nothing significant can be done in Mercosur without Brazil's consent, it is easy to understand why Mercosur has not made significant progress in over a decade.

Conclusion: understanding integration processes in emerging countries

I have made the argument throughout this book that Mercosur integration was fundamentally different from European integration, and much of this difference can be attributed to the fact that the Mercosur project has involved integration in emerging countries that are relatively poor. All the countries in it are outside the main decision-making centers of the international political economy. As a consequence, Mercosur has been a much more vulnerable integration project than either the EU or NAFTA.

In this sense, Mercosur is a model of integration for emerging countries. By calling it a model, I am not implying that other countries should try to emulate it. It is a model in the sense that other emerging countries that decide to integrate will face many of the same dynamics and challenges. There are several lessons that other regions should extract from the Mercosur process, if they decide to embark on a process of vulnerable integration.

First and foremost, vulnerable integration will remain at the mercy of important events in the international political economy. Although the EU has also been heavily influenced by international trends, there is a fundamental difference between it and projects like Mercosur. Emerging nations are more likely to be "infected" by speculative pressures than wealthy nations. International capital views them as more vulnerable, and as a riskier investment, and acts accordingly. Capital flows out at a moment's notice when the climate becomes risky, which makes agreements to integrate more tenuous. It is not surprising that Mercosur nations have not developed more robust institutions to constrain their own behavior; they knew that if they did, they might face circumstances that would force them to change policies drastically. Argentina's failed attempt to hold on to its Convertibility Plan makes this point forcefully.

Second, and linked to the first point, the success of vulnerable integration depends on the decisions of international investors and MNCs. Institutional investors who decide where to place their money internationally will be able to put money into these regions, and pull money out, at the drop of a hat. This was one of the most important changes that took place in the last two decades in the international political economy, and despite recent financial calamity, there is no sign that this dynamic is about to change. Investor behavior can change quickly, with particularly dramatic results for emerging counties. MNCs that invest in productive facilities, on the other hand, face a somewhat different calculus: any money they will be committing to emerging countries will be more long-lasting, since investment in plants and equipment cannot necessarily be removed immediately. Consequently, one of the major dynamics associated with any vulnerable integration process will revolve around the attraction of MNCs, since the success of integration will depend on new investment. Simply put, many emerging countries cannot generate enough investment through their own resources, and must rely heavily on this outside investment. The trick, for such economies, is this: how to attract this investment in such a way that it will help development. The problem revolves around making the region attractive for such investment, while at the same time not giving away the store through excessive subsidies to these MNCs.

Third, emerging country integration is likely to remain an intergovernmental process. In this sense, emerging countries contemplating integration do not need to worry about the power of "faceless international bureaucrats;" vulnerable integration is unlikely to produce them, or if it does, such bureaucrats will not have much power. This means that nations embarking on such a process should concern themselves with strengthening domestic institutions that will allow them to engage in more effective international bargaining.

Fourth, and related to the previous point, democratic accountability in integration may very well be meager, and leaders should aim to increase it. It is only through widespread political support that integration will ultimately be successful, and will be backed up by economic, political, and cultural linkages that are made "on the ground." Mercosur has only been partially successful in this regard; economic links have been made, and business has had increased access to decision makers as the integration process has proceeded. But for integration to take hold and be more stable (and perhaps somewhat less vulnerable), other links must be forged.

Finally, actors in any process of integration in developing countries will face the following question: What do they really want integration to accomplish? Another major argument of this book is that different actors will have different interests and goals when it comes to integration, so it is difficult to come up with a national position on integration. And because of the vulnerability of the integration process in a region like Mercosur, national and sectoral positions can change quite rapidly. An international shock can have an outsized effect on the development of integration processes in emerging countries.

I should emphasize once again that the fact that the countries involved in a process of vulnerable integration are themselves vulnerable does not mean that integration cannot succeed, at least to some degree. Indeed, Mercosur itself has accomplished a great deal, even as it has gone through numerous crises. The fact remains, however, that vulnerable integration will be subject to many more crises of confidence than integration in wealthier countries. What this means is that ambitious integration is unlikely to bear fruit, and will lead to considerable frustration on the part of policy makers if it is pursued. If these limitations are recognized, leaders and societies will have a much better shot at making the integration process work. At the same time, they will need to be quite flexible when it comes to their implementation of integration, since the international context can change so suddenly.

Notes

1 Understanding integration: the European model and a South American case

1 This geopolitical, peacemaking thesis is a standard interpretation of the formation of the European communities, though it has not been unchallenged. Moravcsik, in his sweeping reinterpretation of European integration, makes the case that ideology and geopolitics very often took a backseat to economics when it came to making decisions about integration. For example, he argues that "Whereas the bulk of the literature on the Treaty of Rome negotiations suggests that geopolitical considerations, supranational entrepreneurship, and technocratic or ideological motives for institution-building were critical, I hold that the preponderance of hard evidence demonstrates the greater importance of commercial interest, the distribution of relative power, and the desire to establish credible commitments for future elaboration and implementation of policy." See Moravcsik (1998a: 87). A more standard statement on the role of geopolitics is provided by Keohane and Hoffmann: "Prompted by a desire to prevent another war in Europe, as well as by visions of economic advantage, the postwar generation of leaders in France, Germany, Italy, and the Benelux countries created a remarkable set of institutions, culminating in the signing of the Treaty of Rome in 1957" (1991: 6).

2 While this is generally true, there have been disputes in some agricultural product areas, particularly in sugar and dairy products. Generally speaking, however, the main conflicts and their resolutions have been concentrated in industrial sectors and broader aspects of macroeconomic policy. For a discussion of agricultural issues in Mercosur, see Barbagalo (1998).

3 Economists tend to be much more skeptical of regional agreements than they are of multilateral liberalization. I do not address this debate here, since the goal of this study is not to determine whether a free-trade area, customs union, or unilateral liberalization would have been preferable for the EU or Mercosur. Rather, the focus here is on why Mercosur turned out the way it did. Discussion on the relative merits of different trading arrangements can be found in Viner (1950), Krugman (1996), and Bhagwati (1993).

4 For a general discussion on the economic aspects of integration, see El-Agraa (1997). For a specific consideration of the politics of integration, see Grossman and Helpman (1995) and Milner (1997).

5 The difficulties associated with the politics of monetary union are addressed quite nicely in Jones (1998). See also Garrett and Weingast (1993), who argue that there were indeed many economic reasons to accelerate European integration in the 1980s, though their main argument is that such economic reasons are not enough to progress in the economic integration effort.

6 This is generally true, though as Majone (1998) argues, one of the reasons that the EU has gotten as far as it has is because it has been able, to some degree, to separate economic decisions from the political arena.

7 These arguments on the international motivations for economic integration in Europe are standard and asserted in many places. For an example of this line of argument, see George (1996: Chapter 4). William Wallace argues that in fact these conditions were unique, and cannot be reproduced in other regional integration schemes (Wallace 1995).
8 An impressive treatment of the international context and its explanatory power can be found in Stallings (1992).
9 There is extensive literature on the role of civil society in the integration process in Europe. For a summary of this literature, see Rhodes and Mazey (1995).
10 It should be noted that Moravcsik (1998a) argues that the Commission's importance has been greatly exaggerated. George (1996) makes the argument that the Commission's power has waxed and waned, and has been crucial at some points.
11 For an interesting dependency-focused interpretation of Mercosur, see Cammack (2002).
12 An interesting phenomenon in the scholarly debates over "dependence" and "interdependence" was that there was to some degree a fundamental methodological disagreement over what to measure. Dependency theorists like Cardoso and Faletto did not find it useful to come up with "dependency measures," where interdependence theorists were quite interested in generating specific indicators. A useful focus on hard evidence of interdependence and dependence with specific reference to the difference between developed and developing countries can be found in Gasiorowski (1985).
13 Representative studies along these lines are Haggard (1990) and many of the essays collected in Gereffi and Wyman (1990).

2 A long-standing dream: historical experience with regional integration in Latin America

1 There were also occasionally moves to forge cooperation in all of the Americas; see Corrales and Feinberg (1999).
2 For a good discussion of the history of trade (and the problems associated with it) in Latin America, see Sanderson (1992).
3 For more on the economic policies of the period, see Furtado (1974) and Abreu (1989).
4 There is a voluminous literature on ISI in Latin America. For good overviews of the strategy, see Hirschman (1971) and Kaufman (1990).
5 Kathryn Sikkink (1991) provides an excellent introduction to CEPAL and its developmentalist ideology.
6 Luciano Tomassini makes a similar argument when he notes that "Economic integration was the natural follow-up to the strategy of 'growth turned inwards' pursued . . . by the Latin American countries, and was conceived as a method of removing the 'external barriers' to development by deepening import substitution" (Tomassini 1985: 214).
7 Two of the best summaries of the debt crisis and its implications are Stallings (1987) and Roett (1992).
8 See, especially Hirst and Bocco (1989) and Guilhon Albuquerque (1992), and Moreira (2000). For more on the roots of the change in Brazilian foreign policy, see Hirst (1984) and Fernández (1992).
9 As Manzetti notes, "Argentina and Brazil were no longer divided by any significant dispute, and Argentina had even acknowledged Brazil's prominent political and economical role in Latin America. Both administrations favored demilitarizing the South Atlantic to keep it free of East-West confrontations" (Manzetti 1990: 115).
10 On the "Zone of Peace" in South America, see Kacowicz (1998). On the effect of integration on democratic consolidation, see Cason (2000).
11 From the Argentine side, Felix Peña, who has been a key actor in Mercosur negotiations, argued that there were three main motivations for closer cooperation: "consolidating democracy, transforming our economies by means of technical progress (with greater

social equity, so as to consolidate democracy) and inserting ourselves competitively in international markets" (Peña 1992: 128). From the Brazilian side, a similar perspective was expressed by Celso Lafer, who also was a key player in the integration process: integration in this period "was a series of events derived essentially from the redemocratization of both countries in the middle of the 1980s: the emphasis on development, on democracy, on civilian control of the militaries and the evolution of a transparent and trusting relationship in the nuclear arena" (Lafer 1997: 250).

12 For the clearest early expression of the "Washington Consensus," see Williamson (1990).

13 As Chudnovsky and Porta point out, "[t]he public formalization of the agreements came as a surprise, and their signature was not preceded by a broad debate in either country; on the contrary, it was the debate's starting point" (1989: 15).

14 Araújo Jr argues that the more pragmatic nature of the integration process may in fact make its success more likely (Araújo 1990). For more on the "overnegotiation" of the integration process, see Bresser Pereira (1990).

15 On the problems associated with the heterodox stabilization plans, see Edwards (1995).

16 As Manzetti noted in an article published in 1990, "the ABEIP's future prospects are not rosy. At this point, it is hard to imagine the ABEIP going much further than it already has" (1990: 137). However, as Bouzas pointed out around the same time, "the modest results of the ABEIP in recent years . . . should not be considered negatively. On the contrary, [the ABEIP's] survival in such an unfavorable international context should be considered an important accomplishment" (Bouzas 1990: 37).

17 The term refers to the idea that for integration to proceed, new "protocols" must be negotiated at every turn.

18 LANIC, "GDP deflator," available at http://lanic.utexas.edu/la/region/aid/aid94/Economic/DEFLATOR.html (accessed February 1, 2010).

19 For a good collection of essays on the debt crisis in Latin America, see Stallings and Kaufman (1989).

20 On Argentina, see Tussie (1993). On Brazil's debt problems, see Pang (1989).

21 On the Baker Plan and the debt crisis in the 1980s, see Roett, (1992) and Geske (1991).

3 The launching of Mercosur

1 Mexico's initiative in the NAFTA process has been noted by many, including Corrales and Feinberg (1999) and Feinberg (2002).

2 On this general change, see Stallings (1992, Biersteсker (1995), and Naím (1999).

3 For a broad survey of early and subsequent reforms in Latin America, see Edwards (1995).

4 For an interesting comparative analysis of the adoption of neoliberal reforms in Latin America, see Weyland (1998). On the Argentine case, see William Smith (1992), and on Brazil, see Weyland (1997).

5 Pereira (1999: 9). The changing calculus facing the new governments in Brazil and Argentina is also discussed in Hurrell (1995). The degree to which Mercosur fit into a broader liberalizing tendency in the participant countries is discussed in Richards (1997a).

6 On the changing international context that led to a new emphasis on regionalism, see Fawcett (1995) and Almeida (1993).

7 On the early rationale for Mexican position, see, for example, Luis Rubio (1992), Pastor and Wise (1994), and Golob (2003).

8 For more on the changing relationship between Brazil and Argentina, see Hurrell (1995), Hirst (1990), and Sotomayor Velazquez (2004).

9 On Brazilian foreign economic policy, see Moreira (1996), Abreu and Fritsch (1996), Souto Maior (1996), de Cruz, Jr, *et al.* (1993), Jaguaribe (2003), and Cason and Power (2009).

10 For a discussion of the internal debates in Argentina as to whether to pursue the Mercosur or the hemispheric option, see Onuki (1996).
11 On the diverging foreign policy positions of Brazil and Argentina, see Hirst (1999).
12 A good discussion of the neoliberal position of the Argentine government can be found in Teubal (1998).
13 Peter Evans' classic *Dependent Development* (1979) remains one of the best sources on the relationship between multinational and local capitalists in Brazil. Although these relationships have changed over the last several decades, Evans still provides a nice characterization of the interests of different business actors.
14 As Peter Kingstone (2004) points out in the Brazilian case, industrialists continue to wait for a new industrial policy from the Brazilian state.
15 See Ghezan and Mateos (1995), for example, for an early appraisal of attempts to adjust to integration in Argentine agrobusiness.
16 On Brazilian business, see Schneider (1997); on Argentina, see Lopez (1998).
17 On the business environment of the period, see Nelson (1990).
18 The Menem quote is cited in Smith (1992: 53). Cavallo's speech, which was delivered on February 3, 1991, is quoted in *BBC Summary of World Broadcasts* (1991a).
19 An excellent discussion of the role of labor in trying to influence Mercosur can be found in Vigevani and Veiga (1996).
20 For a discussion of labor politics during and after the transition to democracy in Argentina and Brazil, see Cook (2002). For a comparative analysis of labor relations, see Buchanan (1995).
21 On this process, see Ranis (1998). On Perón (and opposition to Perón), see Garcia Sebastiani (2003).
22 On Brazilian labor, neoliberal reforms, and Mercosur, see de Oliveira (1999).
23 "Tratado de Assunção," Anexo 1. This Annex of the Treaty specified "automatic" tariff reductions every six months, with the expectation that all tariffs among member countries would be removed by the end of 1994.
24 All of these details are laid out in the first Annex of the Tratado de Assunção.
25 For a good summary of what the Mercosur nations agreed to in the Treaty, see Simonsen Associados (1998: 128).
26 See Cardoso and Dantas (1990), Armijo (1996), Richards (1997b), and Smith (1990).

4 Mercosur's day in the sun

1 A useful discussion of trade policy history that is relevant to the issue of trade cooperation can be found in Irwin (1993).
2 For more on the exchange rate anchors of stabilization programs and monetary policy in Argentina and Brazil, see Edwards (2000) and von Mettenheim (2004).
3 For more on both cases, see Flynn (1993) and Gibson (1997).
4 For more on Cardoso's role in the stabilization plan, see Eaton and Dickovick (2004), as well as Cardoso's own accounts (Cardoso 2006a; 2006b).
5 On Brazil in this period, see Kingstone (1998); on Argentina, see Lopez (1998).
6 For an excellent overview of Brazilian foreign policy aspirations and strategies, see Lima and Hirst (2006). See also Cason and Power (2009).
7 For the intellectual underpinnings of this position within Itamaraty, see Guimarães (1999). On the evolution of Brazilian foreign policy during the 1990s, see Mello (2002).
8 The early enthusiasm for Mercosur by multinationals is conveyed in Smith and Pearson (1992).
9 A good discussion on the changing nature of foreign direct investment in Latin America in the 1990s is found in Mortimore (2000).
10 For an example of this in the textile industry, see *Mercosul: Revista de Negocios* (1997).

11 On Brazil, see Cesar (1994); see also Lubetkin (1992).
12 World Bank (n.d.). On the specific effects of trade liberalization on Brazilian industry, see Moreira and Correa (1998).
13 For a comparative discussion of labor in the region, see Paul Buchanan (1995).
14 On Menem's strategy to carry out reforms in labor relations, see Etchemendy (2001).
15 For an excellent discussion of the development of the PT and CUT in a comparative context, see Seidman (1994). On the PT in particular, see Keck (1992).

5 Mercosur in slow-motion crisis

1 In the specific cases of Argentina and Brazil, Argentina's growth rate declined precipitously from the early 1990s to the late 1990s: growth averaged 6.8 percent from 1990 through 1994, and 2.3 percent from 1995 to 1999. In Brazil, average growth rates throughout the decade were anemic, averaging 1.5 and 2.2 percent in the comparable periods, and averaging less than 1 percent per year in 1998 and 1999 (World Bank: *World Development Indicators*).
2 For more on the increase of financial flows to Latin America in the 1990s and their implications, see Welch (1996) and Chuhan *et al.* (1998).
3 The story of the Mexican peso crisis is expertly told in Weintraub (1997).
4 For more on the problem of "contagion" in international financial markets, see Kaminsky and Reinhart (2000).
5 On fast track during the Clinton administration, see Yellen (1998).
6 For a succinct and insightful review of the Asian crisis, see Bosworth (1998).
7 On financial contagion, see Kaminsky *et al.* (2003); Roett and Crandall (1999), and Summers (2000).
8 A good summary (and timetable) of the Russian crisis is provided in Margolin (2000). See also Barrell *et al.* (1998).
9 For a discussion of the devaluation in the broader Mercosur context, see Carranza (2003).
10 For an excellent summary of the causes of the Asian financial crisis and its aftermath, see Stiglitz (2000).
11 This section and the following one draw on Cason (2000a).
12 On the auto industry in Latin America, see Kronish and Mericle (1984).
13 The mere fact that Brazil had opened up its auto market in the first place was surprising in and of itself, as this reversed decades of ISI policies in the sector. For more on the development of the Brazilian auto industry, see Chudnovsky *et al.* (1994) Lee and Cason (1994), and Sánchez (1992).
14 Author interview with a former government minister, July 6, 1995.
15 Author interview with Argentine businessperson, Buenos Aires, August 21, 1997.
16 Daily exchange rate values obtained from Banco Central do Brasil, "Taxas de Câmbio," available: http://www.bcb.gov.br/?TXCAMBIO.
17 On the Brazilian reaction to international financial crisis, see Cason (2001) and Flynn (1999).
18 On Argentina's (failed) strategy to tie the peso to the dollar, see Pastor and Wise (2001).
19 On the election, see Levitsky (2000).
20 See *La Nación* 2002. On the Brazilian election, see Hunter (2003).
21 The intellectual leader of a "southern" strategy for Brazil is Samuel Pinheiro Guimarães. His views are summarized clearly in Guimarães (2002).
22 For more on this period and the repeated initiatives to relaunch the Mercosur process, see Gomez Mera (2005).
23 On EU-Mercosur negotiations, see Bulmer-Thomas (2000); on Mercosur and the FTAA, see Prevost and Weber (2003) and Rios (2003).

6 The future of Mercosur and the challenges of economic integration in the developing world

1. On EU enlargement to the East, see Schimmelfennig (2001) and Zielonka (2004).
2. Paraguay's Congress still has not ratified Venezuela's membership, as of February 2010.
3. On the problems associated with macroeconomic coordination, see Escaith (2004) and Castro and Souza (2001).
4. On the history and practice of European monetary policy coordination, see Kondonassis and Malliaris (1995) and Corsetti and Pesenti (1999).
5. For a brief (and concise) discussion of the conflicting pressures facing Mercosur, see *The Economist* (2004).
6. See Rossi (2004) and Ministério do Planejamento, Orçamento, e Gestão (2006).
7. On the US-Brazil conflict, see Evans (1989).
8. For an early and revealing discussion of the Alliance for Progress, from the perspective of US foreign policy, see Grunwald (1964).
9. On the Latin American enthusiasm for free trade in the 1990s, see Feinberg (2002).

Bibliography

Abellán, J.L. (1972), *La Idea de América: Origen y Evolución*, Madrid: Ediciones Istmo.

Abreu, M. de Paiva (1989), "Crise, Crescimento e Modernização Autoritária: 1930–45," in M. de Paiva Abreu (ed.) *A Ordem do Progresso: Cem anos de Política Econômica Republicana, 1889–1989*, Rio de Janeiro: Editora Campus.

Abreu, M. de Paiva and Fritsch, W. (1996), "Aspectos Estratégicos da Política Comercial Brasileira," in J. A. Guilhon Albuquerque (ed.) *Sessenta Anos de Política Externa Brasileira (1930–1990), Volume II, Diplomacia para o Desenvolvimento*, São Paulo: Cultura Editores Associados.

Agence France Presse (1999), "Argentina Rescinds Protective Measures Against Mercosur Trade Bloc," July 30.

Agência Brasil (2003), "Discurso do senhor presidente da República, Luiz Inácio Lula da Silva, na sessão de posse, no Congresso Nacional." Available http://www2.mre.gov.br/doma/textos/pr_discurso_01_01_2003.htm (accessed January 31, 2010).

Albuquerque, J.A. Guilhon (1992), "Mercosul: Integração Regional Pós-Guerra Fria," *Política Externa*, 1 (2): 112–21.

Alimonda, H. (2000), "Brazilian Society and Regional Integration," *Latin American Perspectives* 27 (6): 27–44.

Almeida, P.R. de (1993), "O Mercosul no Contexto Regional e Internacional," *Política Externa* 2 (2): 86–103.

Amorim, A.B. Nazareth (1994), "O Mercosul e a Integração Latino-americana," *Boletim de Integração Latino-Americana* 14: 62–65.

Andrade, J.P. de (2003), "Limites a integração: o exemplo do Mercosul," in D. Benecke and R. Nascimento (eds), *Opções de Política Econômica para o Brasil*, Rio de Janeiro: Fundação Konrad Adenauer.

Araújo, J.T. de, Jr (1990), "El Programa de Integración Argentina-Brasil y las Tendencias Actuales de la Economía Mundial," in M. Hirst (ed.), *Argentina-Brazil: Perspectivas Comparativas y Ejes de Integración*, Buenos Aires: Editorial Tesis.

Armijo, L.E. (1996), "Inflation and Insouciance: The Peculiar Brazilian Game," *Latin American Research Review* 31 (3): 7–46.

Arza, V. and López, A. (2008), "Introducción al Libro: La Vision Regional," in A. López and V. Arza (eds), *La industria automotriz en el Mercosur*, Montevideo: Red Mercosur. Available: http://www.redmercosur.org/la-industria-automotriz-en-el-mercosur/publicacion/79/es/ (accessed January 31, 2010).

The Associated Press (2004), "Ten Years Later, Mercosur Leaders Meet and Assess Trade Bloc," December 14.

Balassa, B. (1967), "Trade Creation and Trade Diversion in the European Common Market," *The Economic Journal* 77 (305): 1–21.

Baldwin, D.A. (1980), "Interdependence and Power: A Conceptual Analysis," *International Organization* 34 (4): 471–506.

Banchoff, T. and Smith, M. (1999), "Introduction: Conceptualizing Legitimacy in a Contested Polity," in T. Banchoff and M. Smith (eds), *Legitimacy and the European Union*, New York: Routledge.

Barbagalo, E. Brandini (1998), "A Política Agrícola no Mercosul," in Luiz Olavo Baptista, A. de Azevedo Mercandante, and P. B. Casella (eds) *Mercosul: Das Negociações à Implantação*, 2nd edition, São Paulo: LTr Editora.

Barbosa, R.A. and César, L.F. Panelli (1994), "A Integração Sub-regional, Regional, e Hemisférica: O Esforço Brasileiro," in G. Fonseca Júnior e S.H. Nabuco de Castro (eds), *Temas de Política Externa Brasileira II, Vol. 1*, São Paulo: Paz e Terra.

Bardwell, K. (2000), "The Puzzling Decline in House Support for Free Trade: Was Fast Track a Referendum on NAFTA?," *Legislative Studies Quarterly* 25 (4): 591–610.

Barrell, R., Dury, K., Holland, D., Pain, N., and te Velde, D. (1998), "Financial Market Contagion and the Effects of the Crises in East Asia, Russia, and Latin America," *National Institute Economic Review* 166: 57–73.

Basso, M. ed. (1997), *Mercosul: Seus Efeitos Jurídicos, Econômicos e Políticos nos Estados-Membros*, Porto Alegre: Livraria do Advogado.

Batista, P. Nogueira (1994), "O Mercosul e os Interesses do Brasil," *Estudos Avançados* 8 (21): 79–95.

BBC Summary of World Broadcasts (1991a), "Economy Minister explains government's new measures," February 12.

—— (1991b), "The Signing in Paraguay on 26th March of the Treaty of Asunción," March 28.

—— (1992), "Business Association Wants Special Tariffs on Imports from Brazil," July 28.

—— (1994), "Ouro Preto Protocol Makes Mercosur into an 'International Legal Entity'," December 19.

Bernal-Meza, R. (2002), "Política Exterior Argentina: De Menem a de la Rua: Hay una Nueva Política?," *São Paulo em Perspectiva* 16 (1): 74–93.

Bhagwati, J. (1993), "Beyond NAFTA: Clinton's Trading Choices," *Foreign Policy* 91: 155–62.

Biersteker, T. (1995), "The 'Triumph' of Liberal Economic Ideas in the Developing World," in B. Stallings (ed.), *Global Change, Regional Response: The New International Context of Development*, Cambridge: Cambridge University Press.

Bolívar, S. (1965 [1815]), *Carta de Jamaica*, Caracas: Ediciones del Ministerio de Educación.

Bonelli, R. and Hahn, L. (2000), "Resenha dos Estudos Recentes sobre Relações Comerciais Brasileiras," Texto para Discussão No. 708, Rio de Janeiro: IPEA, Available: http://www.ipea.gov.br/pub/td/td_2000/td0708.pdf (accessed January 31, 2010).

Bosworth, B. (1998), "The Asian Financial Crisis: What Happened and What we Can Learn from it," *Brookings Review* 16 (3): 6–9.

Bouzas, R. (1990), "La Crisis de la Deuda, la Vulnerabilidad Externa y el Programa de Integración y Cooperación Argentina-Brasil," in M. Hirst (ed.), *Argentina-Brasil: Perspectivas Comparativas y Ejes de Integración*, Buenos Aires: Editorial Tesis.

Buchanan, P. (1995), *State, Labor, Capital: Democratizing Class Relations in the Southern Cone*, Pittsburgh: University of Pittsburgh Press.

Bulmer-Thomas, V. (1999), "The Brazilian Devaluation: National Responses and International Consequences," *International Affairs* 75 (4): 729–41.

—— (2000), "The European Union and Mercosur: Prospects for a Free Trade Agreement," *Journal of Interamerican Studies and World Affairs* 42 (1): 1–22.

Burns, B. (1993), *A History of Brazil*, 3rd edition, New York: Columbia University Press.

Business Latin America (1993), "Mercosur Presidents Push Forward," January 11.

Bustamante, M.T. (2005), "(Des)Construindo o Mercosul," *Revista de Economia e Relações Internacionais* 4 (7): 5–18.

Caetano, G. and Perina, R., eds (2000), *Mercosur y Parlamentos: El Rol de los Congresos en la democracia y la integración*, Montevideo: CLAEH.

Calvete, C. da Silva (2000), "Acordos Coletivos e Dimensão Social na União Européia e no Mercosul," in Paulo Borba Casella (ed.) *Mercosul: Integração Regional e Globalização*, Rio de Janeiro: Renovar.

Cameron, D. (1992), "The 1992 Initiative: Causes and Consequences," in A. Sbragia (ed.) *Europolitics: Institutions and Policymaking in the "New" European Community*, Washington: The Brookings Institution.

Cammack, P. (2002), "Dependent and Disciplinary Regionalism," in P. van Dijck and M. Wiesebron (eds), *Ten Years of Mercosur*, Amsterdam: Cuadernos del Cedla.

Caporaso, J. (1980), "Dependency Theory: Continuities and Discontinuities in Development Studies," *International Organization* 34 (4): 605–28.

Caporaso, J. and Keeler, J.T.S. (1995), "The European Union and Regional Integration Theory," in C. Rhodes and S. Mazey (eds), *Building a European Polity?* Boulder: Lynne Rienner Publishers.

Cardoso, E.A. and Dantas, D. (1990), "Brazil," in J. Williamson (ed.) *Latin American Adjustment: How Much Has Happened?* Washington, DC: Institute for International Economics.

Cardoso, F.H. (2006a), *A Arte da Política: A História que Vivi*, Rio de Janeiro: Editora Civilização Brasiliense.

—— (2006b), *The Accidental President of Brazil: A Memoir*, New York: Public Affairs.

Cardoso, F.H. and Faletto, E. (1979), *Dependency and Development in Latin America*, Berkeley: University of California Press.

Carranza, M.F. (2003), "Can Mercosur Survive? Domestic and International Constraints on Mercosur," *Latin American Politics and Society* 45 (2): 67–104.

Casella, P.B. (2000), "Integração nas Américas: Uma Visão de Conjunto," in P.B. Casella (ed.), *Mercosul: Integração Regional e Globalização*, São Paulo: Renovar.

Cason, J. (2000a), "On the Road to Southern Cone Economic Integration," *Journal of Interamerican Studies and World Affairs* 42 (1): 23–42.

—— (2000b), "Democracy Looks South: Mercosul and the Politics of Brazilian Trade Strategy," in P. Kingstone and T. Power (eds), *Democratic Brazil: Institutions, Actors, and Processes*, Pittsburgh: University of Pittsburgh Press.

—— (2001), "Brazil: Political Institutions and the Delayed Reaction to International Financial Crisis," in S. Horowitz and U. Heo (eds), *The Political Economy of International Financial Crisis: Interest Groups, Ideologies, and Institutions*, Lanham, MD: Rowman & Littlefield Publishers.

Cason, J. and Burrell, J. (2002), "Turning the Tables: State and Society in South America's Economic Integration," *Polity* 34 (4).

Cason, J. and Power, T. (2009), "Presidentialization, Pluralization, and the Rollback of Itamaraty: Explaining Change in Brazilian Foreign Policy Making in the Cardoso-Lula Era," *International Political Science Review* 30 (2): 117–40.

Castro, A. Barros de and Souza, F.E. Pires de (2001), "A Coordenação Macroeconômica no Mercosul: Reflexões a Partir da Experiência Brasiliera," in J.M. Fanelli (ed.), *Coordinación de Políticas Macroeconómicas en el Mercosur*, Buenos Aires: Siglo Veintiuno de Argentina Editores, Red-Mercosur.

Castro, M.S. Portella de (1996), "Considerações Sobre o Mercado de Trabalho e o Movimento Sindical no Âmbito do Mercosul," in H. Zylberstajn, T. Vigevani, I.J. Rodrigues, and M.S. Portella de Castro (eds), *Processos de Integração e a Sociedade: O Sindicalismo na Argentina, Brasil, México, e Venezuela*, Rio de Janeiro: Paz e Terra.

Castañeda, J. (1993), *Utopia Unarmed: The Latin American Left After the Cold War*, New York: Knopf.

Cesar, A. (1994), "Brazil—Industry: Business Sector Hurt by Lower Tariffs," *Inter Press Service*, September 12.

Chalmers, D. (1977), "The Politicized State in Latin America," in J. Malloy (ed.), *Authoritarianism and Corporatism in Latin America*, Pittsburgh: University of Pittsburgh Press.

Chudnovsky, D. and Porta, F. (1989), "On Argentine-Brazilian Economic Integration," *CEPAL Review* 39: 115–34.

Chudnovsky, D., López, A, and Porta, F. (1994), "Intra-Industry Trade and Regional Integration: The Case of the Auto Industry in Argentina," unpublished ms.

Chuhan, P., Claessens, S., and Mamingi, N. (1998), "Equity and Bond Flows to Latin America and Asia: The Role of Global and Country Factors," *Journal of Development Economics* 55: 439–63.

Clarín (1986a), "Negociaciones paralizadas porque faltan definiciones," June 1.

—— (1986b), "La estrategia hace temer a los sectores empresarios," June 1.

—— (1987), "Preocupación por la integración con Brasil," January 19.

—— (1988), "Crítica al manejo de la integración con el Brasil," July 28.

—— (1999), "Mercosur: Dudas por los Brasileños," April 15.

—— (2000), "Autos: Habrá otros seis años de comercio compensado," March 23.

—— (2002a), "Los Lideres de Mercosur Piden Ayuda para Argentina," February 19.

—— (2002b), "Estrechan Mas Lazos con Brasil," *Clarin*, February 14.

—— (2004a), "Advertencia de Kirchner a Brasil Durante la Cumbre del Mercosur," December 18.

—— (2004b), "Empresarios, Satisfechos con la Propuesta Oficial," July 8.

—— (2009), "Brasil Pidió 'Desdramatizar" los Conflictos Comerciales," December 11.

Comisión Economica para America Latina (CEPAL) (2005), *Anuario Estadístico de América Latina y el Caribe 2004*, Santiago, Chile: Comisión Económica para América Latina y el Caribe, 2005). Available: http://www.eclac.cl/publicaciones/Estadisticas/4/LCG2264PB/p1_2.pdf (accessed January 31, 2010).

Cook, M.L. (2002), "Labor Reforms and Dual Transitions in Brazil and the Southern Cone," *Latin American Politics and Society* 44 (1): 1–35.

Corrales, J. (2002), "The Politics of Argentina's Meltdown," *World Policy Journal* 19 (3): 29–42.

Corrales, J and Feinberg, R (1999), "Regimes of Cooperation in the Western Hemisphere: Power, Interests, and Intellectual Traditions," *International Studies Quarterly* 43 (1): 1–36.

Corsetti, G. and Pesenti, P. (1999), "Stability, Assymetry, and Discontinuity: The Launch of the European Monetary Union," *Brookings Papers on Economic Activity* 1999 (2): 295–372.

de Cruz, A.S., Jr, Calvacante, A.R.F, and Pedone, L.(1993), "Brazil's Foreign Policy Under Collor," *Journal of Interamerican Studies and World Affairs* 35 (1): 119–44.

de la Balze, F. (2002), "The Future of Mercosur: Argentina's Options," in J.S. Tulchin and R.H. Espach (eds), *Paths to Regional Integration: The Case of Mercosur*, Washington, DC: Woodrow Wilson Center for International Scholars.

Deutsch, K. (1954), *Political Community at the International Level*, New York: Doubleday.

Domínguez, J. (1997–98), "A View From Latin America," *Foreign Policy* 109: 48–51.

Duina, F. (2007), *The Social Construction of Free Trade: The European Union, NAFTA, and Mercosur*, Princeton: Princeton University Press.

Eaton, K and Dickovick, J.T. (2004), "The Politics of Re-centralization in Argentina and Brazil," *Latin American Research Review* 39 (1): 90–122.

The Economist (2004), "A Free-Trade Tug-of War: The Future of Mercosur," December 11.

Edwards, S. (1995), *Crisis and Reform in Latin America: From Despair to Hope*, New York: Oxford University Press.

—— (2000), "Twenty Five Years of Stabilization Programs in Latin America: The Exchange Rate Connection," UCLA Anderson School of Management Working Paper. Available: http://www.anderson.ucla.edu/faculty/sebastian.edwards/banxico.pdf (accessed January 31, 2010).

El-Agraa, A.M. (1997), *Economic Integration Worldwide*, New York: St. Martin's Press.

Escaith, H. (2004), "La Integración Regional y la Coordinación Macroeconómica en América Latina," *Revista de la CEPAL* 82: 55–74.

Escude, C. (1988), "Argentine Territorial Nationalism," *Journal of Latin American Studies* 20 (1): 139–65.

Espana, J.R. (1995), "The Mexican Peso Crisis: Impact on NAFTA and Emerging Markets," *Business Economics* 30 (3): 45–49.

Etchemendy, S. (2001), "Constructing Reform Coalitions: The Politics of Compensations in Argentina's Economic Liberalization," *Latin American Politics and Society* 43 (3): 1–35.

Evans, P. (1979), *Dependent Development: The Alliance of Multinational, State, and Local Capital in Brazil*, Princeton: Princeton University Press.

—— (1989), "Declining Hegemony and Assertive Industrialization: U.S. Brazilian Conflict in the Computer Industry," *International Organization* 43 (2): 207–38.

Fanelli, J.M. (2001), "Coordinación Macroecónomica en el Mercosur: Balance y Perspectivas," in D. Chudnovsky and J.M. Fanelli (eds), *El Desafío de Integrarse para Crecer: Balance y Perspectivas del Mercosur en su Primera Década*, Buenos Aires: Red-Mercosur, Siglo Veintiuno de Argentina Editores.

Fawcett, L. (1995), "Regionalism in Historical Perspective," in L. Fawcett and A. Hurrell (eds), *Regionalism in World Politics: Regional Organizations and World Order*, New York: Oxford University Press.

Feinberg, R. (2002), "Regionalism and Domestic Politics: US-Latin American Trade Policy in the Bush Era," *Latin American Politics and Society* 44 (4): 127–51.

Fernández, W. (1992), *Mercosur: Economía, Política y Estrategia de Integración*, Montevideo: Fundación de Cultura Universitaria.

Ferrari Filho, F. (2003), "Uma Agenda Econômica pos-Keynesiana para a Economia Brasileira: da tríade mobilidade de capital, flexibilidade cambial e Metas de Inflação à proposição de uma Estratégia Econômica Alternativa," in D. Benecke and R. Nascimento (eds), *Opções de Política Econômica para o Brasil*, Rio de Janeiro: Fundação Konrad Adenauer.

Financial Times (1996), "Argentina and Brazil Clear the Road: Last Week's Agreement Aims to Help Both Countries Expand their Motor Industries," February 2.

Flecha de Lima, Paulo de Tarso (1988), "Integração Brasil-Argentina," speech delivered at the headquarters of the Federação das Indústrias do Estado do Rio Grande do Sul in Porto Alegre, July 4, 1988. Mimeo.

Flynn, P. (1993), "Collor, Corruption, and Crisis: Time for Reflection," *Journal of Latin American Studies* 25 (2): 351–71.

—— (1999), "Brazil: The Politics of Crisis," *Third World Quarterly* 20 (2) 287–317.

Folha de São Paulo (1985), "América Latina precisa reforçar seu poder de negociação," December 1.

—— (1998), "Mercosul Busca Acordo Para Automóveis," December 10.

—— (1999a), "Mercosul Fará Acordo Temporário," December 22.

—— (1999b), "Brasil Reage a Restrição da Argentina as Têxteis," July 24.

—— (2000), "Essa Vaca não Pode ir para o Brejo," March 27.

—— (2002), "Brasil Abre Fronteira a Produto Argentino," February 7.

—— (2004a), "Reunião para debater salvaguardas é adiada," December 21.

—— (2004b), "Brasil Quer 'Comprar' Paz com a Argentina," December 15.

—— (2006a), "Acordo Automotivo Benficia Argentinos," January 25.

—— (2006b), "Argentina Festeja Acordo de Salvaguardas," February 2.

Frenkel, R. (2004), "Real Exchange Rate and Employment in Argentina, Brazil, Chile, and Mexico," unpublished ms. Available: http://www.g24.org/fren0904.pdf (accessed February 2, 2010).

Furtado, C. (1974), *Formação Econômico do Brasil*, São Paulo: Companhia Editora Nacional.

García Munhoz, D. (2003), "Brasil e Argentina: Desequilíbrios Externos e Inconsistência das Políticas Macroeconômicas," in D. Benecke and R. Nascimento (eds), *Opções de Política Econômica para o Brasil*, Rio de Janeiro: Fundação Konrad Adenauer.

García Sebastiani, M. (2003), "The Other Side of Peronist Argentina: Radicals and Socialists in the Political Opposition to Peron (1946–55)," *Journal of Latin American Studies* 35 (2): 311–40.

Garrett, G. and Weingast, B.R. (1993), "Ideas, Interests, and Institutions: Constructing the European Community's Internal Market," in J. Goldstein and R. Keohane (eds), *Ideas and Foreign Policy: Beliefs, Institutions, and Political Change*, Ithaca: Cornell University Press.

Gasiorowski, M. (1985), "The Structure of Third World Economic Interdependence," *International Organization* 39 (2): 331–42.

Gazeta Mercantil (1999), "Saída de Menem Põe o Mercosul na Era de Redefinições," October 14.

George, S. (1996), *Politics and Policy in the European Union, Third Edition*, New York: Oxford University Press, 1996.

Gereffi, G. and Wyman, D (eds) (1990), *Manufacturing Miracles: Paths of Industrialization in Latin America and East Asia*, Princeton: Princeton University Press.

Geske, M (1991), *The Baker Initiative: An Analysis of the Domestic and International Sources of United States Foreign Economic Policy*, PhD dissertation, University of Wisconsin-Madison.

Ghezan, G.S. and Mateos, M. (1995), "Las Grandes Empresas Agroalimentarias Frente a la Integración Regional: El Caso de Carnes, Aceites, y Lácteos," in S. Cloquell and E. Santos (eds), *Argentina Frente a los Procesos de Integración Regional: Los Afectos sobre el Agro*, Rosario, Argentina: Homo Sapiens Ediciones.

Gibson, E.L. (1997), "The Populist Road to Market Reform: Policy and Electoral Coalitions in Mexico and Argentina," *World Politics* 49 (3): 339–70.

Gilpin, R. (1987), *The Political Economy of International Relations*, Princeton: Princeton University Press.

Ginesta, J. (1999), *El Mercosur y su contexto regional e Internacional*, Porto Alegre: Editora da Universidade/UFRGS.

Goldfajn, I. (2000), "The Swings in Capital Flows and the Brazilian Crisis," Texto para Discussão #422, Pontifícia Universidade Católica, Rio de Janeiro. Available: http://www.econ.puc-rio.br/pdf/td422.pdf (accessed January 31, 2010).

Golob, S. (2003), "Beyond the Policy Frontier: Canada, Mexico, and the Ideological Origins of NAFTA," *World Politics* 55: 361–98.

Gómez Mera, L. (2005), "Explaining Mercosur's Survival: Strategic Sources of Argentine-Brazilian Convergence," *Journal of Latin American Studies* 37: 109–40.

—— (2008), "How 'new' is the 'New Regionalism' in the Americas? The Case of Mercosur," *Journal of International Relations and Development* 11: 279–308.

González-Oldekop, F. (1997), *La Integración y sus Instituciones*, Buenos Aires: Cuidad Argentina.

Griffith-Jones, S. (2000), "International Capital Flows to Latin America," CEPAL, Serie Reformas Económicas No. 55 (2000). Available: http://www.cepal.org/publicaciones/DesarrolloEconomico/1/lcl1351/lcl1351i.pdf (accessed January 31, 2010).

Grossman, G.M. and Helpman, E. (1995), "The Politics of Free-Trade Agreements," *American Economic Review* 85 (4): 667–90.

Grunwald, J. (1964), "The Alliance for Progress," *Proceedings of the American Academy of Political Science* 27 (4): 78–93.

Guerreiro, G. (2009), "Senado Aprova Entrada da Venezuela no Mercosul," *Folha Online*, December 15. Available: http://www1.folha.uol.com.br/folha/brasil/ult96u666908.shtml (accessed February 2, 2010).

Guimarãs, S. Pinheiro (2002), *Quinhentos Anos de Periferia*, 4ª edição, Porto Alegre: UFRGS Editora.

Gunder Frank, A (1967), *Capitalism and Underdevelopment in Latin America: Historical Studies of Chile and Brazil*, New York, Monthly Review Press.

Haas, E. (1958), *The Uniting of Europe*, Stanford: Stanford University Press.

—— (1964), *Beyond the Nation-State: Functionalism and International Organization*, Stanford: Stanford University Press.

—— (1967), "The Uniting of Europe and the Uniting of Latin America," *Journal of Common Market Studies* 5 (4): 315–43.

—— (1975), *The Obsolescence of Regional Integration Theory*, Berkeley: Institute of International Studies.

Haas, E. and Schmitter, P. (1964), "Economics and Differential Patterns of Political Integration: Projections About Unity in Latin America," *International Organization* 18 (4): 705–37.

Haggard, S. (1990), *Pathways From the Periphery: The Politics of Growth in Newly Industrializing Countries*, Ithaca: Cornell University Press.

Haya de la Torre, V.R. (1988), "El Pensamiento de la Nueva Generación antiimperialista latinoamericana contra el enemigo de fuera y contra el enemigo de dentro," in M. Rivarola and P. Planas (eds), *Victor Raúl Haya de la Torre*, Madrid: Ediciones de Cultura Hispánica.

Hirschman, A. (1971), "The Political Economy of Import-Substituting Industrialization in Latin America," in A. Hirschman, *A Bias for Hope*, New Haven: Yale University Press.

Hirst, M. (1984), "Política Externa: A Experiência Brasileira," *Dados* 27: 377–94.

—— (ed.) (1990), *Argentina-Brasil: Perspectivas Comparativas y Ejes de Integración*, Buenos Aires: Editorial Tesis.
—— (1996a), *Seguridad e Integración: América Latina en un mundo en transición*, Buenos Aires: Grupo Editorial Norma.
—— (1996b), "A Dimensão Política do Mercosul: Atores, Politização e Ideologia," in H. Zylberstajn, T. Vigevani, I.J. Rodrigues, and M.S. Portella de Castro(eds), *Processos de Integração e a Sociedade: O Sindicalismo na Argentina, Brasil, México, e Venezuela*, Rio de Janeiro: Paz e Terra.
—— (1999), "Mercosur's Complex Political Agenda," in Riordan Roett (ed.), *Mercosur: Regional Integration, World Markets*, Boulder: Lynne Rienner Publishers.
Hirst, M. and Bocco, H. E. (1989), "Cooperação nuclear e integração Brasil-Argentina," *Contexto Internacional* 4 (9): 63–78.
Hoffmann, S. (1966), "Obstinate or Obsolete? The Fate of the Nation-State and the Case of Western Europe," *Daedalus* 95 (3): 862–915.
—— (1982), "Reflections on the Nation-State in Western Europe Today," *Journal of Common Market Studies* 21: 21–37.
Hornbeck, J.F. (2009), "U.S.-Latin American Trade: Recent Trends and Policy Issues," Congressional Research Service Report for Congress #98–840. Available: http://www.fas.org/sgp/crs/row/98–840.pdf (accessed February 2, 2010).
Hunter, W. (2003), "Brazil's New Direction," *Journal of Democracy* 14 (2): 151–62.
Hurrell, A. (1995), "Regionalism in the Americas," in L. Fawcett and A. Hurrell (eds), *Regionalism in World Politics: Regional Organizations and World Order*, New York: Oxford University Press.
Instituto Nacional de Estadística y Censos de la República Argentina. Available: http://www.indec.gov.ar/ (accessed June 14, 2006).
Inter Press Service (1992), "Brazil: Exporters Fear Loss from Argentine Measures," October 30.
—— (1993), "Latin America: Integration Survives Despite Presidential Changes," December 17.
—— (1994), "Mercosur: Free Trade to Exclude Sugar, Auto Sector," December 15.
—— (1997a), "Mercosur: Business Dissatisfied with Temporary Solution to Crisis," April 4.
—— (1997b), "Integration: Argentina Toughens Up on Brazil," April 21.
—— (1997c), "Integration: Mercosur Credibility Bruised by Brazilian Initiative," April 2.
—— (1997d), "Mercosur: Brazil Caught Between Trade Deficit and Trade Partners," June 17.
—— (1998), Mercosur Nations Sign Auto Accord," December 16.
—— (2006), "Mercosur: Argentina, Brazil Compromise in Trade Squabble," February 10.
International Monetary Fund (1992), *Direction of Trade Statistics Yearbook*, Washington, DC International Monetary Fund.
—— (1998), *Direction of Trade Statistics Yearbook*, Washington, DC International Monetary Fund.
International Trade Reporter (1996), "Brazil-Argentina Auto Agreement Seen as Step to Large Car Industry," February 28.
Irwin, D.A. (1993), "Multilateral and Bilateral Policies in the World Trading System: an Historical Perspective," in J. de Mello and A. Panagariya (eds), *New Dimensions in Regional Integration*, New York: Cambridge University Press.
Jaguaribe, H. (2003), "Perspectivas do Brasil na Política Internacional," in D. Benecke R.

Nascimento, and R. Fendt (eds), *Brasil na Arquitetura Comercial Global*, Rio de Janeiro: Fundação Konrad Adenauer.
Jones, E. (1998), "Economic and Monetary Union: Playing with Money," in A. Moravcsik (ed.), *Centralization or Fragmentation? Europe Facing the Challenges of Deepening, Diversity, and Democracy*, New York: Council on Foreign Relations.
Kacowicz, A.M. (1998), *Zones of Peace in the Third World: South America and West Africa in Comparative Perspective*, Albany: State University of New York Press.
Kahler, M. (1992), "External Influence, Conditionality, and the Politics of Adjustment," in S. Haggard and R. Kaufman (eds), *The Politics of Economic Adjustment*, Princeton: Princeton University Press.
Kaminsky, G.L. and Reinhart, C.M. (2000), "Of Crises, Contagion, and Confusion," *Journal of International Economics* 51 (1): 145–68.
Kaminsky, G.L., Reinhart, C.M., and Veigh, C.A. (2003), "The Unholy Trinity of Financial Contagion," *Journal of Economic Perspectives* 17 (4): 51–74.
Katzenstein, P. (1975), "International Interdependence: Some Long-Term Trends and Recent Changes," *International Organization* 29 (4): 1021–34.
Kaufman, R. (1990), "How Societies Change Developmental Models or Keep Them: Reflections on the Latin American Experience in the 1930s and the Postwar World," in G. Gereffi and D. Wyman, *Manufacturing Miracles: Paths of Industrialization in Latin America and East Asia*, Princeton: Princeton University Press.
Kaufman, R. and Stallings, B. (eds) (1989), *Debt and Democracy in Latin America*, Boulder: Westview Press.
Keck, M. (1992), *The Workers' Party and Democratization in Brazil*, New Haven: Yale University Press.
Keohane, R. (1984), *After Hegemony: Cooperation and Discord in the World Political Economy*, Princeton: Princeton University Press.
Keohane, R. and Hoffmann, S. (1991), "Institutional Change in Europe in the 1980s," in Keohane and Hoffmann (eds), *The New European Community: Decisionmaking and Institutional Change*, Boulder: Westview Press.
Keohane, R. and Nye, J. (eds) (1972), *Transnational Relations and World Politics*, Cambridge: Harvard University Press.
—— (1977), *Power and Interdependence: World Politics in Transition*, Boston: Little, Brown and Company.
Kiguel, M.A. (2002), "Structural Reforms in Argentina: Success or Failure?," *Comparative Economic Studies* 44 (20): 83–102.
Kindleberger, C. (1986), *The World in Depression, 1929–1939, Revised Edition*, Berkeley: University of California Press.
Kingstone, P. (1998), "Corporatism, Neoliberalism, and the Failed Revolt of Big Business," *Journal of Interamerican Studies and World Affairs* 40 (4): 73–96.
—— (1999), *Crafting Coalitions for Reform: Business Preferences, Political Institutions, and Neoliberal Reform in Brazil*, University Park, PA: Penn State University Press.
—— (2004), "Industrialists and Liberalization," in M.A. Font and A.P. Spanakos (eds), *Reforming Brazil*, Lanham, MD: Lexington Books.
Klonsky, J. and Hanson, S. (2009), "Mercosur: South America's Fractious Trade Bloc," Council on Foreign Relations Backgrounder. Available: http://www.cfr.org/publication/12762/mercosur.html (accessed February 2, 2010).
Kondonassis, A.J. and Malliaris, A.G. (1995), "Toward Monetary Union of the European Community: History and Experiences of the European Monetary System," *The American Journal of Economics and Sociology* 53 (3): 291–302.

Kronish, R. and Mericle, K. (1984), *The Political Economy of the Latin American Motor Vehicle Industry*, Cambridge: MIT Press.
Krugman, P. (1996), "Regionalism versus Multilateralism: Analytical Notes," in J. de Melo and A. Panagariya (eds), *New Dimensions in Regional Integration*, Cambridge: Cambridge University Press.
La Nación (Argentina) (1986a), "El Acta de Integración de los dos países," July 30.
—— (1986b), "Los bienes de capital," July 30.
—— (1997a), "Gestión de Fernández para superar la crisis con Brasil," March 29.
—— (1997b), "Mercosur: en Brasil, esperan más límites," April 6.
—— (1997c), "Proponen diseñar políticas comunes," April 15.
—— (1999a), "Mercosur: Se Logró Superar la Peor Crisis," July 30.
—— (1999b), "Menem Propone como Salida que el Mercosur se dolarice," January 16.
—— (2002), "Las Exportaciones a Brasil, en Suspenso," October 8.
—— (2005), "Difieren con Brasil Por el Comercio Automotor," November 17.
—— (2006), "La Argentina y Brasil Pactan Limites al Comercio Bilateral," February 2.
—— (2008), Afirman desde el Gobierno que las medidas proteccionistas no son contra ningún país," October 17.
Lafer, C. (1997), "Relações Brasil-Argentina: Alcance e Significado de uma Parceria Estratégica," *Contexto Internacional* 19 (2): 249–65.
—— (2000), "Brazilian International Identity and Foreign Policy: Past, Present, and Future," *Daedalus* 129 (2): 207–38.
LANIC, "GDP deflator." Available: http://lanic.utexas.edu/la/region/aid/aid94/Economic/DEFLATOR.html (accessed February 1, 2010).
Latin American Regional Report—Brazil (1992), "Argentina 'Threatens' Mercosul: Move to Halt 'Avalanche' of Cheaper Priced Brazilian Goods," November 26.
—— (1993), "What kind of ties within Mercosul? Problems with Argentina Causing Particular Anxiety," November 25.
Latin American Regional Report—Southern Cone (1992a), "Presidents set Timetable for Mercosur at 'most important' Las Leñas Summit," August 6.
—— (1992b), "Argentina's Cavallo Says Extension of Mercosur Timetable Inevitable," December 24.
Latin American Weekly Report (1990), "Private Cartels are Collor's new target: First, Cement Makers; Next the Auto and Appliance Companies," May 7.
—— (1993), "More Rows Looming on Mercosur; Paraguayan State Firms, Uruguayan Cars, Trade Unions," May 13.
—— (1994), "Mercosur Presidents Reach Agreement on Custom's Union From 1 January," December 29.
Lavagna, R. (1998), *Argentina, Brasil, Mercosur: Una Decisión Estratégica*, Buenos Aires: Cuidad Argentina.
Lee, N. and Cason, J. (1994), "Automobile Commodity Chains in the NICs: A Comparison of South Korea, Mexico, and Brazil," in G. Gereffi and M. Korzeniewicz (eds), *Commodity Chains and Global Capitalism*, Westport, CT: Praeger.
Lerda, J.C. and Baumann, R. (1987), "Brasil e Argentina—integração em debate," *Folha de São Paulo*, July 28.
Levitsky, S. (2000), "The 'Normalization' of Argentine Politics," *Journal of Democracy* 11 (2): 56–69.
Lima, M.R. Soares de and Santos, F. (1998), "Brazilian Congress and Foreign Trade Policy," paper presented at the Congress of the Latin American Studies Association, Chicago.

Lima, M.R. Soares de and Hirst, M (2006), "Brazil as an Intermediate State and Regional Power: Action, Choice, and Responsibilities," *International Affairs* 82 (1): 21–40
Lindberg, L. (1963), *The Political Dynamics of European Integration*, Stanford: Stanford University Press.
Lindberg, L. and Scheingold, S. (eds) (1971), *Regional Integration: Theory and Research*, Cambridge: Harvard University Press.
Lopez, J.J. (1998), "Private Investment Response to Neoliberal Reforms in a Delegative Democracy: Reflections on Argentina," *Quarterly Review of Economics and Finance* 38 (3): 441–57.
López-Córdova, E. and Moreira, M. Mesquita (2003), "Regional Integration and Productivity: The Experiences of Brazil and Mexico," Interamerican Development Bank, INTAL-ITD-STA Working Paper #14. Available: http://www.iadb.org/intal/aplicaciones/uploads/publicaciones/i_INTALITDSTA_WP_14_2003_Cordova_Moreira.pdf (accessed February 1, 2010).
Love, J. (1980), "Raúl Prebisch and the Origins of the Doctrine of Unequal Exchange," *Latin American Research Review* 15 (3): 45–72.
Lubetkin, M. (1992), "Southern Cone: Expectations for Common Market Vary," *Inter Press Service*, December 22.
McAllister, R. (1997), *From EC to EU: An Historical and Political Survey*, New York: Routledge.
Mace, G. (1988), "Regional Integration in Latin America: A Long and Winding Road," *International Journal* 43: 404–27.
Machado, J.B. Mesquita and Ferraz, G. (2005), "FTAA: Assessments and Perceptions of the Brazilian Government and Production Sectors," in F. Lorenzo and M. Vaillant (eds), *Mercosur and the Creation of the Free Trade Area of the Americas*, Washington: Woodrow Wilson Center Report on the Americas. Available: http://www.wilsoncenter.org/topics/pubs/Mercosur_final_Web.pdf (accessed February 1, 2010).
Majone, G. (1998) "State, Market, and Regulatory Competition in the European Union: Lessons for the Integrating World Economy," in A. Moravcsik (ed.), *Centralization or Fragmentation? Europe Facing the Challenges of Deepening, Diversity, and Democracy*, New York: Council on Foreign Relations.
Malamud, A (2005a), "Presidential Diplomacy and the Institutional Underpinnings of Mercosur: An Empirical Examination," *Latin American Research Review* 40 (1): 138–64.
—— (2005b), "Mercosur turns 15: Between Rising Rhetoric and Declining Achievement," *Cambridge Review of International Affairs* 18 (3): 421–36.
Manzetti, L. (1990), "Argentine-Brazilian Economic Integration: An Early Appraisal," *Latin American Research Review* 25 (3): 109–40.
—— (1993), "The Political Economy of Mercosur," *Journal of Interamerican Studies and World Affairs* 35 (4): 101–41.
Margolin, R (2000), "The Russian Financial Crisis: From Craze to Crash," *The Stern Journal*, Spring: 9–17.
Mariano, N.C. (1998), *Operación Cóndor: Terrorismo de Estado en el Cono Sur*, Montevideo: Ediciones Lohlé-Lumen.
Martins, L. (1986), "The Liberalization of Authoritarian Rule in Brazil," in G. O'Donnell, P.C. Schmitter, and L. Whitehead (eds), *Transitions from Authoritarian Rule: Latin America*, Baltimore: Johns Hopkins University Press.
Medeiros, M. de A. (2002), "The Institutionalization Question: Mercosur, *Quo Vadis*?," in P. van Dijck and M. Wiesebron (eds), *Ten Years of Mercosur*, Amsterdam: Cuadernos del Cedla.

Mello, F. Campos de (2002), "Política Externa Brasileira e os Blocos Internacionais," *São Paulo em Perspectiva* 16 (1): 37–43.

Mercosul: Revista de Negócios (Brazil) (1997), "Do Mercosul Para o Mundo," January/February.

Milenky, E. (1973), *The Politics of Regional Organization in Latin America*, New York: Praeger.

Milner, H. (1997), "Industries, Governments, and Regional Trade Blocs," in E. Mansfield and H. Milner (eds), *The Political Economy of Regionalism*, New York: Columbia University Press.

Ministério de Desenvolvimento, Industria, e Comércio Internacional (Brasil), *ALICEweb*. Available: http://aliceweb.desenvolvimento.gov.br/default.asp (accessed June 14, 2006).

Ministério do Planejamento, Orçamento, e Gestão (2006), "Visão Estratégica Sul-americana—Informe Nacional: 1ª Rodada de Consultas Estratégicas no Brasil," Brasília. Available: http://www.planejamento.gov.br/arquivos_down/spi/iirsa/IIRSA_informe.pdf (accessed June 15, 2006).

Moravcsik, A. (1991), "Negotiating the Single European Act," *International Organization* 45 (1): 651–88.

—— (1998a), *The Choice for Europe: Social Purpose and State Power From Messina to Maastricht*, Ithaca: Cornell University Press.

—— (1998b), "Europe's Integration at Century's End," in A. Moravcsik (ed.), *Centralization or Fragmentation? Europe Facing the Challenges of Deepening, Diversity, and Democracy*, New York: Council on Foreign Relations.

Moreira, M. Marques (1996), "O Brasil e o Novo Contexto Econômico Internacional," in J. A. Guilhon Albuquerque (ed.) *Sessenta Anos de Política Externa Brasileira (1930–1990), Volume II, Diplomacia para o Desenvolvimento*, São Paulo: Cultura Editores Associados.

—— (2000), "Globalization versus Regionalism: a Brazilian Point of View," in B. Hettne, A. Inotai, and O. Sunkel (eds), *National Perspectives on the New Regionalism in the South*, New York: St. Martins Press.

Moreira, M. Mesquita and Correa, P.G. (1998), "A First Look at the Impacts of Trade Liberalization on Brazilian Manufacturing Industry," *World Development* 26 (10): 1859–74.

Mortimore, M. (2000), "Corporate Strategies for FDI in the Context of Latin America's New Economic Model," *World Development* 28 (9): 1611–26.

Muchnik, D. (2006), "Etapa de Definiciones en el Mercosur," *Clarín*, January 16.

Naim, M. (1999), "Fads and Fashions in Economic Reforms: Washington Consensus or Washington Confusion?," paper prepared for the IMF conference on second generation reforms, Washington, DC. Available: http://www.imf.org/external/pubs/ft/seminar/1999/reforms/Naim.HTM (accessed February 1, 2010).

Nash, N.C. (1992), "Free-Trade Talks in South America," *New York Times*, June 29.

Nelson, R (1990), "Is There a Business Strategy in Brazil?," *Business Horizons* 33 (4): 15–23.

Neunreither, K. (1994), "The Democratic Deficit of the European Union: Towards Closer Cooperation Between the European Parliament and the National Parliaments," *Government and Opposition* 29: 219–314.

Nye, J.S., Jr., (1965), *Pan-Africanism and East African Integration*, Cambridge: Harvard University Press.

—— (1971a), *Peace in Parts: Integration and Conflict in Regional Organization*, Boston: Little, Brown, and Company.

—— (1971b), "Comparing Common Markets: A Revised Neo-Functionalist Model," in L. Lindberg. and S. Scheingold (eds), *Regional Integration: Theory and Research*, Cambridge: Harvard University Press.

O Globo (1986), "Empresários reclamam contra a marginalização," December 12.

O'Keefe, T.A. and Haar, J. (2001), "The Impact of Mercosur on the Automobile Industry," University of Miami North-South Center Agenda Paper #50.

Oliveira, L. J. de (1999), "Neoliberalismo, Integração Econômica e as Organizações de Trabalhadores." Available: http://www.uel.br/cesa/dir/pos/publicacoes/publourivalo.html (accessed June 1, 2006).

Onuki, J. (1996), *O Governo e o Empresariado Argentina: A Percepção do Mercosul*, MA thesis, Universidade de São Paulo, Department of Political Science.

—— (2004), "O Mercosul e a Incoerência da Política Externa Argentina," *Politica Hoje* 1 (14). Available: http://politicahoje.com/ojs/viewarticle.php?id = 91&layout = abstract (accessed February 1, 2010).

Organization of American States (1994), Sistema de Informação de Comércio Exterior, "Mercosul/CMC/Dec. N° 29/94: Adequação ao Regime Automotriz Comum." Available: http://www.sice.oas.org/trade/mrcsrs/decisions/DEC2994p.asp. (accessed February 1, 2010).

Packenham, R. (1992), *The Dependency Movement: Scholarship and Politics in Development Studies*, Cambridge: Harvard University Press, 1992.

Pang, E.S. (1989), "Debt, Adjustment, and Democratic Cacophony in Brazil," in B. Stallings and R. Kaufman (eds), *Debt and Democracy in Latin America*, Boulder: Westview Press.

Pastor, M. and Wise, C. (1994), "The Origins and Sustainability of Mexico's Free Trade Policy," *International Organization* 48 (3): 459–89.

—— (2001), "From Poster Child to Basket Case," *Foreign Affairs* 80 (6): 60–72.

Peña, F. (1992), "Pré-requisitos Políticos e Economicos da Integração," *Política Externa* 1 (2): 122–31.

—— (1999), "Broadening and Deepening: Striking the Right Balance," in R. Roett (ed.), *Mercosur: Regional Integration, World Markets*, Boulder: Lynne Rienner Publishers.

Pereira, L.C. Bresser (1990), "Presupuestos y Obstáculos de la Integración Argentina-Brasil," in M. Hirst (ed.), *Argentina-Brasil: Perspectivas Comparativas y Ejes de Integración*, Buenos Aires: Editorial Tesis.

—— (2004), "A Argentina Pode Ter Razão," *Folha de São Paulo*, December 20.

Pereira, L. Valls (1999), "Toward the Common Market of the South," in R. Roett (ed.), *Mercosur: Regional Integration, World Markets*, Boulder: Lynne Rienner Publishers.

Phillips, N. (2003), "Hemispheric Integration and Subregionalism in the Americas," *International Affairs* 79 (2): 327–49.

—— (2004), *The Southern Cone Model: The Political Economy of Regional Capitalist Development in Latin America*, New York: Routledge.

Pimentel, L.O. (ed.) (1998), *Mercosul no Cenário Internacional: Direito e Sociedade* (2 volumes), Curitiba: Juruá Editora.

Porrata-Doria, Jr., R. (2005), *Mercosur: The Common Market of the Southern Cone*, Durham: Carolina Academic Press.

Prebisch, R. (1959), "Commercial Policy in the Underdeveloped Countries," *American Economic Review* 49 (2): 251–73.

Prevost, G. and Weber, R. (2003), "The Free Trade Area of the Americas in the Context of U.S.-Latin American Relations," *Journal of Developing Societies* 19 (2–3): 114–36.

Protocolo de Ouro Preto (1994), "Protocolo Adicional ao Tratado de Assunção Sobre a

Estrutura Institucional do Mercosul." Available: http://www.mercosul.gov.br/tratados-e-protocolos/protocolo-de-ouro-preto-1/ (accessed May 2, 2010).

Ranis, P. (1998), "Argentine Privatization under Peronism: Consequences for and Responses from Argentine Labor," paper presented at the 1998 Congress of the Latin American Studies Association, September 1998, Chicago.

Rebossio, Alejandro (2009), "La Crisis Reactiva la Pugna entre Argentina y Brasil," *El País*, December 3.

Reuters (1995a), "Menem Could Cancel Brazil Visit Because of Car Row," June 14.

—— (1995b), "Argentina Automakers Bound to Lose Their Edge," June 16.

—— (1995c), "Menem Says Auto Trade Spat with Brazil Overcome," June 16.

Rhodes, C. and Mazey, S. (1995), "Introduction: Integration in Theoretical Perspective," in Rhodes and Mazey (eds), *The State of the European Union: Building a European Polity?* Boulder: Lynne Rienner Publishers.

Richards, D.G. (1997a), "Dependent Development and Regional Integration: A Critical Examination of the Southern Cone Common Market," *Latin American Perspectives* 24 (6): 133–55.

—— (1997b), "Inflation, Unemployment, and Distributional Conflict in Argentina, 1984–90," *Journal of Development Studies* 34 (2): 156–72.

Riethof, M. (2004), "Changing Strategies of the Brazilian Labor Movement: From Opposition to Participation," *Latin American Perspectives* 31 (6): 31.47.

Rios, S. Polonia (2003), "O Desenho das Estratégias Brasileiras de Comercio com os Estados Unidos, América Latina, e a União Européia," in D. Benecke, R. Nascimento, and R. Fendt (eds), *Brasil na Arquitetura Comercial Global*, Rio de Janeiro: Fundação Konrad Adenauer.

Roett, R. (1992), The Debt Crisis and Economic Development in Latin America," in J. Hartlyn, L. Schoultz, and A. Varas (eds), *The United States and Latin America in the 1990s: Beyond the Cold War*, Chapel Hill: University of North Carolina Press.

—— (ed.) (1999), *Mercosur: Regional Integration, World Markets*, Boulder: Lynne Rienner.

—— (2003), "Os Estados Unidos e a ALCA," in D. Benecke, R. Nascimento, and R. Fendt (eds), *Brasil na Arquitetura Comercial Global*, Rio de Janeiro: Fundação Konrad Adenauer.

Roett, R. and Crandall, R. (1999), "The Global Economic Crisis, Contagion, and Institutions: New Realities in Latin America and Asia," *International Political Science Review* 20 (3): 271–83.

Rosecrance, R. and Stein, A. (1973), "Interdependence: Myth or Reality," *World Politics* 26 (1): 1–27.

Rossi, C. (2004), "Lula diz que, se morrer já terá 'valido a pena,'" *Folha de São Paulo*, December 10.

Rozemberg, R. (2002), "Mercosur: Between Skepticism and the Relaunch," in J. S. Tulchin and R. H. Espach (eds), *Paths to Regional Integration: The Case of Mercosur*, Washington, DC: Woodrow Wilson Center for International Scholars.

Rubio, L. (1992), "The Rationale for NAFTA: Mexico's New 'Outward-Looking' Strategy," *Business Economics* 27 (2): 12–16.

Sánchez, E.P. (1992), "The Auto Industry in Latin America: The Challenge of Adjusting to Economic Reform," *Business Economics* 27 (2): 25–30.

Sanderson, S. (1992), *The Politics of Trade in Latin American Development*, Stanford: Stanford University Press.

Schamis, H.E. (2002), "Argentina: Crisis and Democratic Consolidation," *Journal of Democracy* 13 (2): 81–94.

Schimmelfennig, F. (2001), "The Community Trap: Liberal Norms, Rhetorical Action, and the Eastern Enlargement of the European Union," *International Organization* 55 (1): 47–80.

Schneider, B.R. (1997), "Organized Business and Politics in Democratic Brazil," *Journal of Interamerican Studies and World Affairs* 39 (4): 95–127.

Secretaria de Comércio Exterior (Brasil) (1997), "Balança Comercial Brasileira, Julho 1997." Available: http://161.148.1.101/bal97/aspec07.htm (accessed January 15, 1999).

—— (n.d.), "Intercâmbio Comercial Brasileiro—Países e Blocos Econômicos." Available: http://mdic.gov.br/sitio/interna/interna.php?area = 5&menu = 576 (accessed June 7, 2010).

Seidman, G. (1994), *Manufacturing Militance: Workers Movements in Brazil and South Africa, 1970–1985*, Berkeley: University of California Press.

Senhor (1986), "Mano a Mano," August 5.

Shapiro, M. (1992), "The European Court of Justice," in A. Sbragia (ed.) *Europolitics: Institutions and Policymaking in the "New" European Community*, Washington: The Brookings Institution.

Sikkink, K. (1991), *Ideas and Institutions: Developmentalism in Brazil and Argentina*, Ithaca: Cornell University Press.

Simonsen Associados (1998), *Mercosul: The Big Emerging Market*, São Paulo: Makron Books.

Smith, G. and Pearson, J. (1992), "The New World's Newest Trading Bloc," *Business Week*, May 4.

Smith, M.P. (1996), "Democratic Legitimacy in the European Union: Fulfilling the Institutional Logic," *The Journal of Legislative Studies* 2 (4): 283–301.

—— (1999), "EU Legitimacy and the 'Defensive' Reaction to the Single European Market," in T. Banchoff and M. Smith (eds), *Legitimacy and the European Union*, New York: Routledge.

Smith, P. (2008), *Talons of the Eagle: Dynamics of U.S.-Latin American Relations, 3rd edition*, New York: Oxford University Press.

Smith, W. (1990), "Democracy, Distributional Conflicts, and Macroeconomic Policy Making in Argentina, 1983–89," *Journal of Interamerican Studies and World Affairs* 32 (2): 1–42.

—— (1992), "State, Market and Neoliberalism in Post-Transition Argentina: The Menem Experiment," *Journal of Interamerican Studies and World Affairs* 33 (4): 45–82 (1991).

Sotomayor Velazquez, A.C. (2004), "Civil-Military Affairs and Security Institutions in the Southern Cone: The Sources of Argentine-Brazilian Nuclear Cooperation," *Latin American Politics and Society* 46 (4): 29–60.

Souto Maior, L.A. (1996), "A Diplomacia Econômica Brasileira na Pos-guerra (1964–90)," in J. A. Guilhon Albuquerque (ed.), *Sessenta Anos de Política Externa Brasileira (1930–1990), Volume II, Diplomacia para o Desenvolvimento*, São Paulo: Cultura Editores Associados.

Spero, J. Edelman and Hart, J. (2009), *The Politics of International Economic Relations, 7th edition*, Boston: Wadsworth.

Stallings, B. (1987), *Banker to the Third World*, Berkeley: University of California Press.

—— (1992), "International Influence on Economic Policy: Debt, Stabilization, and Structural Reform," in S. Haggard and R. Kaufman (eds), *The Politics of Economic Adjustment: International Constraints, Distributive Conflicts, and the State*, Princeton University Press.

Stallings, B. and Kaufman, R. (eds) (1989), *Debt and Democracy in Latin America*, Boulder: Westview Press.

Stiglitz, J. (2000), "What I Learned at the World Economic Crisis," *The New Republic*, April 17.
Summers, L. (2000), "International Financial Crises: Causes, Preventions, and Cures," *The American Economic Review* 90 (2): 1–16.
Tachinardi, M.H (1995), "Mercosul: Desafios e Oportunidades," *Política Externa* 3 (4): 79–89.
TELAM Noticias (1995a), "Brasil apunta a captar las inversiones automotrizes," June 14.
—— (1995b), "Cavallo confirmó que Brasil suspendió la medida por 30 días," June 15.
—— (1995c), "Brasil y Argentina retoman negociaciones por cupos para autos," June 22.
Terra, M.A. (2008), "Asimetrías en el Mercosur: Un Obstáculo para el Crecimiento?" in F. Masi, M.I. Terra, and R. Bouzas (eds), *Asimetrías en el Mercosur: Impedimiento para el Crecimiento?* Montevideo: Red Mercosur. Available: http://www.redmercosur.org/asimetrias-en-el-mercosur-impedimento-para-el-crecimiento/publicacion/73/es/ (accessed January 31, 2010).
Teubal, M. (1998), "Regional Integration Processes in Latin America: Argentina and Mercosur," in A.E. Fernández Jilberto and A. Mommen (eds), *Regionalization and Globalization in the Modern World Economy: Perspectives on the Third World and Transitional Economies*, New York: Routledge.
Tomassini, L. (1985), "The disintegration of the integration process: towards new forms of regional cooperation," in A. Gauhar (ed.), *Regional Integration: The Latin American Experience*, Boulder: Westview Press.
Tratado de Assunção (1991), "Tratado para a Constituição de Um Mercado Comum Entre A República Argentina, A República Federativa Do Brasil, A República Do Paraguai E A República Oriental Do Uruguai." Available: http://www2.mre.gov.br/dai/trassuncao.htm (accessed February 1, 2010).
Trubek, D.M. and Mosher, J.S. (2003), "New Governance, Employment Policy, and the European Social Model," in J. Zeitlin and D.M. Trubek (eds), *Governing Work and Welfare in a New Economy: European and American Experiments*, New York: Oxford University Press.
Tsoukalis, L. (1997), *The New European Economy Revisited*, New York: Oxford University Press.
Tussie, D. (1993), "Bargaining at a Crossroads: Argentina," in *The Developing Countries in World Trade*, D. Glover and D. Tussie (eds), Boulder: Lynne Rienner Publishers.
Tussie, D., Labaqui, I, and Quiliconi, C. (2001), "Disputas Comerciales e Insuficiencias institucionales: De la Experiencia a la Esperanza?," in D. Chudnovsky and J.M. Fanelli (eds), *El Désafío de Integrarse para Crecer: Balance y Perspectivas del Mercosur en su Primera Decada*, Buenos Aires: Red-Mercosur, Siglo Veintiuno de Argentina Editores.
Vacchino, J.M. (1990), "Organismos Latinoamericanos de Integración: Evolución y Perspectivas," in L. Tomassini (ed.), *Nuevas Formas de Concertación Regional en América Latina*, Buenos Aires: Grupo Editor Latinoamericano.
Vacs, A. (1998), review of Carlos Escude, *Foreign Policy Theory in Menem's Argentina*, *Journal of Interamerican Studies and World Affairs* 40 (1): 97–100.
Vaillant, M. (2005), "Mercosur: Southern Integration Under Construction," *Internationale Politik und Gesellschaft* 2/2005: 52–71.
Veiga, P. de Motta (2000), "Brasil Frente al Mercosur: Economía y Política en el Proceso de Integración," in Celia Barbato, ed., *Mercosur, una Estrategia de Desarollo: Nuevas Miradas Desde la Economía y la Política*, Montevideo: Ediciones Trilce.
Veiga, P. de Motta and Iglesias, R. (2003), "Políticas de Incentivo as exportações no Brasil

entre 1964 e 2002: Resenha de Estudos Selecionados," Ministério da Fazenda, Secretaria de Assuntos Internacionais, Brasília. Available: http://www.fazenda.gov.br/sain/download/Temas%20de%20Economia%20Internacional2.pdf (accessed May 2, 2010).

Vigevani, T. and Veiga, J.P. (1996), "Interesses e Mobilizacão Sindical," in H. Zylberstajn, T. Vigevani, I.J. Rodrigues, and M.S. Portella de Castro (eds), *Processos de Integração Regional a Sociedade: O Sindicalismo na Argentina, Brasil, México, e Venezuela*, Rio de Janeiro: Paz e Terra.

Viner, J. (1950), *The Customs Union Issue*, New York: Carnegie Endowment for International Peace.

von Mettenheim, K. (2004), "From the Economics of Politics to the Politics of Monetary Policy in Brazil," University of Oxford Centre for Brazilian Studies Working Paper #54 (2004), Available: http://www.brazil.ox.ac.uk/_data/assets/pdf_file/0008/9368/Von20Mettenheim2054.pdf (accessed February 1, 2010).

Wade, R. (1990), *Governing the Market: Economic Theory and the Role of Government in East Asian Industrialization*, Princeton: Princeton University Press.

Wallace, W. (1995), "Regionalism in Europe: Model or Exception?," in L. Fawcett and A. Hurrell (eds), *Regionalism in World Politics*, New York: Oxford University Press.

Weintraub, S. (1997), "As Mexico Imploded: Action and Inaction in the United States," University of Miami North-South Center Paper #28.

Welch, J.H. (1996), "Capital Flows and Economic Growth: Reflections on Latin America in the 1990s," *The Quarterly Review of Economic and Finance* 36: 101–14.

Weyland, K. (1996), *Democracy Without Equity: Failures of Reform in Brazil*, Pittsburgh: University of Pittsburgh Press.

—— (1997), "The Brazilian State in the New Democracy," *Journal of Interamerican Studies and World Affairs* 39 (4): 63–94.

—— (1998), "Swallowing the Bitter Pill: Sources of Popular Support for Neoliberal Reform in Latin America," *Comparative Political Studies* 31 (5): 539–68.

Wiarda, H. (1995), "After Miami: The Summit, the Peso Crisis, and the Future of U.S.-Latin American Relations," *Journal of Interamerican Studies and World Affairs* 37 (1): 43–69.

Williamson, J. (1990), "What Washington Means by Policy Reform," in J. Williamson (ed.), *Latin American Adjustment: How Much Has Happened?* Washington, DC: Institute for International Economics.

Wise, C. (1999), "Latin American Trade Strategy at Century's End," University of Miami North-South Agenda Paper #37.

Woo, W.T. (2000), "The Asian Financial Crisis: Hindsight, Insight, Foresight," *ASEAN Economic Bulletin* 17 (2): 113–19.

Wooley, J.T. (1992) "Policy Credibility and European Monetary Institutions," in A. Sbragia (ed.) *Europolitics: Institutions and Policymaking in the "New" European Community*, Washington: The Brookings Institution.

World Bank (n.d.), *World Development Indicators*. Available: http://publications.worldbank.org/WDI/ (accessed February 1, 2010).

World Bank (1987), *World Development Report*, New York: Oxford University Press.

—— (2005), "Argentina: A la Búsqueda de un crecimiento sostenido con equidad social: Observaciones sobre el Crecimiento, la desigualdad, y la Pobreza." Available: http://www-wds.worldbank.org/servlet/WDSContentServer/WDSP/IB/2006/04/13/000160016_20060413145957/Rendered/PDF/325530SPANISH01recimiento0Sostenido.pdf (accessed February 1, 2010).

Yeats, A.J. (1998), "Does Mercosur's Trade Performance Raise Concerns about the Effects of Regional Trade Arrangements?," *The World Bank Economic Review* 12 (1): 1–28.

Yellen, J. (1998), "The Continuing Importance of Trade Liberalization," *Business Economics* 33 (1): 23–26.

Yoffie, D. (1983), *Power and Protectionism: Strategies of the Newly Industrializing Countries*, New York: Columbia University Press.

Zielonka, J. (2004), "Challenges of EU Enlargement," *Journal of Democracy* 15 (1): 22–35.

Index

ROUTLEDGE PAPERBACKS DIRECT

For Product Safety Concerns and Information please contact our EU
representative GPSR@taylorandfrancis.com
Taylor & Francis Verlag GmbH, Kaufingerstraße 24, 80331 München, Germany

www.ingramcontent.com/pod-product-compliance
Ingram Content Group UK Ltd.
Pitfield, Milton Keynes, MK11 3LW, UK
UKHW022124190926
475702UK00013B/1623
* 9 7 8 0 4 1 5 7 4 6 1 5 1 *